A LEVEL
COMPUTING

P.M. Heathcote MSc
Senior Lecturer, University College Suffolk

&

K.R. Bond PhD, BSc
Head of Computing, Aylesbury Grammar School
Chief Examiner for A Level Computing

EDUCATIONAL

Letts Educational
Aldine House
Aldine Place
London W12 8AW
Tel: 0181 740 2266
Fax: 0181 743 8451
e-mail: mail@lettsed.co.uk

Every effort has been made to trace copyright holders and to obtain their permission for the use of copyright material. The authors and publishers will gladly receive information enabling them to rectify any reference or credit in subsequent editions.

First published 1997
Reprinted 1998
Reprinted 1999

Text © P M Heathcote and K R Bond 1997

Design and illustration © BPP (Letts Educational) Ltd 1997

British Library Cataloguing in Publication Data
A CIP record for this book is available from the British Library

ISBN 1 85758 601 8

Typeset by TTP International, Sutton, Surrey

Printed in Great Britain by Progressive Printing UK Ltd

Letts Educational is the trading name of BPP (Letts Educational) Ltd

Acknowledgements
Questions in Chapter 1, 2, 3, 4, 5, 6, 7, 8, 9, 10, 11, 12 and mock exam questions: Reproduced by kind permission of the Associated Examining Board. Any answers or hints on answers are the sole responsibility of the authors and have not been provided or approved by the Associated Examining Board. Questions in Chapters 1, 2, 4, 5, 6, 7, 8, 9, 10, 11, 12 and mock exam questions: Reproduced by kind permission of the Northern Examinations and Assessment Board. The authors are responsible for the solutions given to these questions and they may not necessarily constitute the only possible solutions. Questions in Chapters 1, 2, 4, 5, 6, 7, 8, 9, 10, 11 and mock exam questions: Reproduced from NICCEA/NISEAC examination papers with the permission of the Northern Ireland Council for the Curriculum, Examinations and Assessment. Question in mock exam questions: OCEAC material is reproduced by permission of the University of Cambridge Local Examinations Syndicate. The University of Cambridge Local Examinations Syndicate bears no responsibility for the example answers to questions from past OCEAC question papers which are contained in this publication. Questions in Chapters 1, 4, 7, 9, 10, 11 and mock exam papers: Reproduced by kind permission of the Scottish Qualifications Authority. Solutions to answers do not emanate from the Scottish Qualifications Authority. Questions in Chapters 1, 2, 3, 4, 5, 6, 8 and 9: UCLES material is reproduced by kind permission of the University of Cambridge Local Examinations Syndicate. The University of Cambridge Local Examinations Syndicate bears no responsibility for the example answers taken from its past question papers which are contained in this publication. Question in Chapter 5: UODLE material is reproduced by permission of the University of Cambridge Local Examinations Syndicate. University of Cambridge Local Examinations Syndicate bears no responsibility for the example answers to questions taken from past UODLE question papers which are contained in this publication. Questions in Chapters 1, 2, 3, 4, 6, 7, 8, 9, 11, 12 and mock exam questions: Reproduced by kind permission of London Examinations, a division of Edexcel Foundation. Edexcel Foundation, London Examinations accepts no responsibility whatsoever for the accuracy or methods of working in the answers given.

CONTENTS

STARTING POINTS

In this section

How to use this book
   The structure of the book
   Using your syllabus checklist

Syllabus checklists and paper analysis
   Examination boards and addresses

Studying and revising Computing
   Modular courses
   Study strategy and techniques
   Reading for A/AS level
   Coursework
   Revision techniques

The examination
   Question styles
   Examination techniques
   Final preparation

HOW TO USE THIS BOOK

The structure of this book

The aim of this book is to guide you in how to tackle an A-Level Computing course. It should serve as a study guide, work book and revision aid throughout your A-level course, no matter which syllabus you are following. It is *not* intended to replace, but rather to complement your existing text book by drawing your attention to the key points of each topic and showing you how to apply your knowledge in answering examination questions.

The book is divided into three sections. Section 1, Starting Points, contains study tips and syllabus information – all the material you need to get started on your A-level study – plus advice on planning your revision and tips on how to tackle the exam itself. Use the Syllabus Checklists to find out exactly where you can find the study units which are relevant to your particular syllabus.

Section 2, the main body of the text, contains the core of A-level Computing. It has been devised to make study as easy – and enjoyable – as possible, and has been divided into chapters which cover the subject areas you will encounter on your syllabus. The chapters are split into units, each covering a topic of study.

A list of objectives at the beginning of each chapter directs you towards the key points of the chapter. The Chapter Roundup at the end brings the topics of the chapter into focus and links them to other themes of study. To reinforce what you have just read, there is a Question Bank at the end of each chapter. Recent examinations from all the boards (including Scottish Higher) provide the question practice. The Tutorial notes give you practical guidance on how to answer A-level questions, highlighting important points and possible pitfalls, and providing additional information relevant to that particular topic.

Section 3, Test Run, focuses on the examination you will sit at the end of your course. First, you can assess your progress using the Test Your Knowledge Quiz and analysis chart. Then, as a final test, you should attempt the Mock Exam Questions, under timed conditions. This will give you invaluable examination practice in a variety of question types and, together with the answers and hints specially written by the authors, will help you to judge how close you are to achieving your A-level pass.

Using your syllabus checklist

Whether you are using this book to work step-by-step through the syllabus or to structure your revision campaign, you will find it useful to keep a checklist of what you have covered. Keep the checklist at hand when you are doing your revision; it will remind you of the chapters you have revised and those still to be done.

The checklist for each examination – A, AS or Higher Grade – is in two parts. First there is a list of topics covered by this book which are part of the syllabus. Although the checklists are detailed, it is not possible to print entire syllabuses. *You are therefore strongly recommended to obtain an official copy of the syllabus for your examination and consult it when the need arises.* The examination board addresses are given after the syllabus checklists.

When you have revised a topic make a tick in the column provided and, if there are questions elsewhere in the book, try to answer them.

The second part of the checklist gives you information about the examination, providing details about the time and marks allocated for each written paper.

SYLLABUS CHECKLISTS AND PAPER ANALYSIS

ASSOCIATED EXAMINING BOARD

A-level Syllabus 0643
AS-level Syllabus 0982

Syllabus topic Topics marked with an asterisk are also included in the AS syllabus	Covered in Unit No	✔
1* **Applications and effects**		
1.1* The applications of computing in a variety of contexts. These could include science, education, manufacturing, commercial data processing, publishing, leisure, communication, embedded systems, information systems, on-line services, artificial intelligence and the use of expert systems	1.1, 1.2, 1.4-1.7	
1.2* Generic packages e.g. word-processing and desk-top publishing, graphics packages, spreadsheets, databases, expert system shells, CAD	1.3, 1.8	
1.3* Social, economic and legal consequences of computerisation	1.10	
1.4* Legal implications of computerised data processing	1.9	
2* **Systems development**		
2.1* The systems life-cycle Problem specification, analysis, design, implementation and maintenance	4.2	
2.2* Analysis Feasibility studies. Methods of gathering information	4.3, 4.4	
2.3* Design Systems flowcharts, pseudo-code. Prototyping. Algorithm design. E-R modelling. Dry-run testing. Modular and top-down program design	4.4-4.6, 12.1	
2.4* Testing strategies	4.5	
2.5* Implementation	4.7	
2.6* Evaluation	4.9	
3 **Data representation in computers**		
3.1 Character codes and their representation	6.1	
3.2 The concept of number bases – denary, binary and hexadecimal	6.2	
3.3 Representation of negative integers by twos complement and sign and magnitude method. BCD. Floating point numbers including the concept of mantissa and exponent and the need for normalisation. Comparison of the precision and range of various number systems, according to their representation. Rounding errors and truncation errors.	6.2-6.5	
3.4 Bitmapped graphic representation. Digitised sound representation. Machine code of a stored program.	6.6, 8.1	
4* **Hardware**		
4.1* The generation of bit patterns in a computer. Bits, bytes and words. Program and data.	7.1	
4.2* Internal components of a computer Processor, memory, bus, secondary storage, their purpose and how they relate. Capabilities of processors	7.1	
4.3 Structure and role of the processor ALU, accumulator and control unit. Purpose of	7.2	

Syllabus topic Topics marked with an asterisk are also included in the AS syllabus		Covered in Unit No	✔
	registers. Fetch–Execute cycle and the role of registers within it		
4.4	Processing concepts Interrupts in the context of the FE cycle. Addressing modes. Assembly language instructions and their relationship to memory addressing and the use of the registers. Multiple processor architectures	7.3, 7.4, 8.1–8.9	
5*	**Peripherals**		
5.1	Secondary storage devices	2.1	
5.2*	Input and output methods	2.2–2.4	
6*	**Data communication and networking**		
6.1	Principles of electronic data communication. ADC/DAC. Multiplexors. ISDN. Modems	9.1	
6.2	Communication methods Simplex, half duplex and full duplex transmission. Circuit and packet switching. Sources of error and error detection methods. Data compression. Data encryption. Buffering	9.2	
6.3*	Networking. Rationale for networks. Topologies. Applications of networking. Standard protocols	9.3–9.5	
7*	**System software**		
7.1	The need for an operating system. Memory management. File creation and management. Control of hardware devices. Process control. Interface with user	10.1, 10.8	
7.2*	Operating system classification. Batch mode. Interactive mode. Real-time. Multi-programming, multi-user, and multi-tasking systems	10.2	
7.3	Operating system implementation. The role of the dispatcher. Scheduling and scheduling algorithms. The allocation of memory by the operating system. Virtual memory and paging. Peripheral control. File creation and multi-level directory systems	10.3–10.7	
8*	**Programming concepts**		
8.1*	Low-level and high-level programming	11.1	
8.2*	Methods of program translation. Assemblers, compilers, interpreters	11.6	
8.3	The translation process	11.6	
8.4*	High-level languages The characteristics and classification of high-level languages. Choice of programming languages to develop particular applications	11.1	
8.5	Programming methodologies Structured programming techniques. Procedural-oriented programming. Object-oriented programming. Logic programming	11.3, 11.4	
8.6*	Features of high-level languages. Syntax rules. Data types. Programming statements and comments. Constants and variables. Procedures and functions. Parameters. Modules	11.2, 11.5, 12.2	
8.7*	Data structures Multi-dimensional arrays. Records. Trees. (A-level only) Lists. Linked lists. Queues. Stacks	12.3, 12.4	
8.8	Standard algorithms Serial and sequential searches. Binary search. Insertion and bubble sort. Tree traversal algorithms. Creating and maintaining linked lists. Stack, queue and list operations. Recursive techniques	12.5–12.10	

Syllabus topic Topics marked with an asterisk are also included in the AS syllabus		Covered in Unit No	✔
9*	**Files and databases**		
9.1*	File types Binary e.g. executable files, bitmap. Text files. Physical and logical organisation. Fixed and variable length records	3.1–3.3	
9.2*	File organisation Serial, sequential and direct access Indexed sequential files (A-level only)		
9.3*	File processing	3.5	
9.4*	Security and integrity of data Security: backup files. File generation. Archiving. Transaction logs. Authorisation tables. Encryption. Integrity: Check digits. Parity. Control totals. Batch totals. Hash totals	3.6, 9.2	
9.5*	Database concepts	5.1	
9.6	Relational databases	5.3	
9.7	Database design. Entity relationship modelling. Normalisation techniques	5.2, 5.3	
9.8	Techniques of database management Role of a Database Administrator. (DBA). Databases in multi-user and distributed systems. Concurrent access to data. Database recovery	5.4–5.6	

Scheme of assessment

Paper 1: *Project – centre-assessed and board-moderated. (30% of the total marks)*

Paper 2: *Written Paper   2.5 hours   (35% of the total marks)*

This paper will also form Paper 2 of the AS examination.

The paper will be divided into two sections, both testing those areas of the syllabus common to both AS and A-level.

All questions will be compulsory.

Section A will consist of up to 15 short answer questions and will carry 70 marks.

Section B will be a structured, applications-based question, testing comprehension of syllabus topics, ability to analyse a problem and the quality of the language used. This question will carry 30 marks.

Paper 3: *Written Paper   2.5 hours   (35% of the total marks)*

The paper will be divided into two sections.

Section A will consist of up to eight compulsory, short-answer questions drawn from any area of the syllabus. This section will carry 40 marks.

Section B will require candidates to answer three out of five structured questions from any area of the syllabus. This section will carry 60 marks.

EDEXCEL, LONDON EXAMINATIONS (FORMERLY ULEAC)

A-level Syllabus 9105

Syllabus topic	Covered in Unit No	✔
Section 1 Applications of computers and their social and economic implications		
1.1 (a) General application areas: communication and information systems; commercial and general data processing; industrial, technical and scientific uses; monitoring and control systems; automation, embedded systems and robotics; expert systems and artificial intelligence; miscellaneous areas such as education and training, entertainment. (b) Specific applications: a detailed study of one particular application. Particular applications for detailed study are not prescribed by the Council.	1.1–1.8	
1.2 The social and economic implications of the use of computers. Social and economic effects on people and organisations associated directly with the application, on other individuals and organisations, and on society in general; economic reasons for the use of computers; changes to existing methods, products and services; changes in the working environment; changes in employment, retraining; privacy and integrity of data; data protection legislation; security, reliability and resilience of systems; consequences of system failure; computer crime.	1.9–1.10	
Section 2 Systems analysis and design		
2.1 Systems analysis	4.2–4.4	
2.2 Systems design	4.3	
2.3 Types of system: batch, single-user on-line, multi-user on-line, distributed systems, control systems, automated and embedded systems.	4.1	
Section 3 Problem formulation and solution		
3.1 Problem formulation Detailed specification and design of input and output, including the user interface; specification of processing requirements; documentation.	4.5–4.8	
3.2 Problem solution Evaluation of alternative proposals; top-down analysis of the problem solution selection of appropriate tools and methods for solving the problem; decomposition of the solution into self-contained modules; design of test strategy.	4.5	
Section 4 Structure and representation of data		
4.1 Database systems Purpose of a DBMS; physical organisation of a database as a set of files related through links and/or common fields.	5.1–5.3	
4.2 File organisation Files, records and fields; fixed and variable length records; serial and direct access to records; serial, sequential, indexed sequential and random files;	3.1–3.6	

Syllabus topic		Covered in Unit No	✔
	file security and backup; file privacy, passwords, encryption blocks and buffers.		
4.3	Data structures	12.6-12.10	
	(a) Data structures to suit application requirements: lists, tables, records, strings, stacks, queues, binary trees, hash tables.		
	(b) Representation of data structures using arrays and pointers.		
4.4	Data types and representations	12.2, 6.1-6.5	
	(a) representation of complex data types by structures of standard types; Boolean data; characters; integers; real numbers.		
	(b) Binary, octal and hexadecimal notation; BCD; range and accuracy of representations, overflow, truncation and rounding errors.		
Section 5	**Algorithm design and programming concepts**		
5.1	Methods of describing algorithms; expression of algorithms making use of modules, selection, repetition, iteration and recursion; algorithms for accessing and updating files and for the management of indexes; merging two or more sequential files; sorting; searching ordered arrays (sequential, binary); hash table searching.	11.2, 12.1, 12.4, 12.5 3.4, 3.5	
5.2	Structured algorithm design Modularity; top-down design; algorithms for parallel tasks; testing, evaluation and analysis of algorithms.	11.3 7.4	
5.3	Programming methodology Debugging techniques; program traces; types of program error.	11.3	
5.4	High-level programming languages Language features; block structure; local and global variables; functions and procedures; parameters passed by value and by reference; input, output and file-handling operations. Types of high-level language; imperative and declarative, special- and general-purpose languages; criteria for selecting a suitable language.	11.1, 11.2 11.4	
Section 6	**System software and architecture**		
6.1	System software and packages	1.8	
	(a) The need for and use of general software packages: word-processing packages; spreadsheet packages, graphics packages; information retrieval packages; data management packages; program and sub-routine libraries.	11.5, 11.6	
	(b) The need for and use of system utility programs: editors; linking loaders; debugging tools; file creation, reorganisation and transfer programs.		
	(c) Compilers and interpreters; reverse Polish form the stack mechanism for procedure calling and parameter passing.	10.1-10.8	
	(d) Operating systems: the nature of batch, on-line, multi-access, real-time transaction processing, network and process control operating systems; the form of interface between the operating system and the user;		

Syllabus topic		Covered in Unit No	✔
	management of files and filestore; multiprogramming; scheduling; store protection and management; resource allocation; spooling; time slicing; swapping; interrupt handling.		
6.2	Computer architecture and operation Comparison of mainframe; microcomputers; parallel processing computers; processor configuration; control unit; arithmetic and logic unit; registers; buses; store access; address mapping; input and output transfers; the machine instruction cycle; detection of interrupts; the form of machine code instructions; the range of functions – transfer, logical shift, arithmetic, branch, input and output; registers; modes of operand addressing (immediate, direct, indirect, indexed, relative); mnemonic form of instructions with symbolic addressing (assembly language); the nature and purpose of an assembler.	7.1-7.4 8.1-8.9	
6.3	Hardware and communications Processor hardware; standard processor chips; standard chips for store, store access, input and output; standard buses and interfaces; the functions and characteristics of storage media; the characteristics and performance of a range of peripheral equipment (including control devices); the suitability of different peripherals for various applications; peripheral device control; use of buffers; interrupts and interrupt priorities; polling; handshaking; transfer checks – parity bits, check sum; communications; the need for standard protocols; networks of computers; shared access to central facilities (e.g. common filestore, printer); message passing; data transmission via modems and telephone lines or other means; electronic mail systems; distributed information systems.	2.1-2.4 3.1, 3.2 9.1-9.5	

Scheme of assessment

The examination will consist of two written papers with equal weighting, each of three hours.

The project assessment will count for one third of the final assessment in the subject as a whole.

Paper 1   Written Paper   3 hours   ($\frac{1}{3}$ of the total marks)
The paper will be divided into two sections.
Section A will consist of compulsory, short-answer questions. This section will carry 40 marks.
Section B will require candidates to answer four out of six questions. This section will carry 60 marks.

Paper 3   Written Paper   3 hours   ($\frac{1}{3}$ of the total marks)
The paper will be divided into two sections.
Section A will consist of compulsory, short-answer questions. This section will carry 40 marks.
Section B will require candidates to answer four out of six questions. This section will carry 60 marks.

Paper 3   Project – centre-assessed and board-moderated.   ($\frac{1}{3}$ of total marks)

NORTHERN EXAMINATIONS AND ASSESSMENT BOARD

A-level Syllabus End of Course Examination 4446
A-level Syllabus Modular 4447
AS-level Syllabus End of Course Examination 3446
AS-level Syllabus Modular 3447

Syllabus topic The AS syllabus consists of the CORE modules 1–3	*Covered in Unit No*	✔
CORE 1 (CP01) Software and System Development		
C1.1 **Systems analysis and design**	4.2–4.9	
C1.1.1 Problem analysis	11.3	
C1.1.2 Structured system design	4.3, 4.4	
C1.1.3 Human–computer interfaces	4.5	
C1.1.4 Changeover	4.7	
C1.1.5 Maintenance	4.9	
C1.1.6 Documentation	4.8	
C1.2 **Algorithms**		
C1.2.1 Algorithm constructs	11.2, 12.1	
C1.2.2 Scope of variables	11.2	
C1.2.3 Logical operations	8.5	
C1.2.4 Algorithm testing	12.1	
C1.3 **Data types and data structures**	12.2–12.10	
C1.4 **Sorting and searching**	12.5	
C1.5 **Program production**		
C1.5.1 Levels of computer language	11.1, 11.4	
C1.5.2 Translation programs	11.6	
C1.5.3 Program errors	11.3	
C1.6 **Nature and type of software**		
C1.6.1 Software packages	1.8	
CORE 2 (CP02) The Computer, Data and Applications		
C2.1 **Computer architecture**	7.1	
C2.2 **The operating system**	10.1	
C2.2.1 Modes of operation	10.2	
C2.3 **Storage hierarchy**	7.1, 7.2	
C2.3.1 Secondary storage	2.1	
C2.3.2 File management	10.6	
C2.4 **Input/output peripheral equipment**	2.2–2.4	
C2.5 **Interfacing**	7.1	
C2.6 **Communication networks**	9.2–9.4	
C2.7 **Representation of data as bit patterns**	6.1	
C2.7.1 Characters	6.1	
C2.7.2 Numbers	6.2	
C2.7.3 Truncation and rounding, overflow and underflow	6.5	
C2.8 **Logical operations**	8.5	
C2.9 **File organisation**	3.1–3.5	
C2.10 **Data capture, verification and validation**	2.2, 4.1	
C2.11 **Typical computer applications and their associated hardware**	1.1–1.7, 4.4	
C2.11.1 Business and commerce	4.1, 5.1	
C2.11.2 Communication and information systems	9.5	

Syllabus topic The AS syllabus consists of the CORE modules 1–3		*Covered in Unit No*	✔
C2.12	**Consequences of current trends in the uses of computers**	1.9, 1.10	
C2.13	**Privacy and security**	1.9, 5.5	
C2.13.1	Software and data misuse legislation	1.9	
C2.13.2	Data protection legislation	1.9	
CORE 3 (CP03) PROJECT (Coursework)			
EXTENSION 1 (CP04) Software and Software Development			
E1.1	**System design**		
E1.1.1	Human–computer interface	2.2	
E1.1.2	Design validation		
E1.1.3	Design evaluation		
E1.2	**Sorting**	12.5	
E1.3	**Logical operations**	8.5	
E1.4	**Algorithms**		
E1.4.1	Algorithm constructs	11.2, 12.1	
E1.4.2	Algorithm testing and data	12.1	
E1.5	**Data types and data structures**	12.2–12.10	
E1.6	**Software engineering**		
E1.6.1	Software tools	11.6	
E1.6.2	Computer languages	11.4–11.5	
E1.6.3	Program translation	11.6	
E1.6.4	Program construction	11.6	
E1.7	**Spreadsheets**	1.8	
EXTENSION 2 (CP05) The Computer, Data and Applications			
E2.1	**The operating system**		
E2.1.2	Interrupts	10.3	
E2.1.3	Memory management	10.5	
E2.1.4	Input/output	3.2	
E2.1.5	Accounting and security		
E2.1.6	File management	10.6	
E2.1.7	Scheduling	10.4	
E2.2	**Secondary storage**	2.1	
E2.3	**Input/output**	2.4	
E2.4	**Data transmission**	9.1, 9.2	
E2.5	**Communication networks**	9.2	
E2.5.1	Communication standards	9.2	
E2.6	**Databases**	5.1-5.6	
E2.7	**Distributed systems**	4.1, 10.1	
E2.8	**File organisation**	3.1	
E2.9	**Typical applications of computers and communications systems**		
E2.9.1	Information systems	9.5	
E2.9.2	Control systems		
E2.9.3	Simulations		
E2.9.4	Artificial intelligence	1.6	
E2.9.4.1	Expert systems	1.6	
E2.10	**Data security and integrity processes**	5.4, 3.6	
E2.11	**Disaster planning**		

Syllabus topic The AS syllabus consists of the CORE modules 1–3		Covered in Unit No	✔
E2.12	**Malpractice**		
E2.13	The regulatory framework	1.9	
E2.13.1	Software and data misuse legislation	1.9	
E2.13.2	Data protection legislation	1.9	
E2.13.3	Codes of practice	1.9	
EXTENSION 3 (CP06) Project (Coursework)			

Scheme of assessment

In order to accommodate both a modular and linear approach for A and AS level, a written paper will be set each year on each of CORE 1 (CP01), CORE 2 (CP02), EXTENSION 1 (CP04) and EXTENSION 2 (CP05) modules. All papers will have a range of types of question.

Where appropriate, candidates' answers in continuous prose will be assessed for quality of language.

Candidates for Computing (AS) will attempt:

CORE 1 (CP01)	Written paper	30%	2 hours
CORE 2 (CP02)	Written paper	30%	2 hours
CORE 3 (CP03)	Coursework	40%	

Candidates for Computing (Advanced) will attempt:

CORE 1 (CP01)	Written paper	15%	2 hours
CORE 2 (CP02)	Written paper	15%	2 hours
EXTENSION 1 (CP04)	Written paper	15%	2 hours
EXTENSION 2 (CP05)	Written paper	15%	2 hours
CORE 3 (CP03)	Coursework	20%	
EXTENSION 3 (CP06)	Coursework	20%	

NORTHERN IRELAND COUNCIL FOR THE CURRICULUM EXAMINATIONS AND ASSESSMENT

A-level Syllabus

Syllabus topic		Covered in Unit No	✔
Module 1.	**Computer systems**		
1.1	**System software**		
(i)	Operating system software The need for and functions of operating systems. A general understanding of process scheduling – multi-programming, interrupt handling, time slicing; memory management – store protection, program swapping and paging; file store management – file directories, control of access to files, program and subroutine libraries, disk and file utilities; input/output control system – spooling; job control – command language, job scheduling, accounting. Describe and distinguish between the different types of system in terms of hardware, software and the user interface. Modes of operation: batch processing systems, single and multi-user on-line systems, distributed and networked systems, control and real-time systems, interactive systems. User interfaces including GUI.	10.1–10.8	

Syllabus topic		Covered in Unit No	✔
(ii)	Compilers and interpreters Distinguish between compilers and interpreters. Be able to describe the need for and function of language translators. A general understanding of the algorithms used in the following: lexical, syntactic and semantic analysis – symbol tables, EBNF, handling of errors; generation of code – simple data structures, reverse Polish form of expressions, simple program structures, stack mechanism for procedure calling and simple parameter passing, run time support routines.	11.5, 11.6	
1.2	**Data types and representation**		
	Represent elementary data as patterns of bits and bytes. Character codes: ASCII. Integer representation and arithmetic up to 16 bits. Sign and magnitude, two's complement, addition and subtraction. Detection of overflow. Floating point representation including range and accuracy. Overflow and underflow, truncation and rounding errors, loss of significance.	6.1-6.5	
1.3	**Computer systems architecture and software**		
(i)	Processor architecture The internal organisation of a conventional processor. Processor components: control unit, memory unit, arithmetic and logic unit, registers. Memory access: data and address buses, memory mapped input and output. Machine instruction cycle. Detection of interrupts. An awareness of the processes involved in the execution of machine language programs.	7.1-7.3	
(ii)	Assembly language A basic knowledge of assembly language programming techniques (not a detailed knowledge of assembly language programming). Instruction formats, address formats, addressing modes (immediate, direct, indirect, indexed, fixed). Techniques: machine instruction cycle, sequences, jumps – conditional and unconditional, iteration, subroutine calls.	8.1-8.9	
(iii)	Memory: functions and characteristics Primary memory: RAM, ROM, PROM and EPROM memory units. Secondary memory: tapes, disks, optical disks.	7.1	
(iv)	Input and output devices: features and uses Common I/O devices. I/O interface unit; control of I/O devices using programmed I/O; interrupt I/O and direct memory access (DMA); analogue representation and analogue/digital conversion.	7.1-7.3, 2.1, 2.4	
(v)	Computer networks and distributed systems Technical features and the role of computer networks in decentralising and distributing data processing activities.	9.3-9.5	
(vi)	Communication Data transmission, packet switching, message switching, communications protocols.	9.1-9.2	
Module 2.	**Software techniques and tools**		
2.1	**Algorithms**	3.4, 3.5, 12.5	
	Derive and describe suitable algorithms for given tasks using suitable data structures: searching, sorting, merging, updating, accessing.	11.2, 11.3	

Syllabus topic	Covered in Unit No	✔
2.2 Structured design		
Problem identification, analysis and definition. Appropriate use of algorithmic concepts of: sequencing, selection, repetition, recursion. Top-down design and modularity. Testing, evaluation and analysis of algorithms.	11.2, 11.3	
2.3 Programming methodology		
The principles of structured programming. Module and program testing, testing strategy, debugging techniques, types of error. The need for program documentation. Use of self-documenting identifiers and code.	11.3	
2.4 High-level programming languages	11.4, 11.5, 12.1-12.10	
Facilities provided by different languages. Types of high-level language: imperative, declarative, applications generators, special purpose, general purpose. 4GLs. Language definition in the form of syntax diagrams and Extended Backus–Naur Form (EBNF). Fundamental concepts of programming in a high-level language. Data types and structures: arrays, stacks, queues, trees, strings, records.		
2.5 Files		
Difference between the logical structure of a file and its physical organisation, and the manipulation of files.	3.1-3.6	
2.6 Database systems		
The nature of a database and the need for such systems. DBMS, data dictionaries, purpose of normalisation, DBA, report generators.	5.1-5.6	
Module 3. System evolution		
3.1 System life cycle		
An appreciation of different life cycle models such as cascade (waterfall) and prototyping.	4.2	
3.2 The analysis and design of the system		
Requirements and system specifications; personnel involved; feasibility studies and report; methods of fact finding; methods of fact recording such as DFD, ER models, decision tables, flowcharts, organisational charts. System information requirements; description of the user interface design including the form of any input and output; file design; system documentation. Tools such as prototyping, applications generators, CASE tools. Choice of appropriate hardware/software. Data normalisation to 3NF.	4.2-4.6 5.3	
3.3 Implementation and maintenance of the system		
Stages in installation/implementation: file conversion, system testing, staff training, changeover strategies such as parallel running, pilot running, direct changeover. The purpose of systems maintenance: user need for change, external impetus for change. Benefits of good systems design; clear and complete documentation. The role of the systems review.	4.7-4.9	
3.4 Evaluation of solutions to problems		
Evaluate alternative solutions on the basis of effectiveness, costs, usability and maintainability.		

Syllabus topic		Covered in Unit No	✔
Module 4.	**The study of applications**		
4.1	**Range and scope of computer applications**		
(a)	General applications. Describe and explain the main aspects of a range of typical applications of computing. The place of the application within the overall business system. The purpose of the application. The information requirements, i.e. the required outcome, and consequently the required input information, plus any necessary processing. Processing modes and requirements. Data integrity, privacy and data security. File design and organisation. Specialist output devices. User/system communication. **Typical applications:** Communication, information, multimedia, leisure, commercial, financial, billing, industrial and scientific, monitoring, selection and reservation.	2.2-2.4 1.1-1.8	
(b)	Particular applications Describe, explain, comment on and evaluate, in detail, the main aspects of two particular specified applications. In 1998 these are Billing Systems and Leisure Systems.		
4.2	**Implications of the use of computers**		
	Economic implications: increased reliability, increased productivity, the new technologies, twenty-four hour working. Social and ethical implications: changes in the working environment, health and safety, data protection, depersonalisation, de-skilling, privacy and confidentiality, security, the Data Processing Management Association's Code of Ethics, data protection legislation. Current trends: the information technology age.	1.9-1.10	

Scheme of assessment

The total assessment is composed of four written papers and one project. The allocation of marks to each component will be as shown in the table below.

Component	Paper title	Module number	Duration of paper (hours)	%
Paper 1	Computer systems	8.1	2	20
Paper 2	Software techniques and tools	8.2	1.5	15
Paper 3	System evolution	8.3	1.5	15
Paper 4	The study of applications	8.4	2	20
Project				30

Modular assessment

Under the modular scheme Papers 1 and 2 may be taken at a time other than the end of a two-year course, e.g. June of year 1, February of year 2. Module results may be used for up to four years.

OXFORD & CAMBRIDGE EXAMINATIONS & ASSESSMENT COUNCIL

A-level and AS-Level Syllabus 9953

Syllabus topic		Covered in Unit No.	✔
MODULE 1.	**Computing system fundamentals**		
1.1	**The need for and function of system software appropriate for a variety of applications**		
(a)	Operating regimes. Single user and multi-user systems (multi-access and multi-tasking); windowing systems.	10.1, 10.2, 10.5 10.4	
(b)	Control. Resource allocation; protection; accounting for resources consumed, user budgets; utilities.		
1.2	**The need for and attributes of programming tools and techniques**		
	Language processing and the use of libraries. Source code, object code and executable versions of a program. Subroutines (procedures). Parameters, local and global variables and appropriate storage organisation. System, public and private libraries. Error detection and reporting.	11.1-11.3 11.6	
1.3	**Data structures and the representation of data types; their implications for software development**		
(i)	Binary representation. Relation between number of digits and number of patterns available. Hardware representation of binary data.	6.1	
(ii)	Data types: Boolean, character, integer, real number, string.	6.2	
(iii)	Files. Items, records, fields.	3.1	
(iv)	Implementation of data structures. Ways of storing and manipulating one-dimensional and multi-dimensional tables; arrays; linked lists; trees; queues; stacks.	12.1-12.10	
1.4	**The capabilities of processors**		
(a)	Conventional processor architecture. Instruction register, program counter, accumulator(s). Interrupts.	7.1-7.3	
(b)	Speed; cycle time; ability to handle file store; networking capability.		
1.5	**The features of contemporary storage methods and devices**		
(a)	Store organisation. Main and backing stores, transfers, buffers. Sequential (serial), indexed sequential and random access to stored information. Physical block size; logical record size. Some typical storage devices.	3.2-3.4, 2.1	
(b)	File-store control. File-control and file-processing utilities; back-up copies of files; archiving.	3.5, 3.6	
1.6	**The need for, and means of, communication between devices and within networks, and the importance of adopting standards**	9.1, 9.2	
	The need for computers to communicate with one another, protocols, switching.	9.2	
MODULE 2.	**Common applications**		
2.1	**Systems analysis**		
	Identification of the purpose of the application; identification of the information system processing and communication requirements; investigation of problem; recognition of hardware needs; choice between packages and purpose-built systems.	4.1-4.9	

	Syllabus topic	Covered in Unit No.	✔
	Top-down design, documentation and implementation of system. Testing and maintenance.		
2.2	**Presentation of data and user interface**		
	Reports; transactions; capturing data; interactive user interfaces; presentation graphics; text and tabular material.	4.5	
2.3	**The features and uses of a range of contemporary input and output devices**		
	Means of input and output for text, numerical and graphical data using on-line and off-line devices. Matching the interface between the tasks to be performed and the skills of the human user. Dealing with errors.	2.2, 2.3	
2.4	**Effects**		
	The social, economic, legal, ethical and other consequences of current usage. Physical and logical protection of data and reasons for this.	1.9, 1.10	
Option 31.	**Business applications**		
3.1	**A knowledge of the common applications of computing in business.**	1.1-1.3	
3.2	**Batch processing and rapid response applications. Response time**	4.1	
3.3	**Text processing**		
	Types of text to be processed; letters, tabular material, text indexed by line numbers; software for text processing; editors; report generators; spreadsheet packages; word-processing packages; spelling checkers; business graphics; integrated packages; fonts.	1.8	
3.4	**Databases and files**		
	Applications in which large quantities of data are required, and techniques for handling the data.		
3.5	**Methods of accessing files. Fixed and variable length records. Primary and secondary keys, sequential, indexed-sequential and multi-keyed files. Database access, views**	3.3–3.5, 5.1, 5.2, 5.5	
Option 32.	**Graphical and real-time applications**		
Option 33.	**Distributed systems**		
Option 34.	**Information applications**		

Scheme of assessment

Advanced Level

Paper 9953/1   Written Paper   15%   1.5 hours

This paper will cover the topics covered in Module 1: Computing System Fundamentals.

Paper 9953/2   Written Paper   15%   1.5 hours

This paper will cover the topics covered in Module 2: Common Applications.

Candidates must choose two option papers from Modules 31/32/33/34. Each paper accounts for 15% of the total marks and occupies 1.5 hours.

Paper 9953/3 Exercises. The exercises are set by the Board and account for 20% of the total mark.

Paper 9953/6 Project. The project accounts for 20% of the total mark.

Advanced Supplementary Level

Candidates sit Papers 9953/1 and 9953/2 (each worth 30% of total mark) and complete a project (Paper 9953/6). (40% of total mark).

SCOTTISH QUALIFICATIONS AUTHORITY (FORMERLY SEB)

Scottish Certificate of Education Higher Grade in Computing Studies

Syllabus topic		Covered in Unit No.	✔
31	**General-purpose packages**		
3131	**Matching the package to the application**		
	Within each class of package, identify different types of data objects that can be manipulated and the operations that can be performed upon them.		
	Word-processing: data objects include (1) document, section, paragraph, sentence, word, character, footnote. Operations include create, insert, delete, select, search, format. (2) page, line, header, footer – set sizes, annotate. (3) continuous segment – cut, paste, change style.	1.8	
	Database: objects include file, record, field, report. Operations include copy, search, select, update, compute field, sort.	3.1, 5.2	
	Spreadsheet: cells of three types (constant text, constant value, formula), row, column, area. Operations include enter, copy, edit, evaluate, sort, select, output.	1.8	
	Graphics: line, arc, area, shape, diagram, picture. Operations include draw, select, delete, insert, scale, translate, rotate.		
	Pattern matching, calculation of values, editing.		
3132	**Languages**		
	Be aware that carrying out operations in a general-purpose package requires the use of a defined language. Distinguish between the syntax and semantics of a language. Use of 4GLs in a variety of application areas.	11.4, 11.5	
3133	**Human–computer interface**		
	Evaluate in terms of ease of use and ease of learning, a variety of HCI styles, e.g. character displays; low to medium resolution graphics interfaces, use in teletext and videotext; high resolution graphics: iconic interfaces, with mouse, tablet, touch screen or joystick.		
3134	**Package integration**		
	For example: mail-merge from database into word-processing document; transfer a table from a spreadsheet into a WP document; transfer a set of fields from a database to a spreadsheet; add pictures from a graphics package into a WP document; draw graphic charts from data in a database.		
	Evaluate integrated packages. Implications for employment and reorganisation of businesses.		
32	**Computer systems**		
3231	**Single-user systems**		
	Describe methods of data representation including: graphic (bitmapped and object attributes), text (ASCII) and number (integer, floating point).	6.1-6.4	
	Explain and illustrate the organisation of the computer as a system of components.	7.1	
	Explain the purpose of registers within the CPU.	7.2	
	Describe the information flow during the execution of an instruction and the selection of instructions for execution.	7.2	

Syllabus topic		Covered in Unit No.	✔
	Assembly code instructions and instruction formats *Details of a particular assembly language are not required and only a knowledge of immediate and direct addressing will be required.*	8.1–8.8	
	Buses and interfaces between CPU and peripherals; buffers, interrupts, polling, direct memory access, spooling.	7.1, 7.3	
	Transmission of data in serial and parallel form.	9.2	
	Backing store including disk and tape.	2.1	
	Single-user operating system.		
	Explain how an operating system may be enhanced, in particular by graphical methods, to produce a better human–computer interface.	10.3, 10.8	
	Explain the additional tasks of an operating system in a multi-tasking environment.	10.4	
3232	**Multi-user and networked systems**		
	Understand the difference between multi-user, batch, real-time, multi-processor and networked environments.	10.2	
	Need for and methods of achieving file security in a multi-access environment.	9.2, 5.5	
	Typical topology of a local area network and its hardware requirements.	9.3	
	Examples of wide area networks, both national and international.	9.5	
	Compare the relative capacities of transmission media, e.g. coaxial and fibre optic cable; explain how errors can occur; parity and checksums.	9.2	
3233	**Past trends and current developments**		
	Stages in development of computers and effects on society.	1.10	
	Current developments; RISC architectures, optical technologies, artificial intelligence.	1.6, 8.7	
	Assess system requirements for a given application.		
	Compare computing capability, efficiency, reliability and cost of micro-, mini- and mainframe computers, past and present.		
33	**Programming**		
3331	**Programming and problem solving**		
	Top-down design. Language constructs of a high-level language such as Pascal or COMAL.	11.2	
	Testing and documentation. Program specification.	11.3	
	Design and coding of a number of fundamental algorithms.	11.2, 12.1	
3332	**Program design aspects and programming style**		
	Understand the meaning and importance of the following desirable characteristics of programs: correctness; reliability; maintainability; readability; portability; efficiency.		
	Structure diagrams and pseudocode.	12.1	
	Choosing a suitable user interface.	4.5	
3333	**Programming languages and environments**		
	Major characteristics of high-level languages in areas of education, science, commerce and industry.	11.4	
	Programmer support tools: translators and their ease of use; error handling and reporting facilities	11.6	

Syllabus topic		Covered in Unit No.	✔
	(syntax and run-time errors); structured listings; editors; trace facilities; module libraries.		
34	**Investigation**		
41	**Communication systems and networks (optional)**		
4131	**Development**		
	Factors, both technological and economic, which have led to the development of networked systems and distributed computing.	4.1	
4132	**Networks**		
	Explain with reference to actual applications how networks allow the efficient exchange of information between local or remote computers. Implications of the use of networks.	9.1, 9.2	
	Various topologies of both LANs and WANs including bus, star and ring and factors relating to suitability of each.	9.3	
	Computer hardware and software relating to networks.	9.1	
	Compatibility factors within and between networks in terms of the need for standards, protocols and the provision of gateways.	9.2	
4133	**On-line information services**		
	Describe facilities offered by on-line information services.	9.5	
4134	**Data transmission**		
	Modes of transmission; error detection techniques.	9.2	
	Private and public lines; limitations of analogue methods; multiplexing; packet switching.	9.2	
	Need for international standards.	9.2	
42	**Knowledge based systems (optional)**		
4231	**General introduction to artificial intelligence**		
	Describe some of the difficulties of defining intelligence and be aware that AI consists of the study of ideas which enable computers to simulate intelligence.		
	Main areas of development in hardware and software including natural language processing, pattern and voice recognition, expert systems, heuristics, intelligent robots, parallel processing.		
4232	**Knowledge representation and processing**		
4233	**Expert systems**		
	Main components of an expert system.	1.6	
	Principal difficulties of expert system development.		
	Use of an expert system shell.		
	Common applications of expert systems.	1.6	
	Effect of expert system development on society.		
43	**Interfacing and control (optional)**		

Scheme of assessment

The course involves practical activity as well as theoretical study. The practical element of the course will be internally assessed and contributes 30% towards the overall award; the external examination contributes 70%.

Two papers will be set:

Paper 1 (core)	1.5 hours	60 marks
Paper 2	2 hours	140 marks (divided into two sections)

WELSH JOINT EDUCATION COMMITTEE

Assessment Pattern

A Level:	4 modules each worth 17.5%
	2 Project modules 30%
AS Level:	2 modules each worth 35%
	1 Project module 30%

The overall syllabus coverage is similar to NEAB, with the material being divided differently between the modules.

EXAMINATION BOARD ADDRESSES

AEB
The Associated Examining Board
Stag Hill House, Guildford, Surrey GU2 5XJ
Tel: 01483 506506

EDEXCEL
Edexcel, London Examinations
Stewart House, 32 Russell Square, London WC1 5DN
Tel: 0171 331 4000

NEAB
Northern Examinations and Assessment Board
12 Harter Street, Manchester M1 6HL
Tel: 0161 953 1180

NICCEA
Northern Ireland Council for the Curriculum Examinations and Assessment
Clarendon Dock, 29 Clarendon Road, Belfast BT1 3BG
Tel: 01232 261200

OCEAC
Oxford & Cambridge Examinations and Assessment Council
Syndicate Buildings, 1 Hills Road, Cambridge CB1 2EU
Tel: 01223 553311

SQA
Scottish Qualifications Authority
Ironmills Road, Dalkeith, Midlothian EH22 1LE
Tel: 0131 663 6601

WJEC
Welsh Joint Education Committee
245 Western Avenue, Cardiff CF5 2YX
Tel: 01222 265000

STUDYING AND REVISING COMPUTING

Computing is a practical-based subject. It is important, therefore, that you have lots of opportunities for practical work in order to learn how to design and develop computer-based solutions to a range of problems.

All A/AS syllabuses in computing are designed to encourage students to:

- develop an understanding of the nature and principles of computing, the range of applications of computers and the effects of their use;

- develop an understanding of the main principles of system analysis and design, methods of problem formulation and planning of solutions using computers, and systematic methods of implementation, testing and documentation;

- develop an understanding of the organisation of computer systems including software, data, hardware and communications;

- acquire the skills necessary to apply this understanding to the development of computer-based solutions to problems.

Modular courses

Most examining boards now offer modular courses which allow credits to be accumulated for either AS- or A-level. The syllabus is divided into small units (modules), each of which is examined by an end-of-module test. These tests may be taken at appropriate times throughout the course or, if preferred, at the end of the course. The advantages of taking the tests throughout the course are that there is regular feedback on how well you are doing and there is the possibility of retaking modules in order to improve your grade. Furthermore, the results of modular tests may be 'banked', and then 'cashed-in' at some time within four years to obtain an AS- or A-level. This allows for a break in a course of study without loss of the credit already obtained. Some modules are compulsory, others may be selected from a list of optional ones. However, at least 30% of the total assessment by written paper must take place in the year in which the award is to be made. All the modular courses must involve a *synoptic element* in the overall assessment. This involves sitting a module or modules which test an understanding of the subject as a whole. The project work is an ideal candidate for such an assessment.

By varying the number of modules studied you can obtain an AS- or an A-level in computing. Currently, an AS is three modules and an A-level is four or six modules, depending on the examining board.

Study strategy and techniques

When and where to study
Whether you are studying for your A-level computing at college, school, evening class or at home, you will need to spend a considerable amount of time working on your own, possibly without a great deal of guidance. A/AS-levels expect students to be able to think for themselves and to take more responsibility for managing their own learning than GCSE does. This means showing more initiative with regard to finding out how to do something, exploring and experimenting with a programming language or a particular package as much as possible and not relying on your teacher to teach you everything about the package or programming language.

In order to be successful you must learn first to plan ahead, possibly as much as a week. It is bad strategy to plan to carry out a piece of A/AS-level work the day before it is due to be handed in. Whilst this strategy might have worked for GCSE it is likely to lead to several problems if repeated at A/AS-level. Firstly, the nature of the work means that you will often encounter difficulties that will need advice from your teacher or access to information that is unobtainable until the following day. Secondly, the work may require access to a fully working computer system which you discover is for some reason not available. Thirdly, the demands of A/AS-level are unpredictable and you may find that you have unexpectedly been given some other tasks to complete overnight.

Computing is also a skills-based subject. In order to be successful you must regularly practise the skills that you learn. Therefore, it is vital that your planning incorporates weekly practice sessions during which you make use of the computing facilities on which you will eventually carry out your A/AS-level project work. You should aim to become proficient in these computing facilities by the time this project work begins.

For successful planning you must decide how much work you need to do and how much time you intend to spend on it. You will not study effectively if you work for long periods without a break. After about 40 minutes concentration begins to wane. A break of a few minutes, in which you do something completely different, can soon recharge your batteries and enable you to continue your studying to greater effect. So, try to plan your work so that you fit in these breaks at convenient intervals. The eyes should be rested during these breaks especially after reading text books or working at a VDU. Focusing on a distant object for a minute will do this. *When* you work is very much a personal matter. Some people find that they work best early in the morning, others seem to work better late at night – find out when suits you best and plan accordingly. If you are doing practical work and you do not have your own computer then you will have to find a suitable time to use the facilities at your institution.

Where you work is also important. It is helpful if you have somewhere that you can call 'your own', even if it is only a table in the corner of your bedroom, where you can work without being disturbed. Make the area welcoming. Tidiness plays an important role in maintaining a business-like attitude to the task of studying and reduces the chances of mislaying important notes or references – a situation which can result in increased levels of stress. It should be somewhere away from noise that disturbs but you may find music helpful – some people do actually work better accompanied by background music, despite popular opinion to the contrary. Your surroundings should be comfortable, warm, and most importantly, well lit.

Make sure that you have essential materials readily at hand; writing paper, pencils and pens (several colours are helpful), calculator and books should be kept conveniently nearby.

Reading for A/AS–level

Students who have read too little frequently run into time trouble in written examinations, and have an unfortunate habit of misinterpreting questions. There isn't enough time in an A/AS-level course for your teacher to provide you with all the information you need. You must therefore be prepared to spend time, regularly, just reading. The reading should be wide-ranging and include the course text books, library books and any manuals for the packages and programming languages used. Computer magazines and quality newspapers are also good sources of articles on computing topics, especially applications and devices. The Internet is also a very good source of relevant information.

Coursework

Coursework forms an important and integral part of all A/AS-level syllabuses in computing, so you should have lots of opportunities to develop the necessary practical skills during your course. All A-level and AS-level syllabuses assess a candidate's ability to analyse, design, implement, test, document and evaluate a solution to a practical problem. This is done via a substantial project (for A-level candidates sitting OCEAC computing this is a project plus board-set exercises) carried out over an extended period of time. The coursework element is allocated a significant number of marks representing between 30% and 40% of the overall assessment.

Project
Candidates are expected to tackle a real problem and provide an appropriate computer-based solution. A-level candidates are expected to carry out the work for a *real* user, whilst it may be possible for AS candidates to consider that the work is for a *potential* user. In a two-year course, planning for project work should begin in the second half of the first year with the identification of a problem to be solved and of the user for whom a solution is to be provided. The problem must be one that can be solved using the computing resources that are available and the user must be prepared to submit to an investigation of his/her needs which might take several hours spread over two or three meetings. For an A-level project the user is expected to use the developed system so that feedback may be obtained for evaluation purposes. For AS this requirement may be relaxed, depending on the examining board. Check with your teacher. You should not carry out project work until you have sufficient knowledge and understanding of the techniques, tools and skills that apply.

For analysis, this means methods of fact finding and techniques for modelling the data flow, processing and data requirements such as data flow and entity relationship diagrams. For design, this means methods of processing, file structures and organisations, database theory, pseudocode, algorithms and structure charts, class diagrams for objects and methods, input/output methods and devices, application generators, general-purpose packages, expert system shells. For implementation, this means skill in using a programming language, an application generator, a general-purpose package or an expert system shell. The development of the project must be carefully planned in stages: analysis, design, implementation, testing, documentation, evaluation. A prototype version of the system can be developed first so that ideas can be tried out and user feedback obtained early in the development. Projects must be completed, usually, by the end of the second term in a two-year course.

Internal Assessment of Coursework

Coursework is assessed by your teacher according to a scheme of assessment supplied by the examining board and externally moderated unless you are sitting the NEAB examination, in which case your project will be externally marked. Your teacher will tell you at the start of your course what the planned timetable for coursework assessments is.

Schemes of assessment differ in detail from one board to another, but broadly assess the same range of skills. You will need to obtain a copy of your syllabus if you want to see how the skill areas are organised and marked.

The project report is the primary means by which you are assessed. It is vitally important that the report communicates the effort you have expended and the success you have achieved in producing a working solution. The marks awarded to your coursework will be for the evidence presented in the report. Remember that an external moderator will not sit down at a computer and try your program.

The report should be presented in a tidy and well-organised manner with numbered pages and a list of contents which references the main sections by page number. If it is possible to word-process the document then do so, and make use of a spellchecker. The report should be concise. The main sections of the report should be clearly defined and labelled, and ideally, linked to the assessment sections, e.g. problem definition, analysis, design, implementation, testing, user documentation, evaluation. Evidence must be provided which demonstrates the reliability of the solution and its effectiveness in meeting the end-user's requirements. A comprehensive test plan which lists test data together with expected and actual outcomes is essential. The test data should be chosen carefully so as to demonstrate that normal operations work correctly and anything else such as attempting to enter incorrect data is trapped. A sample in the form of a screen dump or hard copy, video or audio or photographic material of actual output should be included to demonstrate that the system works. The end-user should be involved in testing the system so that direct feedback can be obtained and reported upon.

Revision techniques

Revision is not something that should be left until a few weeks before you sit your A/AS-level examination or module test. In fact, you should be engaged in preparing for revision from your very first lesson. The basis for successful revision is to have a well-organised set of notes on the topics that you are to be examined on. The notes that you make during the course should be legible with any diagrams drawn neatly. The use of coloured pens is recommended so that key facts or words can be made prominent. Reading references should be recorded so that they can be referred to again and a summary made. New notes should be filed immediately in the correct place so that they are not lost. The amount of knowledge to be accumulated is large and must therefore be absorbed and understood as you go along. Make sure that you have tested your understanding of each new concept or piece of knowledge by tackling a few exercises. Always try to be active in your learning by applying your newly gained knowledge in some exercise.

Revision must be planned and must take place regularly to be effective. It is an important part of the learning process. As the examination approaches it will have to become more concentrated.

First of all get *organised*. Devise some form of revision timetable, bearing in mind that learning periods of about 30–40 minutes produce the best recall. Set yourself definite goals, e.g. completion of a specific topic, the attainment of which provides you with satisfaction and encouragement.

Secondly, ensure you *test* yourself regularly. This may take the form of writing out a summary of a topic from memory or the tackling of an actual examination question from a past paper. You will find many examination questions to try in this book.

Thirdly, construct a *list of definitions* that have to be learned and constantly refer to this list until the definitions are memorised.

THE EXAMINATION

Question styles

Before reading on, check your syllabus to confirm the question styles you will meet. Both terminal examinations and module tests include one or more of the following question styles.

Short answers

You are usually expected to answer all the questions, in which case there is no need to read right through the paper or section of the paper; this advice can be important to the many who have time troubles on short-answer papers. However, you should read through each question completely. Frequently, the questions are in several parts which are linked. Ideas from later parts of the question may help you follow the earlier parts. You may avoid the pitfall, for example, of giving an answer in part (a) that is expected in part (b).

Long answers

Most long-answer papers offer you a choice of questions. It is therefore important that you read through the whole of the section containing the long-answer questions before choosing the questions you intend to attempt. If the question itself is long it can often be tackled without much planning; the structure of the question will, in effect, generate the plan for you. However, some parts of long-answer questions carry a significant number of marks. For example, the writing of a sorting algorithm in pseudocode might carry 7 or 8 marks. The answer will need planning, which will involve a significant amount of thinking time as well as time roughing out a solution. This time is allowed for when setting questions. Time troubles are invariably due to either a failure to stick to the terms of reference of the question or a failure to be concise.

Examination techniques

It is vital that you read each question very carefully and think just as carefully before you answer. Take note of the number of marks allocated to the question and gauge the length of your answer accordingly. If *two* points are asked for and you can think of three put all *three* down if it will take little extra effort and time to do so. Your three points may, in fact, only be two distinct points. It may help to underline key phrases and words in each question in the question paper as you read them. This should draw your attention to the need, for example, to make *three different/distinct* points if the question requires it. Remember that the examiners will be assessing the depth of your knowledge and understanding of computing so they expect your answers to reflect this. Simply stating, for example, that it is 'more efficient' for a lending library to use a computer reveals little understanding and knowledge of the advantages of using a computer for such an application. Avoid using words and phrases such as *faster, cheaper, more efficient* on their own. When you have to use them, make sure you show a knowledge of computing to A/AS standard. For example, an answer 'using a faster computer speeds up access to a database' is less likely to gain credit than an answer such as 'using a faster processor can speed up access to a database'. Avoid the trap that many students fall into of simply turning the words of the question around when answering the question. For example, to the question 'what is a *local area network*' the response 'it is a network in a local area' will gain no credit. Some types of question are best answered with the aid of a diagram or the aid of an example even though the question does not request one. For example, 'what is a linked list' can be answered more clearly if reference can be made to a diagram. Make sure that your diagrams are labelled clearly.

Before each examination, make sure that you know what aspects or areas of the syllabus you are going to be tested upon and how long you can afford to spend on each question. For example, writing a pseudocode solution to a problem under examination conditions can be quite tricky. It is very easy to overrun on time with such questions.

Plan how much time you can afford to spend on thinking about, then planning, and finally writing the solution. Use techniques such as structure diagrams and tables to plan the major steps first and use pencil initially to map out a solution. If you get bogged down on a question, leave space on your answer paper/booklet to enable you to return and complete it later, and move on quickly to the next question. It is quite likely that your subconscious will unravel a tricky problem for you as soon as you have set to work on something else.

Finally, make sure that you are answering the question. This is a skill that will only gradually be perfected as you practise throughout your course, and the tutorial notes with the sample questions and answers in this book contain many suggestions that are specifically designed to help you develop this technique.

Name, state, suggest, define, describe, discuss, explain, outline, list, draw, calculate, comment, compare

Questions on all types of examination paper (except multiple choice) may use any of these key words in a question. They all have different meanings and interpreting them incorrectly can be very expensive in terms of marks or time lost.

- *Name* This usually requires a technical term or its equivalent. Answers to this type of question normally involve no more than one or two words. For example, 'name one register involved in the fetch–execute cycle' has as a possible answer: 'the program counter register'.

- *State* falls short of describing and amounts to no more than making bullet points. For example, 'state one advantage of writing programs as a collection of modules' has as a possible answer: 'teams of programmers are able to work on producing individual modules'.

- *Suggest* is used when it is not possible to give the answer directly from facts that form part of the subject material detailed in the syllabus. The answer should be based on general understanding rather than on recall of learnt material. For example, 'suggest a suitable operating system for producing gas bills' has as a possible answer: 'a batch processing operating system'.

- *Define/What is meant by..?* 'Define' requires a statement giving the meaning of a particular term. 'What is meant by.. ?' is used more frequently as it emphasises that a formal definition as such is not required.

- *Describe* means no more than it says: so, 'describe one feature of a graphical user interface (GUI) which is likely to be helpful to a non-technically minded user' requires a description of a feature such as a pictorial icon, in terms of how it makes the selection and execution of an application easier. 'Describe briefly' or 'describe concisely' requires you to report only on the key features.

- *Discuss* Usually you are given something to consider that may or may not be true. You need to indicate the various possibilities, giving evidence for and against each proposition. For example, 'discuss the use of smart cards as all-purpose identity cards' has as a possible answer: 'a single card could replace some or all of the cards that people have currently to carry and in addition could hold additional information such as medical history which might be useful in a medical emergency. However, it is a problem if you lose your card because you lose everything'.

- *Explain* A reason or an interpretation must be given, not a description. Often, an example or a diagram may form part of the explanation.

- *Outline* A brief summary of the main points is required. The best guide to the amount of detail required lies in the mark allocations; approximately one to one and a half minutes should be allowed per mark. This generally works out at around two or three lines in a standard answer booklet for each mark.

- *List* A number of features or points, each often no more than a single word, with no further elaboration or detail is all that is required.

- *Draw* A properly labelled diagram is required.

- *Calculate* This term is reserved for use where the only requirement is a numerical answer. The additional instruction 'show your working' is used if details or method are required.

- *Comment* Usually you are being asked to think about something unusual or slightly strange. You must relate the information supplied for comment to your own knowledge of the topic and draw some conclusion. Answers to these questions are rarely longer than a sentence or two.

- *Compare* Two or more items have to be compared with each other. You must describe similarities and differences between them. It will not be necessary to describe each item in detail unless the question asks you to 'compare and describe' or 'compare and discuss'.

Taking module tests

If you are taking a modular syllabus, you will sit module tests set by the board during your course. Although these tests cover the limited range of content comprising the relevant module, the questions are A-level standard and therefore preparation for a module test must be just as careful as for terminal examinations. Most of the comments made in the section 'Final preparation' therefore apply to module tests as well as to terminal examinations. However, there are some important differences:

- Revision for a module test involves only coverage of topics in the module.
- On-going revision from the start of a module is crucial since extensive revision time is unlikely to be available before a module test.
- Module papers are A-level standard.
- Module results are reported on higher education references and therefore it is important to do as well as possible in a module test, even though you may be allowed a further attempt at the module at a later date.
- In a modular course, there is unlikely to be much time between a mock module paper and the actual paper. It is therefore important to analyse your mock performance rapidly and to act on gaps in knowledge pinpointed by your answers.

Final preparation

You will need to plan and prepare carefully for your final examinations. Your mock examinations or previous module tests will give you an estimate of where you have reached in your preparations. If you plan this last stage carefully and stick to your plans, you should be able to fit in some social activities to prevent mental fatigue setting in. Examinations are a test of stamina, organisation and resilience, in addition to the obvious test of knowledge.

Before your mock examinations

Revise thoroughly all the work you have covered from the start of the course. Use the syllabus checklist as a 'ticklist' for revising work covered and don't attempt to revise topics not yet covered in class. Pay particular attention to the topics you covered in the first year of your course as these form the foundation for later topics. Make sure that you check your understanding by attempting past paper questions.

After your mock examinations

Go over your mock papers and pinpoint gaps in your knowledge and make sure you fill them. Look for strengths and weaknessess in terms of performance on different sections of your papers. Your teacher should give you feedback on where you can improve and where you are doing well. With careful and thorough revision between the mocks and the final exams, you can improve considerably if your marks were not as good as you'd hoped for.

As your syllabus reaches completion

- Make out a revision timetable covering all your subjects. Allocate set times for each subject on a weekly timetable and make sure you allow some time for relaxation.

- Within your overall revision timetable, make up a computing revision schedule on a topic-by-topic basis, with a full round of detailed revision to be completed by at least one week before the examination. This will leave time for a further round of targeted revision in the final week.

- Stick to your revision schedule and tick off the topics as you revise them. Use the questions in this book to check your grasp of the subject and your answer techniques. The question commentaries should prove useful and the answers to all questions are supplied. Your teacher should be able to supply you with past papers and mark schemes. Use these as you do your topic-by-topic revision, keeping a checklist of the questions you have answered. The mark schemes are published by most boards. They are the documents that the examiners use when marking candidates' scripts. They show what marks are to be awarded for. They are necessarily brief and are not written in the style of model answers but they clearly indicate what is expected.

In the last few weeks

Once you have completed the cycle of detailed revision, try some past papers under exam conditions. Section 3 is designed for this purpose and you can check your performance against the answers. Use the commentaries *immediately* after you have tackled the questions to make sure your approach to each was appropriate.

In the last week

Make out a further revision schedule, taking account of when your exams are and what type of questions are on each paper. There is not much point revising options after the first paper if the options were on the first paper. You should aim to revise as much of the syllabus as possible at a broad level for those papers where all questions have to be attempted and then target specific topics with detailed revision for those papers with longer questions where you have a choice of which to answer.

The night before the exam

Everyone is agreed that the night before the exam you should be as relaxed as possible. We do not recommend any revision, nor do we recommend a late night which will leave you tired and jaded for the exam the next day. Go to bed early in the knowledge that any further revision will only diminish your performance.

The day of the exam

- *Don't* enter the exam room without a plan for tackling that specific examination paper. This will enable you to avoid time trouble or choosing the wrong questions.

- *Do* ensure that your calculator batteries will not run out during the exam, that you have spare pens (blue or black ink) and sharpened pencils and a ruler and a rubber. All boards have banned the use of correction fluids. Do not write in any colour other than blue or black.

- *Be* early for the examination so you can check the location of the exam room and be in the correct state of mind to tackle the exam.

- *Don't* drink (alcohol) before an exam, or eat too little or too much.

- *Don't* sit an examination if you are unwell without informing the invigilator *before* the start of the paper.

- *Don't* sit an examination without a convenient means of keeping track of the time that is elapsing.

During the examination

- *Do* read all the questions. Many students form too early an opinion of a question after reading only the first part when a more careful reading of all parts would have revealed much that could have been tackled successfully.

- *Don't* spend too much time on one question.

- *Don't* dive into a question without reading the entire question and devoting a little thought as to how best to answer the question.

- *Do* leave plenty of space to finish questions that you leave when you run into difficulties.

- *Do* write in short sentences, avoiding too many 'ands' and 'buts' in mid-sentence. This leads to greater clarity of expression.

- *Do* read through your answers and check for mistakes when you have completed the required number of questions.

- *Do* call the invigilator *immediately* you have any problem, or if you have an urgent need to leave the room.

- *Do* take great care to make sure that any loose sheets of your script are securely tied to your answer booklet, and that all sheets/booklets bear your name and all the relevant information before you hand them in.

After the examination

- *Don't* fret over the many 'obvious' mistakes you will have made and should have avoided. All the other candidates will have made similar errors, and there is nothing you can do to retrieve the situation.

- *Do* forget the paper and start to prepare for the next one. Think positively and only carry out an inquest on a paper you have just sat if similar material may appear on a paper you have still to sit (i.e. if you can learn from your mistakes).

- *Do* remember that if you have found a paper hard, it's likely that so will the rest of the candidates (whether they are ready to admit it or not); this could simply mean that the 'pass mark' on this paper could be correspondingly lower.

- *Don't* get overconfident if you found the paper easy (for the opposite reasons to the previous piece of advice).

A-LEVEL COMPUTING

Each chapter features:

- *units in this chapter:* a list of the main topic heads to follow;

- *chapter objectives:* key ideas and skills which are covered in the chapter are introduced;

- *the main text:* this is divided into numbered topic units for ease of reference;

- *chapter roundup:* a brief summary of the chapter;

- *question bank:* exam questions with tutorial comments on the pitfalls to avoid and points to include in framing your own answers.

APPLICATIONS OF COMPUTERS

Units in this chapter

Chapter objectives

After working through the topics in this chapter, you should be able to:

- describe how computers are used in a variety of contexts;
- describe the main features and capabilities of CAD/CAM systems, robots and expert systems;
- describe the main features and use of common application packages such as word-processing, desk-top publishing, spreadsheets and graphics packages;
- distinguish between bitmapped and vector graphics;
- describe the benefits and drawbacks of computerisation to an organisation, its employees and members of the public;
- discuss the effects of computerisation from a social, legal or economic point of view;
- describe the main clauses of the Data Protection Act and copyright laws.

1.1 GENERAL APPLICATION AREAS

The range of computer applications is vast, covering all the areas mentioned in this chapter as well as a great many more, and you need to develop a general knowledge and awareness of a variety of application areas. The best way of doing this is to read widely, – newspapers, relevant magazines and textbooks, and to watch documentary programs such as Tomorrow's World on TV.

For any application, you should be prepared to explain

- the purpose of the application;
- the overall system design;
- how data is captured and input to the computer;
- what hardware is used;
- what provision could be made for system failure;
- the effect of the computer system on individuals in organisations and on society in general.

For example, you could be asked how computers are being used to

- increase the safety of people travelling in cars on a motorway;
- help catch criminals;
- design aircraft, etc.

1.2 COMMUNICATION AND INFORMATION SYSTEMS

Computers are widely used for communications using local and wide area networks. *Electronic mail* is used by both individuals and organisations, and is discussed in more detail in Chapter 9.

The *World Wide Web* is a huge collection of data stored on computers throughout the world and accessible to anyone with a computer, a modem and a subscription to a service provider such as Compuserve.

When discussing in general terms the advantages to a business of computerisation, don't forget that the ability to communicate with other parts of the organisation via e-mail, and the ability to access relevant information via the Internet are good points to make.

1.3 COMMERCIAL AND GENERAL DATA PROCESSING

All businesses face keen competition from others in the same field, and all medium and large businesses are constantly implementing new and innovative uses of computers and information technology to help them gain a competitive edge over their rivals. The way in which computers are used and the benefits that accrue fall into several different categories:

1. *Applications that are common to the majority of businesses,* e.g. payroll and company accounts. The advantages of using computers for these applications include faster and more accurate data processing, a possible reduction in staff costs from the

corresponding manual methods, more information available to management on, for example, bad debts, payroll costs, trends within the company.

2. *Applications that result in a competitive advantage*, e.g. the gathering of information about customer purchases by a large grocery chain using a loyalty card, or the use of market research surveys to establish buying patterns.

3. *Applications specific to a particular industry or organisation*, e.g. hospitals may install sophisticated administration systems, hotels may have computerised booking systems, banks have automated procedures for handling cheques and paying-in slips as well as numerous other types of transaction. Advantages of computerisation include reduction in staffing costs, better service to customers and reduced paperwork.

1.4 CAD/CAM

Computer-aided design (CAD)

Computer-aided design (CAD) systems generally consist of a complete hardware and software package, ranging from micro systems available from around £1,000 to sophisticated systems used in aircraft and automobile design costing hundreds of thousands of pounds. The benefits of CAD can be summed up as

- accuracy;
- repeatability;
- speed and flexibility of production.

Specialised hardware for CAD systems

A CAD workstation may be a stand-alone system, possibly linked to other workstations so that peripherals can be shared, or it may be connected to a mini- or mainframe computer. A powerful processor is required because showing an object in three dimensions, rotating it and manipulating it requires thousands of calculations to be made by the software. In addition, a range of devices described below may be used:

- a high resolution CRT display;
- an additional monitor for displaying commands entered by the operator;
- a keyboard for entering commands;
- a graphics tablet which contains a grid that corresponds to the resolution of the CRT, so that, using a hand-held cursor or stylus (pen), coordinates on the tablet can be mapped directly onto the screen;
- a light pen, which allows the user to pick up a point or character on the screen and cause some action to be taken;
- a plotter to produce high-quality drawings;
- a printer, typically laser or inkjet.

CAD software

CAD systems vary enormously in their capabilities. The more sophisticated systems allow a user to:

- use real-world coordinates; if you were drawing the plan for a room, you would enter the actual room dimensions;
- draw straight lines and polygons, shading them if required;
- draw mathematically defined curves including circles, arcs, ellipses, parabolas and hyperbolas;
- move sections of a drawing to a different location;
- scale an object (i.e. increase or decrease its size);

- rotate an object;
- zoom in on a section of drawing;
- show a drawing from any angle;
- calculate the centre of gravity of an object.

Computer-aided manufacturing

A complete CAD/CAM (*see* Computer-aided manufacturing) system will enable, say, an engineering component to be designed and manufactured using numerically controlled machine tools. The computer performs the calculations for defining the tool path and generates the instructions necessary to produce the part.

1.5 ROBOTICS AND CONTROL SYSTEMS

Robots are used in hundreds of applications from car assembly and spray painting, maintenance of overhead high-voltage cables or underwater maintenance on oil rigs, to testing blood samples and patrolling buildings at night to check for build-up of gas, smoke or humidity.

Robots all have the same basic hardware components:

- **sensors** which detect changes such as temperature, speed, position, pressure etc. These are all things which vary continuously in time;
- **transducers** which convert these analogue signals into analogue voltages;
- **analogue-to-digital converters** which convert the voltages into discrete digital values which can be processed by the computer;
- a **microprocessor** to process the information;
- **actuators** to produce movement or alter the environment in some way, for example by turning a switch on or off.

The advantages of robots are

- They can work in environments that are hazardous to humans, such as underwater or in radioactive environments.
- They can tirelessly perform repetitive and monotonous tasks.
- Quality of work produced is consistent, since they never get bored or have an off-day.
- They can work to a greater level of accuracy than humans.
- Robots can work 24 hours a day, resulting in increased productivity.

However, robots are expensive to buy and install, and often production methods and factory layouts have to be completely redesigned. In some cases people may be easier to retrain than robots for a one-off, low-volume order, for example.

1.6 ARTIFICIAL INTELLIGENCE AND EXPERT SYSTEMS

One definition of artificial intelligence proposed in 1977 is 'the science of making machines perform tasks that would require intelligence if done by people'. However, this definition breaks down because computers can do many things such as performing lightning-fast computations, spell check a long document or remember thousands of telephone numbers and none of these is a good example of what is commonly meant by artificial intelligence. Perhaps a better definition is the following:

Artificial intelligence (AI) is the study of how to make computers do things which, at the moment, people do better.

AI encompasses many fields such as pattern recognition, (used in recognising handwriting, people's faces and speech patterns, and in robot vision), natural language processing (getting a computer to understand ordinary English) and neural computing which attempts to mimic the way in which the human brain works. One aspect of artificially intelligent computers is that they should be *capable of learning and therefore improving their performance at a given task.*

Expert systems

An expert system is a computer program that encapsulates the knowledge of one or more human experts. It can store facts and rules about a specific area of knowledge, and can then use this knowledge base to deliver advice to a user. For example, an expert system used by the construction industry stores thousands of facts and rules governing costs associated with constructing various types of building, taking into account type of ground, floor area, number of storeys, type of heating required and so on. When a construction company wants to work out the estimated cost of a new building, they enter the requirements and the expert system comes up with a cost. (This is traditionally the job of a quantity surveyor, who would take several days to perform the complex calculations manually that the expert system can do in a matter of seconds.)

Medical diagnosis is another field well suited to the capabilities of an expert system.

Components of an expert system

An expert system has three basic components:

* a *knowledge base* containing all the facts and rules associated with the subject;
* an *inference engine*, which is the means of using that knowledge. This could be, for example, a program written in Prolog;
* a *user interface* to provide straightforward communication between the user and the computer.

   An expert system has the following facilities:

* It stores the facts and rules associated with a particular field of knowledge.
* It asks the user questions relevant to the problem (e.g. 'How many storeys will the building have?').
* It can handle 'don't know' answers.
* It allows the user to change an answer to explore a 'what-if' situation.
* It makes reasonable deductions.
* It explains how it reaches its conclusions.

Advantages of an expert system

* The knowledge is always 'on tap' (available) whereas a human expert is not always there when you need one.
* The knowledge is not lost if the expert falls under a bus.
* An expert system may, in a few seconds, be able to reach a conclusion based on complex calculations that would take a human days or weeks to perform.
* It bases its decisions purely on logic; emotion does not come into play.

Disadvantages of an expert system

* It is inflexible: in certain circumstances, the application of pure logic may be detrimental. For example, if an expert system were used to determine sentences for criminal offenders, it may not take account of exceptional circumstances which it has not encountered.

- A human expert who uses an expert system may be reluctant to contradict a decision even though his/her instincts may dictate otherwise. For example a doctor may accept a diagnosis for fear of litigation.
- A human may become over-reliant on the expert system, and rubber-stamp its decisions without thinking about them.

1.7 COMPUTERS IN EDUCATION

Computer-aided learning is used in numerous different situations from teaching multiplication tables to primary school children to teaching airline pilots to handle the latest model of a jumbo jet. Many applications make use of **multimedia**, meaning that the software training package will include some or all of the following: text, graphics, animation, video clips, scanned photographs and sound.

In order to produce interactive educational software, an **authoring package** (e.g. *Authorware*) may be used. This allows the programmer to import sound and graphics files, create animations, and program questions and responses.

The benefits of computer-aided learning include the following:

- The student can work at his/her own pace, and go over material as many times as needed.
- In a work situation, learning can often take place at an employee's own desk, saving the expense of sending him/her away on a course.
- In the case of a flight simulator, for example, real-life situations can be simulated and the student can learn without the danger of crashing an aircraft.

1.8 GENERIC PACKAGES

Word-processing

Word-processing software is used to write letters, technical reports, books and articles and any other documents that in the past would have been typed on a typewriter. Below is a summary of the facilities offered by a typical word-processor.

- type, correct, delete and move text;
- change font and font size, align text left, right or centre, set tabs, set italics and bold;
- find and replace text;
- insert graphics;
- check spelling and grammar;
- set up templates with type styles for different types of document;
- work in tables or columns;
- add headers or footers to each page;
- automatically create indexes and tables of contents;
- type equations with maths symbols;
- integrate with a database to send personalised letters to people selected from a database (mail merge).

Desk-top publishing

Desk-top publishing is an extension of word-processing, allowing the user to lay out each page exactly as he or she wants it. Frequently text is prepared using a word-processor and then imported into a DTP package to be laid out in, for example, a newspaper format. Additional facilities provided by a desk-top publishing package include the ability to

- work in columns (more easily than in a word-processor);
- wrap text around a graphic;
- design complex page layouts;
- control the spacing between characters to achieve the best possible page layout.

Spreadsheets

Spreadsheets are used by people who work with numbers: accountants, bank and building society employees, engineers, financial planners and teachers keeping student results. The user enters the data and the formulae to be used in manipulating or summarising the data and the program calculates the results.

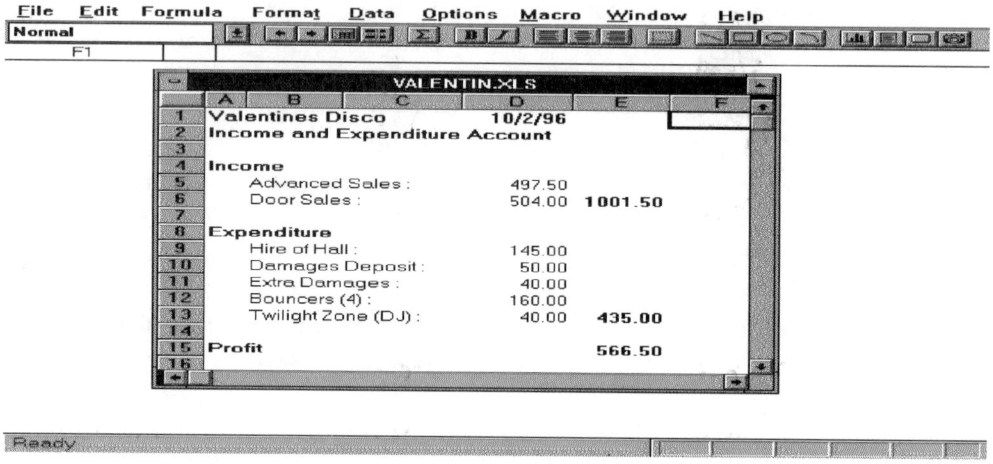

| File | Edit | Formula | Format | Data | Options | Macro | Window | Help |

Normal

F1

VALENTIN.XLS

	A	B	C	D	E	F
1	Valentines Disco			10/2/96		
2	Income and Expenditure Account					
3						
4	Income					
5		Advanced Sales :		497.50		
6		Door Sales :		504.00	1001.50	
7						
8	Expenditure					
9		Hire of Hall :		145.00		
10		Damages Deposit :		50.00		
11		Extra Damages :		40.00		
12		Bouncers (4) :		160.00		
13		Twilight Zone (DJ) :		40.00	435.00	
14						
15	Profit				566.50	
16						

Ready

Figure 1.1: Example spreadsheet

Facilities offered by a typical spreadsheet package include the ability to:
- increase or decrease column width;
- insert or delete cells, rows and columns;
- copy or move blocks of cells;
- display numbers in a particular format, e.g. to two decimal places;
- use many built-in mathematical and statistical functions;
- automatically recalculate results when a field value is changed;
- create a graph or bar chart from figures in the spreadsheet;
- automate a series of steps using a **macro**, i.e. a sequence of instructions typed into the spreadsheet.

A particularly useful feature of a spreadsheet is its ability to allow the user to perform 'What-if' calculations; that is, quickly try out a number of different possibilities for say, budgeted sales figures to look at the consequent profits.

Graphics packages

Graphics packages fall into either one of two categories: **bitmapped** (*see* Fig 1.2) (also known as **pixel-based**) and **vector-based** (*see* Fig 1.3) (also known as object-oriented). Paint programs and scanners produce bitmapped images in the form of a collection of pixels, the smallest visual unit the computer can address. These applications create images by altering the colours or attributes of each individual pixel, and the amount of memory taken up by the image is dependent on the resolution of the display adaptor where the image was first created. As a result, finished bitmap images are difficult to edit when you transfer them from one application to another. If you increase the size of a finished bitmap image, you see unsightly white spaces and jagged edges. If you greatly decrease the size of a finished bitmap image, parts of the image may 'smudge' because of the compression involved. Distortion can occur if you transfer bitmapped images to another computer with a different resolution.

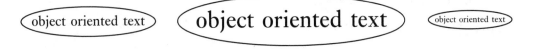

Figure 1.2: Bitmapped graphic image

Object-oriented graphics, on the other hand, have none of these limitations. The information used to create and represent a drawing is geometric data, rather than graphic data. For example, a line is defined by its endpoints, length, width, colour and so on. A vector-based graphics package then uses this information to create a representation of the line on the computer screen. Since this method of storing information has nothing to do with the resolution of a given display adaptor, line-art is considered to be device-independent. No matter what computer you use to create an object-oriented graphic, you can stretch, scale and resize it flexibly without distortion. Object-oriented graphics also tend to create smaller files than bitmapped images because the computer does not have to store the attributes of each individual pixel.

object oriented text   object oriented text   object oriented text

Figure 1.3: Vector-based graphic image

1.9 LEGAL IMPLICATIONS OF THE USE OF COMPUTERS

The Data Protection Act 1984

In the 1970s and early 1980s, the number of institutions such as banks, hospitals, department stores and police forces which stored data about people on computers continued to increase. Concern grew that an individual could be harmed by the existence of data that was inaccurate or misleading, and which could be transferred to a third party without the knowledge or permission of the individual.

The Data Protection Act is an attempt to protect individuals from misuse of data that is held about them on various computer systems. It contains eight principles, summarised as follows:

Personal data must:

1. be obtained and processed fairly and lawfully;
2. be held for specified purposes;
3. not be used for any reason incompatible with its original purpose;
4. be relevant and adequate;
5. be accurate and up-to-date;
6. not be kept longer than necessary;

7. be made available to the individual concerned and provision made for corrections;

8. be kept secure.

'Personal data' means any data relating to a living person who can be identified by it, for example by name.

The Act established the office of Registrar, whose duties include administering a public register of data users, investigating complaints and initiating prosecutions for breaches of the Act. All data users have to register, giving:

1. their name and address (or that of their company);

2. a description of the data held and its purpose;

3. a description of the sources from which the data is obtained;

4. a description of the persons to whom it is intended to disclose data.

Exemptions from the Act

- The Act does not apply to payroll, pensions and accounts data, nor to names and addresses held for distribution purposes.

- Subjects do not have a right to access data if the sole aim of collecting it is for statistical or research purposes, or where it is simply for backup.

- Data can be disclosed to the data subject's agent (e.g. lawyer or accountant), to persons working for the data user, and in response to urgent need to prevent injury or damage to health.

In addition, there are exemptions for special categories, including data held

- in connection with national security;

- for prevention of crime;

- for the collection of tax or duty.

Copyright

Computer software is covered by the Copyright, Designs and Patents Act 1988. For the purposes of the Act, a computer program is a literary work, and copyright is infringed if it is 'stored or adapted' without permission. This means it is illegal to

- copy software;

- run pirated software;

- transmit software over a telecommunications line, thereby creating a copy.

The Computer Misuse Act 1990

This Act was passed in response to the growing threat to computer systems of hacking and viruses. A **virus** is a computer program which is able to copy itself without the user intending it, and usually without being noticed, until it causes some damage such as corrupting or deleting files or directory entries.

The Act created three new offences:

1. unauthorised access to computer programs or data;

2. unauthorised access with a further criminal intent;

3. unauthorised modification of computer material (i.e. programs and data).

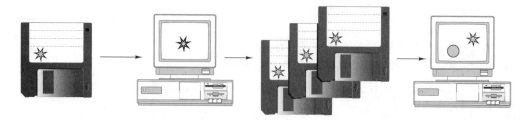

Figure 1.4: How a virus works

1.10 SOCIAL, ETHICAL AND ECONOMIC IMPLICATIONS OF COMPUTERISATION

Computers have found their way into every type of job, and have changed the work environment for millions of workers. Many jobs have disappeared for ever (such as many factory production line jobs), other jobs such as secretarial work have changed, and many new jobs have been created (computer programming and analysis, manufacturing and repairing new products, teaching new skills).

Some jobs may be de-skilled, for example a clerical worker who had a varied office job doing filing and typing may be re-hired as a data entry clerk doing a mindless repetitive job eight hours a day. In other cases, computerisation may bring an increase in skills required and job satisfaction; some clerical workers may be given responsibility for using word-processors, spreadsheets and databases, e-mail and fax machines. While some may enjoy the new challenges, others may be frustrated doing highly technical work with inadequate training.

Codes of practice

Codes of practice, such as those produced by the British Computer Society, set professional standards of competence, conduct and ethical practice for computing in the United Kingdom. The code is separate from any legal requirements, but professionals within the industry are expected to follow the code.

Health hazards

Health hazards from spending long hours keying in data include

- repetitive strain injury (RSI), resulting in painful arms and wrists and an inability to perform simple tasks like picking up a teapot or doing any further typing;
- eyestrain from staring at a screen for long periods;
- backache from sitting too long in one position on an uncomfortable chair.

A European Community directive on the health requirements for working with VDUs includes clauses such as those outlined below:

- Employees' work must be planned in such a way that VDU work is periodically interrupted by breaks or changes in activity.
- All employers must undertake an analysis of workstations to evaluate the risks to eyesight, physical problems and mental stress, and take appropriate action to remedy any risks found.
- Technical requirements for the design of workstations are laid down – for example, the keyboard must be separate from the screen, the chair must allow freedom of movement, be adjustable in height and tiltable.

The future

The number and variety of computer applications is continually growing. We are already seeing the beginnings of

- automobile navigation systems;
- electronic shopping;
- computer-controlled artificial limbs;
- telephones and televisions integrated into computer terminals;
- a cashless society.

We can no longer live in our society without computers, but most people would agree that they have contributed to a rise in our standard of living and would be reluctant to give up the conveniences they bring.

Chapter summary

Chapter 1 has covered just some of the applications of computing that you may be asked to discuss. It gives a brief overview of CAD/CAM, robotics, artificial intelligence and expert systems and commonly used software packages. The legal implications of computing have been discussed, and the benefits and drawbacks that computers bring.

Illustrative questions

1 Give three points a user should consider before deciding to purchase a software package. (3)
(*NEAB*)

Tutorial note
In this sort of question try and draw on your own experience or imagination, and think in terms of specifics rather than generalities. For example, what would *you* consider before buying a word-processing package, a graphics package, a database package? In general, avoid one-word answers such as 'cost', 'suitability', 'availability' which rarely score marks unless some explanation or justification is given.

Suggested answer

Three points:
- Will the software run on existing hardware, or will the hardware have to be changed or upgraded, resulting in extra expense?
- Is the software 'user-friendly' or will it be extremely difficult to master?
- Will it integrate, if required, with other packages already purchased?

2 Describe the main components of an expert system. (4)
(*EDEXCEL*)

Tutorial note
Remember the three basic components of an expert system. It is not essential to write down the technical terms such as 'inference engine' so long as you can *describe* the components.

Suggested answer
An expert system consists of a knowledge base of facts and rules, and facilities to deliver advice to a user by successively applying the facts and rules to answers which the user gives in response to questions posed by the software. It should be able to deal with 'don't know' answers and explain its reasoning to the user.

3 A computer chess game is described by a magazine as using artificial intelligence. Describe what you would look for in the game to decide whether the claim was correct. (4)
(*NEAB*)

Suggested answer
Going by the definition of artificial intelligence as 'the science of making machines perform tasks that would require intelligence if done by people', a chess game that can beat an average player is using artificial intelligence. However, another definition of an artificially intelligent computer is that it should be capable of learning and improving its performance. Therefore if the human player made a given series of moves and beat the computer once, would the computer try a different strategy against the same moves until

it eventually won? If so it is definitely using artificial intelligence.

4   An expert system attempts to automate the knowledge and reasoning of a human
    expert.
    (a) An expert system has at least three components, a knowledge base, an inference
        engine and a user interface.
        Describe the function of *each* component.   (3)
    (b) The knowledge base is separate from the inference engine and the user
        interface. What are the advantages of keeping the knowledge base separate?
                                                                                (2)
    (c) Why is it important that an expert system is able to justify its reasoning?   (2)
    (d) State *two* differences between an expert system and a human expert.   (2)
                                                                            (SQA)

Suggested answer
(a) The knowledge base stores the facts and rules provided by a human expert.
    The inference engine makes use of the facts and rules to help a user come to a
    decision or solve a problem.
    The user interface is the means by which the user and computer communicate, for
    example the computer asks questions in ordinary English and the user responds
    appropriately.
(b) The advantages of keeping the knowledge base separate are that
    • the same inference engine and user interface can be used with many different
      fields of knowledge
    • changes and additions can be made to the knowledge base without affecting the
      other components of the system.
(c) During the development of the expert system, the designer will be able to trace errors
    in the knowledge base or the inference engine by examining how the expert system
    arrived at its conclusions. Secondly, a user needs to know how the expert system
    reached its conclusions in order to have confidence in those conclusions, and so that
    he or she can change certain answers to perform 'what-if' calculations where
    answers are perhaps uncertain.
(d) A human expert may ignore certain relevant facts because of an in-built prejudice or
    bias, whereas an expert system will always be entirely logical. On the other hand
    a human expert may be able to jump to an immediate correct conclusion because of
    some intuitive understanding of a situation, whereas nothing is 'obvious' to a
    computer, which has to follow the facts and rules given.

5   **Teleworking** describes people using computers, telephone lines and related
    technologies to work from their own homes rather than travelling to a central office.
    (a) Describe the recent technological developments that have made teleworking
        possible.   (4)
    (b) Summarise briefly the major effects of teleworking on the workers and on society
        in general.   (4)
                                                                          (UCLES)

Tutorial note
Part (a) demands some knowledge of the recent history of computers and also telephone
systems and how they are changing. Part (b) is asking you to use your imagination
and/or demonstrate a good general knowledge of computer-related issues. As well as
the suggested answer, you could consider the downside of teleworking, such as having
no social contact with colleagues, and no-one to ask for help when needed.

Suggested answer
(a) The number of circuits that can be put onto a single memory chip has vastly
    increased and continues to increase every year, making it economic to have a
    powerful computer at home.
    The capacity of hard disks has also increased enormously from a typical 32 Mb a

few years ago to 1 Gb and more, making it possible to store complex software and large amounts of data.

High-speed digital telecommunications links have been developed, with optic fibre replacing conventional cable, resulting in vastly increased capacity for data transfer. Better and faster modems and ISDN connections mean that large files can be transferred between office and home much faster, making it more economical to access a company database, for example.

(b) The teleworker is able to work to a more flexible schedule, and can more easily fit work around other commitments such as picking children up from school. Time is saved by not having to travel to work, and this also saves pollution and means less traffic on the road and less congestion in car parks. Having people work at home means fewer offices are required.

6 Give three categories of crime identified under the Computer Misuse Act. (3)
(NEAB)

Tutorial note
This is a 'recall' type of question, but even if you have not studied the Computer Misuse Act, you may be able to make some intelligent guesses!

Suggested answer
Unauthorised access to computer programs or data (hacking).
Unauthorised access with a further criminal intent (e.g. unauthorised copying).
Unauthorised modification of computer material (i.e. programs and data) – introducing a virus would come into this category.

7 Many Health Areas are introducing computerised systems to manage the scheduling and routing of ambulances. Give *two* different reasons why computerised systems are particularly suitable for this use. Justify each answer. (4)
(AEB)

Tutorial note
Try to think of specific tasks that computers could perform in this context, and explain why each is useful. For example, a computer could *find the fastest route to a destination* and this would be helpful because it would *minimise response time*. Can you think of two other tasks?

Suggested answer
The software can search for the nearest ambulance, which will ensure that resources are used as efficiently as possible and minimise response time. The computer can organise the scheduling of outpatients to make maximum use of available ambulances.

8 The use of video cameras, linked to computers, for the control and monitoring of traffic and road use is increasing. Suggest and briefly explain *two* ways in which such systems can help to make driving on our roads safer and less frustrating. (4)
(AEB)

Tutorial note
As in Question 4, think of specific examples. For example, cameras linked to computers *can detect accidents* and *notify the police immediately*.

Suggested answer
Video cameras can automatically record the number plates of cars exceeding the speed limit, and the computer can search the DVLC database to find the owners and send out speeding fine notices.

Video cameras can detect potential traffic jams and change the phase of traffic lights to defuse the situation.

9 A national chain of garages requires a vehicle exhaust-fume monitoring system suitable for installation on its forecourts. The system is to be coin operated by customers, producing a printed analysis of exhaust gas composition, a report of engine efficiency and a statement of whether or not the vehicle complies with environmental standards. Describe a suitable hardware configuration, assuming that an appropriate probe is available. (4)
(EDEXCEL)

Tutorial note
Sensing devices are used in hundreds of applications and you need to know the basic components of a system that accepts analogue measurements and transforms them to the digital format that a computer can process. The term 'hardware configuration' simply means the individual components of hardware that make up the complete system – some of them should be fairly obvious!

Suggested answer
The hardware required will be
- a money slot to activate the computer;
- a coin-weighing device producing digital input for the CPU;
- a probe connected to the CPU via an interface;
- an analogue-to-digital converter to translate the analogue input to binary;
- a printer to print the report for the customer.

10 State an appropriate application for a spreadsheet package in the office of a small manufacturing company, and describe three features of the package which would be beneficial within the context of this application. (4)
(EDEXCEL)

Tutorial note
Avoid one-word generalities such as 'Accounts' and try to add in some specifics. Remember that spreadsheets are often used in budgeting as well as keeping current accounts.

Suggested answer
A **spreadsheet** may be used in comparing monthly sales and profits with budgeted figures.
Three features of the package which would be beneficial are
- ability to produce graphs and charts;
- macros for automatic data entry into the correct cells;
- formulae to give totals, averages etc.

11 A mail-order book club holds its customer data on a computer file. The club wishes to contact those customers who have not ordered a book for one year or more. Briefly describe the stages involved in the necessary mail merge. (3)
(NEAB)

Tutorial note
It is very helpful to have done a mail merge yourself in order to answer this type of question. In Word 6, for example, select Tools/Mail Merge and you will see that there are three stages involved: create document, get data, merge data.

Suggested answer
The standard letter is typed in the word-processor using field names from the database instead of actual names; e.g.

Dear <Title> <Surname>.

The customer database is then queried to find all customers whose last order date is more than one year ago, and these records placed in a separate temporary file.

The file is then linked to the letter so that the correct fields are inserted on each letter to all the selected customers.

12 Many governments have passed laws which restrict the uses that may be made of data stored in computers.

(a) Identify the problems such legislation is designed to overcome, and describe the main features of the legislation which cover these problems. (6)

(b) Why is there not, usually, similar legislation for data held in other forms? (2)

(EDEXCEL)

Tutorial note

Part (a) is a question about the Data Protection Act. You will not be required to give *all* the clauses – but you should be able to write down at least four. Part (b) requires you to think why it would be impractical to have similar legislation for data held, say, in filing cabinets.

Suggested answer

(a) With the rapid proliferation of networked computers and databases, there have been growing fears that information about individuals stored on computer files could be misused without the individual's knowledge. There were also fears that misleading or inaccurate information about an individual could be held and passed on to other organisations, such as wrong financial information which could lead to a bad credit rating.

The Data Protection Act 1984 has clauses to ensure that

- personal data must be obtained legally and fairly;
- personal data may only be held for one or more specified purposes;
- the data must be accurate and up to date;
- an individual is entitled to examine the data held about him/her and have it corrected where necessary.

(b) The main danger with computerised data is that large volumes of data can be sent anywhere in the world at very high speed and little cost, whereas it would be so time-consuming and expensive to photocopy and post manual files of information to other organisations that this is unlikely to happen. Therefore there is no need for similar legislation for non-computerised data.

13 A designer in a sector of manufacturing industry is using a workstation with a CAD package. As the designer develops a 2D drawing on the screen, at regular intervals each stage can be added to a hard copy *on the same single sheet of paper* so that at any time this sheet of paper reflects the current state of the designer's drawing as it appears on the screen. The workstation utilises a co-processor to enable the designer to manipulate the 3D image of a drawing.

(a) Outline two advantages which CAD offers manufacturing industry. (4)

(b) Describe, with the aid of examples, the fundamental difference between an object-oriented CAD package and a pixel-based general drawing package. (6)

(c) Describe, and explain the need for, three features of a CAD workstation which distinguish it from a workstation used in a typical business application. (6)

(d) Compare the operation of a plotter and a dot-matrix printer in producing hard copy of a line drawing. Indicate, giving reasons for your answer, the suitability or otherwise of each for producing hard copy required by the designer in this case. (8)

(e) Describe briefly the operation of a co-processor and explain why it is likely to be needed for the manipulation of 3D images. (6)

(NICCEA)

Tutorial note

This is a fairly straightforward question testing your knowledge of CAD systems – be sure to avoid answers such as 'CAD is faster and more accurate' which while true are too superficial to score marks. Make sure you know the difference between object-oriented CAD packages ('vector graphics') and pixel-based 'Paint' packages for part (b).

Suggested answer

(a) Engineers and designers make extensive use of drawings and plans which frequently have to be changed or re-scaled as the design process proceeds. The use of CAD can eliminate much of this tedious and time-consuming work. Once the drawings and plans have been created using CAD they can be manipulated and re-scaled in all sorts of ways.

Libraries of standard components can be purchased or created and reused as appropriate in any design.

(b) In a pixel-based drawing package the points on the screen (pixels) which make up the shape are calculated directly using formulae and lit up. Thus, when a circle has to be drawn the formula for the equation of a circle will be used to light up the circle of points on the screen. The circle exists only as a series of pixels – no other record is kept. With an object-oriented package, the graphical relationships between parts of a drawing are stored mathematically. Thus a circle will be stored using its central position and its radius. This defines the circle uniquely when it is displayed and applies even when zooming in or out takes place.

(c) A puck and graphics tablet to enable fast and simple data entry into the CAD system. The graphics tablet contains a template showing function boxes and grids. The puck can be used for accurate positioning on these grids and hence for accurate positioning of a cursor on the screen.

A very high-resolution full colour screen/monitor with a sophisticated graphics adapter to enable design details to be displayed accurately and realistically.

Very large capacity hard disk drive (perhaps as part of a network) for the storage of a large number of images/designs each of which will require large amounts of storage space.

(d) A plotter operates by moving a pen in two dimensions over a page. The computer feeds the plotter with appropriate *x* and *y* coordinates and the pen is moved accordingly.

A dot-matrix printer produces a line of output (character by character) at a time. When one line is complete the paper is advanced and the next line produced. Output is produced as a series of tiny pinpoints of ink on the paper.

The plotter is ideally suited for this application. As the pen can be moved anywhere on the paper, shapes can be drawn in any order and shapes can be drawn on top of others which have already been drawn. In addition, the smooth movement of the pen when drawing results in high quality lines.

As the dot-matrix produces one line at a time it cannot be used to draw a shape on top of one which is already there. The nature of dot-matrix printing means that quality is relatively poor and so 'straight' lines are usually not smooth.

(e) A co-processor is a special chip designed to perform some of the processing tasks carried out by the computer. It is usually designed to perform intensive number-crunching work at hardware level rather than by use of software algorithms. This leaves the standard processor free to carry out routine processing such as input/output and screen displays.

CAD processing involves the manipulation and re-scaling of drawings. This requires a lot of mathematical processing: even limited rotation of simple 3D images requires hundreds, if not thousands, of complicated calculations. These calculations would occupy nearly all of the standard processor's time and even the fastest standard processor would be very sluggish in displaying the results of these calculations as well as performing them. The co-processor is used to do all the calculations while the standard processor can concentrate on continuously displaying the results.

PERIPHERALS

Units in this chapter

Chapter objectives

After working through the topics in this chapter, you should be able to:

- explain the need for secondary storage;
- describe the physical characteristics of various storage media;
- compare capacity and speed of access of various storage media;
- give examples of how each may be used;
- describe various input methods and situations in which they may be used;
- describe various output methods and their uses;
- discuss choice of input and output methods in relation to particular applications;
- describe the use of analogue input devices and the conversion to digital format.

2.1   SECONDARY STORAGE DEVICES

Secondary storage devices are used as a more permanent form of data storage, in contrast with primary storage (main memory) which loses its contents when power is switched off. Storage media include:
1. magnetic disk (hard disks and floppy disks);
2. magnetic tape;
3. CD-ROM;
4. WORM disks;
5. magneto-optical disks;
6. microfiche.

Hard disks

There are two types of **hard disk**: exchangeable and fixed. As the names suggest, exchangeable disks can be removed from the drive and another disk inserted, whereas fixed disks, like those in a microcomputer, cannot be removed except for repair or replacement. Exchangeable disks are gradually being superseded by fixed disks which are faster and more reliable.

A hard disk unit consists of several platters each of which is attached to a central spindle and has two recording surfaces. There is a read–write head for each surface, with all the read–write heads being mounted on a single unit and moving in and out together.

Each surface has a number of concentric **tracks**, with each track being divided into a number of **sectors**. A sector (typically 256 bytes) is the smallest unit that can be read or written in a single operation.

All the tracks that are accessible from a single position of the read–write heads form a **cylinder**; data is recorded cylinder by cylinder to minimise movement of the read–write heads, thereby minimising access time.

A hard disk typically has a storage capacity of between 512 Kb and several gigabytes.

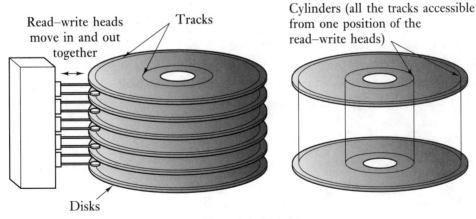

Figure 2.1: Disk drive

Floppy disks

Floppy disks consist of a thin piece of mylar plastic coated with ferric oxide, enclosed in a protective jacket. The disk is read through an opening in the jacket, protected in the standard 3½" disk by a metal sleeve until the disk is inserted in the drive and accessed. The disk has a small hole in the corner, which when open causes the disk to be **write-protected** so that the data on the disk cannot be accidentally overwritten.

Floppy disks, like hard disks, are divided into tracks and sectors. A high–density disk can store 1.44 Mb of data.

Before being used, a disk has to be formatted, a process which checks the disk for unusable areas, marks out the tracks and sectors, and creates the disk directory.

Magnetic tape

Magnetic tape is now principally used as a backup medium. It is also used to archive records of past transactions for long-term storage, as it is cheap, robust and easily used to store large quantities of data. Modern tape units generally use cartridge tape (similar to video tape) rather than reels of tape.

Data is recorded in 'frames' across the tape, with one frame representing one byte. The frames form tracks along the length of the tape, with 9 tracks being common, giving 8 data tracks and one parity track.

Data can only be read from a tape (or written to it) when it is running at full speed. This means that when an instruction is given to read a record, the tape has to accelerate from rest to full speed, continue at that speed while the data in the block is transferred and then decelerate to rest again. Blocks of data on the tape have to be separated by **inter-block gaps** to allow for the acceleration and deceleration.

Because the inter-block gaps are essentially wasted space, records are usually written several to a block, so that several records are transferred to memory in one operation.

Record 1	Record 2	Record 3	Record 4	Inter-block gap	Record 5	Record 6	Record 7	Record 8	Inter-block gap	Record 9	Etc.

BLOCK 1   BLOCK 2

Figure 2.2: Blocks and inter-block gaps on a magnetic tape

Header labels and trailer labels

In addition to data, each tape will generally contain a header record (**header label**) at the beginning of the file and a **trailer label** at the end of the file. The header label will contain:

• a field identifying the record as the header label;

• the file name;

• the date written;

• the purge date, before which the information on the tape cannot be overwritten.

The trailer label will contain:

• a field identifying the record as the trailer label;

• a count of the number of records on the file;

• the reel number if the file occupies more than one reel of tape.

Magnetic tape is a **serial** medium, meaning that an individual record can only be accessed by starting at the beginning of the tape and reading through every record until the required one is found. Likewise, it is impossible to read a record, amend it in memory, then backspace to the beginning of the block and overwrite the old record. Therefore, updating a magnetic tape file always involves copying the file to a new tape with the amendments made.

Uses of magnetic tape

It is a cheap and convenient medium for backup, and is also used for **archiving** past transactions or other data that may be needed again, such as weather records collected over a number of years.

Cartridge tape drives are in common use for backing up the hard disk of personal computers, being much more convenient than using dozens of floppy disks. A single 36-track, 12 in tape cartridge can store up to 2.4 Gb.

CD ROM

CD ROM (Compact Disk Read Only Memory) is one of the three main forms of optical disk, the other two being WORM disks and magneto-optical disks, discussed below. A CD is created using a mastering facility (just as audio CDs are created in a recording studio) and copies of the master are duplicated or 'pressed' at a factory. They are used for many different applications including

- software distribution (e.g. Word for Windows, Windows 95);
- games;
- reference material such as encyclopedias, telephone directories, past copies of newspapers, art catalogues, dictionaries;
- advertising, such as the free CDs commonly distributed with computer magazines.

The capacity of a CD ROM is around 650Mb, about 500 times as much as a high-density floppy disk. Their high capacity allows storage of photographic images, sound and video, making them ideal for **multimedia** applications.

When the master disk is created, a laser beam burns tiny holes in the surface of the disk, which (unlike a magnetic disk) has a single spiral track divided into sectors. To read data from the disk, a laser beam is reflected off the surface of the disk, detecting the presence or absence of pits which represent binary digits.

WORM disks

Write Once, Read Many optical laser disks (**WORM** disks) look similar to CD ROM disks, but they are often gold rather than silver in colour. An end user company can use these disks to write their own material, typically for archiving or storing say, graphic or photographic images which will not be changed.

These disks are also widely used for pirated software; whereas silver CDs are pressed in factories, gold CDs are usually written one at a time on PCs in garages and back bedrooms. A £5 blank disk can hold £20,000 worth of software and sell for £50 to £80, and they are sometimes used by less reputable PC manufacturers who install the software on their PCs to make a more attractive deal for the unknowing customer. However, because there is a lot of competition among pirates, these CDs sometimes carry viruses which can cause havoc on a hard drive.

Magneto-optical disks

Magneto-optical disks integrate magnetic and laser technology to enable read *and* write magnetic storage. A 5½" disk can store up to 1000 Mb. These disks may in the future replace current magnetic disks, but at present the technology is still developing and the disks are too expensive, slow and unreliable to be in widespread use.

Microfiche

Computer output on microfilm (COM) devices are used to prepare **microfiche**, a 4 in by 6 in hard-copy film that is sometimes seen in libraries and bookshops being used for reference purposes. Each microfiche sheet is divided into as many as 270 frames, each containing a page of information which can be read using a special viewer. COM is also extensively used for archiving material such as old cheques or income tax returns.

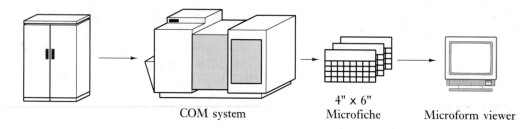

COM system   4" x 6"
                    Microfiche   Microform viewer

Figure 2.3: Computer Output to Microfilm

2.2   INPUT METHODS

The most common input devices are the traditional **keyboard** and **mouse**. **Joysticks** and **track balls** are also in common use with personal computers. For large volume data entry, a key-to-disk system as described below is often used.

Key-to-disk system

This is a stand-alone computer system used solely for entering data in large-scale batch operations. It has the following components:

* several VDUs or keystations;
* a dedicated mini- or microcomputer;
* a fixed disk drive where data is stored;
* a tape drive onto which completed batches of data are transferred;
* a supervisor's console.

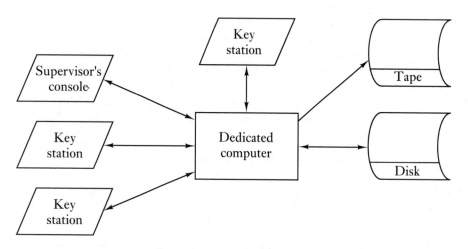

Figure 2.4: A key-to-disk system

Using a key-to-disk system, each operator loads the data entry program appropriate to his/her batch of data, and then keys in the data from the source documents. The data is validated by the program as it is being entered, and errors are reported by an audible bleep and an error message on the screen.

When the batch of data has been entered and stored on disk, the source documents are passed to another operator who switches his/her machine to **verify** mode and keys in the batch a second time. Any discrepancies can then be checked and corrected.

Completed batches are transferred from disk to magnetic tape, which is then physically taken to the main computer for processing. In some systems the transfer to the main computer is done via a data link instead of using a magnetic tape.

The supervisor's console will record the progress of each batch through the system, and also record statistics such as the number of keystrokes per hour and the number of errors made at each station.

Optical character recognition (OCR)

OCR devices are particularly well suited to applications such as credit card billing systems where data such as customer account number and amount due is encoded by the computer on a **turnaround document** – that is, a document which is produced by the computer and sent to the customer, who returns the bottom tear-off slip with their payment. A clerk checks that the payment enclosed is the same as the payment due, and manually keys in the amount paid if it is different. The machine-readable document is then input to the computer with no further keying required.

Scanners

Scanners come in a variety of shapes and sizes, from **bar-code** scanners which scan bar codes on labels in supermarkets or libraries, to hand-held and page scanners which scan a complete page, pixel by pixel.

A scanner works by shining a bright light onto the image being scanned while the scan head moves from the top to the bottom of the document at an even rate. As it moves over each 'line' of the image, the scan head collects data by measuring the intensity of light that is reflected back from the document. Each scanned line therefore results in a stream of data which the scanner translates into digital information, with a certain number of bits representing each tiny area on the scanned picture. For a black-and-white image, only one bit will be required; for 256 shades of grey, 8 bits will be required.

The resolution of the scanner is measured in dots per inch (dpi) along the x and y axes; the higher the resolution, the sharper the image, but the more memory it will occupy.

With appropriate OCR software, scanned text can be turned into a form that the computer can process, making this an alternative to keyboard entry for long text documents, or for forms where hand-printed characters are written in specified boxes.

Magnetic ink character recognition (MICR)

MICR is used mainly by banks for processing cheques. Special characters encoded along the bottom of a cheque are used to identify the bank number and the customer's account number. When the cheque is processed, the amount is also encoded by a bank operator, using a special ink containing ferric oxide which can be magnetised during processing.

MICR has several advantages for cheque processing:

- speed: over 1000 cheques per minute can be processed;
- smudged cheques can still be read;
- the characters are hard to forge.

Optical mark recognition (OMR)

An optical mark reader is a scanning device which can detect marks in preset positions on a special form. **OMR** is frequently used to score multiple-choice tests and for market research questionnaires like the one shown below (Fig 2.5).

We value your views on the service we provide here at QuickShop. If you could spare a few minutes to answer this short questionnaire, your answers will help us to make sure we are meeting your needs in the future.

1. QuickShop Direct Service	Excellent	Good	Average	Poor
If ordering by post				
Ease of ordering	☐	☐	☐	☐
If ordering by telephone				
Ease of ordering	☐	☐	☐	☐
Courtesy of telephone operators	☐	☐	☐	☐
Product knowledge of operators	☐	☐	☐	☐
For all orders				
Speed of delivery	☐	☐	☐	☐
Packaging of goods	☐	☐	☐	☐
Product quality	☐	☐	☐	☐

2. What newspapers do you buy on a regular basis?

The Times	☐	The Independent	☐
The Daily Telegraph	☐	The Daily Mail	☐
The Guardian	☐	The Daily Express	☐

3. *etc.*

Figure 2.5: An OMR document

Magnetic stripes and smart cards

Cards with magnetic stripes are widely used as charge cards, telephone cards, railway tickets etc. A bank card used for withdrawing cash from an automated teller machine (ATM), for example, will have encoded in the stripe

- the customer's account number;
- the personal identification number (PIN) in encrypted form;
- the bank's sort code;
- the customer's withdrawal limit;
- the amount withdrawn in the last time period (e.g. day).

To use the ATM, the customer inserts the card and is then requested to enter the PIN, which is checked against the encrypted PIN on the card and the PIN held in the customer's record on the bank's computer. The customer then presses a key to indicate the type of transaction desired, and if cash is required, types in the amount. This is checked against the account balance on the bank's computer and the information held on the card. If all is satisfactory the card is returned and the notes issued.

A **smart card** can hold more information than a magnetic stripe card, and contains a processing chip, making it extremely hard to forge or duplicate. They may eventually replace magnetic stripe cards.

Touch screens

A **touch screen** allows a user to enter commands or data by touching an area of the screen. Touch screens are used in many situations including industrial environments, theatre booking offices, fast food outlets for registering the customer's order, and tourist offices, where a tourist can touch a particular area of the screen to have information displayed on theatres, restaurants or other attractions. Several electronic techniques change a touch on the screen into electronic impulses that can be interpreted by software. In one such technique, beams of infra-red light are projected across the screen surface. A finger or other object touching the screen interrupts the beams causing an electronic signal to be generated. This signal identifies the location on the screen where the touch occurred.

Voice data entry

Speech recognition has a number of applications, being particularly suitable for limited data entry in situations where the user's hands are occupied such as a surgeon performing an operation, or a baggage handler at an airport who can simply state the three-letter destination identifier (e.g. LHR for London Heathrow) to have the luggage routed to the right conveyor system.

Speech recognition works as follows:

1. The word is spoken into the microphone and the sound broken down into its various frequencies.
2. The sounds are digitised using an analogue-to-digital converter so that they can be processed by the computer.
3. The digitised version is compared with a database of digitised sounds in the computer's dictionary until a match is found. If no match is found, the user is asked to repeat the word.
4. The word is displayed or spoken for confirmation, or the command is obeyed.

In speech recognition, the creation of the database is called *training*, and is achieved by having someone speak each word several times into the computer. Most speech recognition systems are speaker-dependent, only responding to the voice of one individual. Speaker-independent systems generally have a very limited vocabulary – obvious problems include the fact that different people say words with different accents, and the same person may speak the same word in many different ways, for example if they have a cold. ("Tudes!")

2.3 OUTPUT METHODS

Visual display unit (VDU)

A **VDU** has three basic attributes: size, colour and resolution. It has its own fixed amount of RAM associated with it to store the image being displayed on the screen, and the amount of RAM it has will determine the resolution and the maximum number of colours that can be displayed. Note that:

- The resolution is determined by the number of pixels (addressable picture elements) used to represent a full-screen image.
- The number of colours that can be displayed is determined by how many bits are used to represent each pixel. If only one bit is used to represent each pixel, then only two colours can be represented. To display 256 colours, 8 bits per pixel are required, and to display 65,536 (i.e. 2^{16}) colours, 16 bits (2 bytes) per pixel are needed. It is usually possible to adjust both the resolution and the number of colours – *if a high resolution is selected you won't be able to have as many colours because of the memory limitations of the VDU.*

For example, if a resolution of 800 x 600 pixels is selected together with 65,536 colours, the amount of video RAM required will be 800 x 600 x 2 bytes = 960,000 bytes, i.e. almost 1Mb. If 1Mb is all the video RAM supplied by the manufacturer, the resolution cannot be increased to say, 1000 x 800 unless the number of bytes used to represent each pixel is reduced, thus limiting the number of colours which can be displayed.

Printers

There are many different kinds of printer, including the following:

1. **Laser printer**. These printers give high-quality output, are quiet in operation and relatively inexpensive to run, although they are fairly expensive to purchase. Major running costs include toner (powdered ink), occasional drum replacement and possibly a maintenance contract.

2. **Inkjet printer**. These are inexpensive and can give good quality colour images. An inkjet printer would be a suitable choice for a school to purchase, for example for student projects, posters etc. The ink is expensive and special paper is required for best results.

3. **Dot-matrix printers**. These are among the cheapest printers, and have the advantage that carbon copies can be produced, but the quality is not as good and they are noisy.

Plotters

Plotters are used to produce extremely accurate, high-quality drawings in, for example, engineering or architectural applications. The two basic types of pen plotter are the **drum plotter** and the **flatbed plotter**, each of which have one or more pens that move over the surface of the paper under computer control to produce the drawing. Several pens may be used to vary the width and colour of each line, and the computer selects and manipulates them under program control. On the drum plotter, the pens move along one axis while the drum moves the paper along the other axis, making it possible to draw lines and curves in any direction to an accuracy of a few thousanths of an inch.

2.4 ANALOGUE TO DIGITAL CONVERSION

In many cases input devices generate signals which are analogue in nature rather than digital; that is they vary continuously between two values. Temperature, pressure, sound and movement are all analogue in nature, so that for example the movement of a mouse generates an analogue signal. A computer cannot process analogue signals and therefore a special interface known as an **analogue to digital converter** is required to convert the continuously varying analogue signal to a digital form. The basic process is as follows:

1. The input signal range is divided up into a number of discrete levels, with the number of levels determining the resolution with which the analogue signal can be accurately reproduced.

2. Samples of the analogue signals are taken at frequent intervals and converted in real time to digital values.

Chapter summary

In Chapter 2, the characteristics of storage devices have been described and compared. Input and output devices have been described and examples of their uses given.

Illustrative questions

1 Explain what is meant by a cylinder on a magnetic disk pack and indicate how this concept can influence the efficiency of reading data from the disk pack. (6)
(NICCEA)

Tutorial note
Remember that a fully annotated diagram is quite acceptable as an explanation for the first part of the question.

Suggested answer
A cylinder refers to all the data area that can be reached in a magnetic disk pack from one position of the read–write heads. It consists of one track per disk surface directly above or below the next.

It is more efficient to store data cylinder by cylinder because no time is wasted moving the read–write heads to get to the next track.

2 In designing a file it has been determined that there will be 75,000 records and that each record is 200 bytes long. The file is to be stored on a disk pack which has 200 cylinders. Each cylinder has 10 tracks and each track has a capacity of 16,000 bytes. Calculate how many cylinders the file will require. (3)
(NEAB)

Tutorial note
Make an estimate first, then get your calculator out and make sure you come up with an answer that looks reasonable!

Suggested answer
$(75,000 \times 200) / (16,000 \times 10) = 93.75$ or approximately 94 cylinders.

3 A typical business microcomputer stores all its software and datafiles on hard disk. It also has a floppy disk drive. Outline *two* different reasons why the floppy disk drive may still be needed. (4)
(NICCEA)

Tutorial note
There are at least six or seven answers that should spring to mind here and any two are acceptable!

Suggested Answer
Any two from:
- to copy new software or restore software onto the hard disk;
- to make backup copies of data files to store away from the hard disk;
- to restore data from the backup copy if the data file becomes corrupted;
- to try out sample software;
- or any other reasonable suggestion.

4 The use of **point-of-sale** (POS) terminals in supermarkets is now commonplace. What is meant by *point-of-sale*?
Suggest *two* advantages to the customer of POS terminals connected to a central computer. (3)
(AEB)

Suggested Answer
POS: place where a shop transaction takes place (e.g. the checkout).
Advantages: (any two from) faster checkout service, itemised receipts, price errors unlikely, daily special offers ('Buy two get one free'), cash back facility.

5   'In the future computer keyboards will be obsolete as every computer will be capable of direct speech input.'
State whether or not you agree with this claim and give two distinct reasons to support your answer.   (2)
(AEB)

Tutorial note
You must make two points for or against the claim, not one of each. Do read the question carefully and don't be side-tracked into an irrelevant discussion of the relative speed of speaking and typing. It is frankly difficult to see how keyboards could become completely obsolete; for example in a noisy environment it is easier to write something rather than shout it to a human, let alone to a computer! You would be given marks for making points such as: 'developments in processing power will make speech-processing in real time possible and economic'.

Suggested Answer
Difficult to teach a computer to recognise all voices (e.g. accents, dialects). Certain operations would be harder such as punctuation and text formatting.

6   Although large disk storage devices are now readily available for computer systems, the use of magnetic tape is still widespread. Describe two distinct uses of magnetic tape and explain its suitability in each case.   (4)
(EDEXCEL)

Suggested answer
Tape can be used for backing up large files in a computer system – suitable because it is compact and easy to store. It can be used for transporting files or software by post – more suitable than floppy disks because a large volume can be stored on a single tape and posted. Also tapes are less vulnerable to corruption than disks.

7   A mail order company uses a computer system to produce about three thousand invoices daily. Choose a suitable type of printer for this computing application. Give reasons for your choice.   (3)
(EDEXCEL)

Tutorial note
Work out that if the printer is operating for 6 hours a day, that's 500 invoices an hour or about 8 per minute so it's got to be a reasonably fast printer. Inkjet is too slow and costly on ink cartridges. You could justify a dot–matrix printer.

Suggested answer
A laser printer would be suitable – it is fast enough, good enough quality print for invoices and quiet in an office environment.

8   Describe two essentially different methods of direct data capture and state the applications in which they are used.   (4)
(NICCEA)

Tutorial note
Direct data capture implies that the data is not first *written* on a form of some kind, for example, and *then keyed in* from the form. Have you ever watched the electricity meter being read in your house? Or done a multiple-choice exam marked by computer?

Suggested answer
Meter readings are recorded on a hand-held computer which displays the customer name and address, location and number of the meter and previous reading. When the meter reader has finished his round he returns to the central office, connects his computer into the main computer and the data is transmitted to a transaction file.

Multiple choice exams may be marked by using an optical mark reader together with appropriate software to scan the scripts and process the marks.

9 Give an application in computing which makes use of an analog(ue) to digital converter, indicating precisely how it is used within the application. (4)

(*NICCEA*)

Tutorial note
An analogue to digital converter transforms data in analogue or continuous form to digital form which can be represented by a coded series of electrical impulses. Temperature, pressure, humidity, wind speed and direction, sound and the movement of a mouse or joystick, for example, are all analogue in nature.

Suggested answer
A temperature sensor in a greenhouse may be connected to an analogue to digital converter. The magnitude of the analogue signal is monitored at frequent intervals and converted to a binary value by comparison with pre-set readings. The reading is then stored in the computer's memory and if it falls below a certain value, or rises too high, appropriate action may be activated.

10 Describe briefly the operation of a bar code reader and indicate the contents of the bar codes commonly used in supermarkets. (4)

(*NICCEA*)

Tutorial note
Note that a supermarket bar code does not contain information such as description.

Suggested answer
The bar code reader scans by light or laser beam a bar code which consists of light and dark lines. The sequence is converted into a binary pattern and passed into the computer.

The bar code used in supermarkets contains a start, middle and end marker and specific details about the item such as the country of origin, the manufacturer, product identification and check digit.

11 The music stored on a compact disc (a CD) is in digital form, whereas that on a vinyl disc is in analogue form.

  (a) What is the essential difference between these two forms? (2)

  (b) Explain the advantages of recording music digitally. (4)

  (*UCLES*)

Tutorial note
Sound in analogue form may be represented by wave forms. The height of these wave forms may be sampled at regularly spaced time intervals, with the height being represented, say, by a 16-bit code. The more frequently the samples are taken, the more faithfully the sound will be represented.

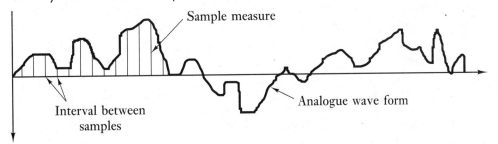

Suggested answer
(a) The analogue sound on a vinyl disc is a reproduction of a continuous wave form. The digital form on a CD consists of binary codes representing the wave height at specified time intervals, typically 40,000 samples per second for high-quality sound.

(b) The advantages of recording music digitally is that the recording can be exactly reproduced. A further advantage is that the sound can be processed or altered in different ways, for example to remove scratches from an old recording, or sounds of coughing from an audience. It also means that it can be played using a CD attached to a computer, and combined with graphics or text for a multi-media presentation.

12 A school is intending to implement a computerised registration system. The headteacher is considering using one of the following systems.

- Option 1: mark sense cards. Each teacher has a pack of cards and he/she registers each class by placing pencil marks in columns which correspond to absent pupils.

- Option 2: badge readers stationed at every entrance to the school, linked on-line to the school's administration computer. Every pupil has a badge which is used to 'clock' in or out.

- Option 3: microcomputers in every classroom linked to a central administration computer. Each teacher registers the class by displaying the class register and selecting the absentees with a mouse.
  Discuss the relative merits and drawbacks of each system. Pay particular attention to security, effectiveness and relative costs. (9)
  (NEAB)

Tutorial note
The question gives clear guidelines as to what points to cover, but remember to justify each point. Saying 'this system is secure' or 'this system is costly' will not score any marks unless you say *why*.

Suggested answer
- Option 1 is cheap to implement, not requiring sophisticated hardware. It would be fast to register absent pupils and quite secure as only the teachers would have access to the cards which would be centrally stored, say, in the school office. It offers the opportunity to register pupils in every class, not just at the start of the day.
- Option 2 needs more hardware and cabling to link the badge readers to the central computer, so is more costly. Students could clock in and then disappear for the rest of the day, or get a friend to clock in for them. It is not possible to take registers for individual classes.
- Option 3 is costly because every classroom would need a micro. It would not be very secure because even if teachers had passwords, these might become known and pupils could hack in and change the data.

13 During the 1980s plastic cards with a magnetic stripe became very popular, particularly in the banking and credit card industries. More recently this technology has begun to be replaced by so-called 'smart cards' which have a microprocessor and memory built into them. It is predicted that the magnetic stripe card will be completely replaced in the financial sector (banking and credit card industries) within a relatively short period of time.

(a) In one type of magnetic stripe system, cards are encoded with the following information:
  - customer account number;
  - personal identification number (PIN) held in encrypted form;
  - customer's bank branch identification code;
  - customer's daily cash withdrawal limit.
  The data is stored on two separate tracks within the magnetic stripe. One of these tracks is read only, the other is a read–write track.
  (i) Identify *two* other items of data which are likely to be stored on the stripe, and explain why they are necessary.
  (ii) State which of the six items of data would be stored on the read only track and which would be stored on the read–write track.
  (iii) Describe the processing stages which follow when a card is inserted into a cash dispenser with the intention of withdrawing some cash. (10)

(b) Discuss the reasons why magnetic cards became so popular in the financial sector during the 1980s, and yet are likely to be replaced by smart cards. (4)

(c) A particular type of smart card is designed for use in the financial sector. Its construction includes three distinct types of memory:
- read–write;
- read only;
- programmable read only.

Describe how each of these is likely to be used in this smart card, and describe why it is appropriate for this particular use. (6)

(EDEXCEL)

Suggested answer

(a) (i) Examples are:
- amount being withdrawn today so that maximum not exceeded;
- date of withdrawal because of maximum daily limit;
- expiry date to check that card is valid.

(ii) R/O – account number, branch, limit, PIN;
R/W – amount withdrawn, date.

(iii) The card is inserted and the PIN read. The PIN is compared with the one on the card to verify card off-line. The account number is used to validate account on-line. User enters requirements, which are validated on-line, and the details of transaction written back to card/centre.

(b) Reasons for widespread use of magnetic cards:
- convenience, no need to carry large sums of cash;
- requirement for increased security;
- supports on-line and off-line activities.

Why it is likely to be replaced?
- stripe can be read/amended illegally;
- stripe is easily damaged;
- storage capacity low.

(c) R/W – temporary storage during processing, e.g. decryption, allows data to be written to it;
R/O – operating system/algorithms. Does not depend on maintenance of power supply;
PROM – ID details can be added after card is manufactured.

14 Describe and explain the operation of the following peripherals. For each one suggest an appropriate application of its use:
(a) a touch-sensitive screen; (4)
(b) a graphics tablet; (4)
(c) a speech synthesiser; (4)
(d) a graphics printer. (4)

(AEB)

Suggested answer

(a) A **touch-sensitive screen** is a VDU screen on which a range of options is displayed. The user chooses by touching the appropriate option. The screen may respond to pressure or have a capacitive overlay or be scanned by a light beam or have electrical resistance. It could be used in a Tourist Information office.

(b) A graphics tablet is a flat rectangular slab on to which a stylus is placed. The position of the stylus is sent to the processor in the form of x and y coordinates. It could be used for the input of line drawings or CAD applications generally.

(c) A speech synthesiser is a 'spoken' word output device. Words from the system vocabulary are electronically generated from phonemes (the sounds that make up a particular language) and output through a small speaker; unknown words may be spelt out. Application: spoken computer response to a telephone enquiry (e.g. bank balance).

(d) A graphics printer is a device which can print pictures and diagrams as well as text. It could be dot-matrix, inkjet or laser operation. The image is bitmapped in memory and resolution depends on the dots per inch printed. Application: Desk-top publishing.

FILES

Units in this chapter

Chapter objectives

After working through the topics in this chapter, you should be able to:

- define a file;
- explain the concept of an addressable block and the use of the file buffer in accessing data on files;
- describe the use of fixed and variable length records;
- illustrate how key fields are used to locate or index records;
- describe the organisation of serial and sequential files;
- explain hashing and describe the organisation of random files;
- describe indexed sequential file organisation and the purpose of the index and overflow blocks;
- explain the principle of master and transaction files and the methods used to retrieve, insert, edit and delete data;
- describe security and backup measures.

3.1 FILE STRUCTURE

In a manual filing system, data is often stored in individual folders in a filing cabinet. Each individual folder may contain information pertaining to one particular person or project. The contents of that folder is a **record** which will contain discrete pieces of information (known in computer terminology as **fields**) such as name, address, and so on.

Information in a computer system also has to be organised in a logical manner so that any item of data can be retrieved when it is needed.

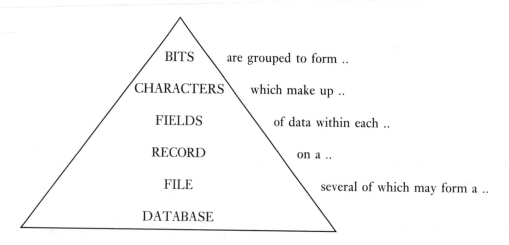

A **file** is often defined as a collection of records, usually held on a secondary storage medium such as disk or magnetic tape. So for example a stock file is a collection of records each of which contains data about a particular item of stock, and a customer file is a collection of records each of which holds data about a particular customer. Within each record are a number of fields such as Name, Address line 1, Address line 2, Town, Post Code, and so on.

However, the term **file** is also used in a broader sense to mean a data structure which could hold, for example

- a source code program written in a high-level language;
- a binary file containing executable code;
- a bitmapped graphics file;
- a word-processed letter;
- an ASCII text file.

For the rest of this chapter, the word **file** will be used in the sense of a *collection of records*, e.g. a customer file containing one record for each customer. A card index file is the manual equivalent of this type of file.

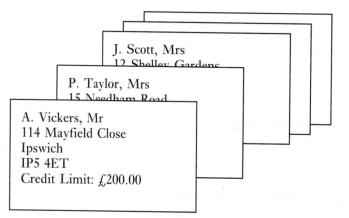

Figure 3.1: A card index file

The way in which a file is **physically** organised on disk or tape is generally transparent to the user, who is concerned only with the **logical** file organisation, which determines how individual records can be accessed.

3.2 PHYSICAL ORGANISATION

Data is held in a similar manner on disk and tape, being organised into **physical blocks** (also known, confusingly, as **physical records**). This is the amount of data that is actually read into memory at one go when an instruction to read the file is given. On a disk, a physical block consists of one or more sectors.

The physical block is read into a **buffer**, i.e. a space set aside in memory as a temporary store. The operating system then separates the data into the **logical** records required by the application.

For example, the records in a customer file may be 100 bytes each, but the physical block size may be 512 bytes. When a user issues an instruction to read a particular customer record, the entire block is transferred to the memory buffer. The operating system then copies the record requested into a record buffer area being used by that particular program. When the user issues the next read instruction, no physical data transfer from the disk will occur if the relevant record happens to be in the same block.

Double buffering

Because processing is so much faster than reading from or writing to a storage device, a system of double buffering is used, meaning that there are two buffers, so that while data is being transferred into one buffer from the storage device, the other buffer is being emptied and the records processed.

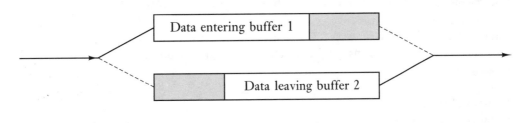

Figure 3.2: Double buffering

3.3 LOGICAL ORGANISATION

Logical organisation is the term used to mean the organisation as perceived by the user, who does not need to be aware that the records are held in physical blocks. To the user, it appears as though every time an instruction is given to read, a single record is copied from the disk or tape into memory. It appears this way because the operating system is working very hard in the background to separate out logical records and present them in the order requested.

Fixed and variable length records

A file such as a customer file may contain either fixed or variable length records. If the file consists of fixed length records, then every record has exactly the same number of fields, and every field contains exactly the same number of bytes. Of course, since people have names and addresses of different lengths, some fields have to be padded out with spaces or may be completely filled with spaces.

Some files use variable length records, in which

- The number of bytes in any particular field may vary from record to record.
- The number of fields may vary from record to record.

Many database packages, for example, use variable length records, though this is transparent to the application developer who can specify a maximum length for each field.

In order to implement variable length records, either

- each field is separated from the next with a predefined special character, or
- a byte count is held at the start of each field.

In addition an end-of-record marker has to be held to show where each record ends.

Advantages and disadvantages of variable length records

The advantage of variable length records are

- Less space is wasted on the storage medium.
- It enables as many fields as necessary to be held on a particular record; for example subjects taken and exam results for different pupils.
- It may reduce the time taken required to read a file because more records can be packed into each physical block.

The disadvantages are

- The processing required to separate out the fields is more complex.
- It is harder to estimate file sizes accurately when a new system is being designed.

3.4   FILE ORGANISATION

There are several different ways of organising files, with each method being suited to particular uses or applications. Types of file organisation include

- serial;
- sequential;
- indexed sequential;
- random.

Serial file organisation

The records on a serial file are not stored in any particular sequence; they are stored one after another in the order in which they are written. Serial files are suitable for *transaction files*, for example all cash withdrawals made at a particular cashpoint machine.

- To *access* a particular record on a serial file, each record on the file must be read, starting from the beginning of the file, until the required record is found.
- To *add* a record to a serial file, the file can be opened at the end and a new record appended.
- To *delete* a record from a serial file, the whole file has to be copied over to a new serial file, omitting the record that is to be deleted.

Sequential file organisation

Each record on a sequential file has a *key field* such as employee number which uniquely identifies the record. The records are held one after another in *key sequence*.

Sequential organisation is suitable for master files such as payroll files which have a high hit rate. The term hit rate refers to the percentage of records accessed in a particular run of a program. In a payroll system the hit rate will typically be almost 100% since every employee will be paid.

- To *access* a particular record on a sequential file, each record on the file must be read, starting from the beginning of the file, until the required record is found.
- To *add* a record to a sequential file, each record must be copied over to a new file, adding in the new record at the appropriate place.
- To *delete* a record from a sequential file, the whole file has to be copied over to a new sequential file, omitting the record that is to be deleted.

Indexed sequential organisation

An indexed sequential file contains
- one or more levels of index, depending upon the size of the file;
- a home area where the records are stored;
- an overflow area for records which will not fit into the correct home block.

The indexes
A large file which occupies several disk cylinders (see figure 2.1) may have

- a cylinder index which has an entry for each cylinder, giving the highest record key on the cylinder. This is the 'top-level' index;
- on each cylinder, a second level of index giving the highest record key in each block within that cylinder. This is a 'lower-level' index.

(This is rather like the indexes on a set of encyclopedias, where the back of each volume may be marked 'AAR–BER', 'BES–CAR' etc. This is equivalent to the **top-level index**, and within each volume, there is a further **lower-level index** telling you which page to look on to find a particular entry such as 'Argentina'. Having two levels of index makes it quicker to find what you are looking for.)

Once the file has been set up, the index entries do not change, even when records are added or deleted. The index specifies which block a new record should be written to.
e.g. Cylinder index:

Cylinder	Highest Key
34	1460
35	2360
36	4112
..	..

Cylinder 34 will have its own block index, perhaps occupying Blocks 1 and 2 on the cylinder:

Block	Highest key
3	0065
4	0321
5	0455
..	..

The home area
The 'home area' is where the actual records are stored in key sequence. The records are stored in physical blocks of say 512 bytes. Thus, if each record is 90 bytes long there will be room for 5 records in each block, with a bit of space left over. However, the file may be set up with say 3 records per block, allowing for two more records to be added into each block. The **packing density** is then said to be 60%.

The overflow area
If the situation arises where there are already 5 records in a particular block, and a sixth one has to be added, it will be put into the overflow area and a pointer or 'tag' written in the home block to say which block the new record is in.

e.g. Block 4 on cylinder 34 contains the following records:

0101	Harrison Bernard	45 St Edmunds Road Colchester	CO3 5RT
0124	Bradman Henrietta	12 Gloucester Way Sudbury	SU6 5FC
0192	Brooke Donald	3 Papermill Lane Bramford	IP7 5JB
0263	Kettless Neil	8 Oakview Dovercourt	C06 5KL
0321	Henke Maria	23 Newnham Court Ipswich	IP8 7HG

Now a new record is to be added:

| 0311 | Pointon Leslie | Fishers Farm Stonham | IP3 4ES |

Since Block 4 is already full, this record will be put in the overflow area (which starts, say, at Block 121) and a 'tag' is left in the home block:

Block 4

0101	Harrison Bernard	45 St Edmunds Road Colchester	CO3 5RT
0124	Bradman Henrietta	12 Gloucester Way Sudbury	SU6 5FC
0192	Brooke Donald	3 Papermill Lane Bramford	IP7 5JB
0263	Kettless Neil	8 Oakview Dovercourt	C06 5KL
0311	0121		
0321	Henke Maria	23 Newnham Court Ipswich	IP8 7HG

Block 121

| 0311 | Pointon Leslie | Fishers Farm Stonham | IP3 4ES |

Indexed sequential file organisation is suitable for applications that sometimes require the file to be accessed randomly and sometimes require the file to be processed sequentially. For example, a customer file may be processed sequentially when statements are to be sent out to all customers, but randomly when a customer has a query on his/her account, or changes address.

- to *access* a record on an indexed sequential file, the cylinder index is read to find which cylinder the record is on, then the block index is read to find which block the record is in. The block is then read into memory and searched to find the record. If a 'tag' is found instead of the record, the overflow block pointed to by the tag is read into memory and the record copied to a buffer area.
- to *add* a record to an indexed sequential file, the indexes are read as above to determine which block the record should be written to. That block is then read into memory, and if there is space, the new record is inserted in the correct sequence in the block, which is then written back to the same place on the disk. If there is no room in the block, a tag is left in the block specifying a new location in overflow, where the record is written. (If there is no room for even a tag, then another record may be moved from the block to the overflow area to make room for both tags.)
- to *delete* a record from an indexed sequential file, the indexes are read as above to determine which block the record is in. The block is read into memory, the record deleted (e.g. overwritten with 0s) and the block rewritten to its original location.

File reorganisation

After a lot of records have been added and deleted, many records will be in overflow rather than in their correct home block, resulting in slower file access and processing. The file then needs to be reorganised by reading the records sequentially, copying them to a new indexed sequential file, with for example a 60% packing density, and recreating the indexes. This would typically be done using a **utility** program.

Random (hash file) organisation

In a random file, each record is stored at an address calculated from the record key using a **hashing algorithm** or **randomising function**.

For example, if 1000 spaces have been allocated in an empty file to hold records with six digit keys, one way of calculating the address would be to take the last three digits of the record key as the address and store the record at that address.

e.g.

Record key	Block address
645231	231
742477	477
689000	000
538477	477

As demonstrated above, more than one record key may hash to the same address. Assuming that only one record is to be stored per block, the second record is said to cause a 'collision' and must be stored somewhere else, for example in the next free block on the file. When the end of the file is reached, the computer continues searching for a free block from the first address on the file.

Referring to the example above, the record with key 538477 will be stored at address 478.

Random file organisation allows extremely fast access to individual records, but the file cannot be processed sequentially. It is suitable for on-line enquiry systems where a fast response is required.

- To *access* a record on a random file, its address is calculated from the record key using the hashing algorithm. The record at that address is then read. If it is not the required record, then the next record is read and examined until either the record is found, or a blank record is encountered.
- To *add* a record to a random file, its address is calculated using the hashing algorithm and then the relevant block is read into memory. If the block is empty, the record is written to the file. Otherwise, the next block is read and examined until an empty space is found.
- To delete a record from a random file, the record *must not be physically deleted* because this would result in any records which caused collisions being inaccessible. Therefore, the record is *flagged as deleted* by setting an extra field (e.g. a boolean field) in the record to indicate that this is a deleted record.

3.5   FILE PROCESSING

Files in a computer system may be categorised as
- master files, for example a customer file containing details of all customer accounts;
- transaction files, containing for example all purchases made by customers in one day;
- reference files, containing for example rates of interest, VAT rates or other information that is common to all records on a master file.

Grandfather–father–son method of updating

The method used to update a master file will depend on its organisation. In order to update a sequential master file, the transactions must first be sorted into the same sequence as the master file. A record from each file is then read and the record keys compared. If the master record has no matching transaction it is copied across unchanged to the new master file and another one read into memory until a match is found. The master record can then be updated in memory and another transaction record read. If it is for the same record, the master record in memory is updated again, and so on until a transaction for a different record is read. Then the updated master record can be written to the new file and another one read into memory and compared with the current transaction.

This method of updating is known as the **grandfather–father–son** method, with a new file being created each time an update is carried out. Normally at least three 'generations' of master file are kept for backup purposes. If the latest version of the master file is corrupted or destroyed, it can be recreated by re-running the previous update, using the old master file and matching transactions.

Figure 3.3 illustrates the grandfather–father–son update process.

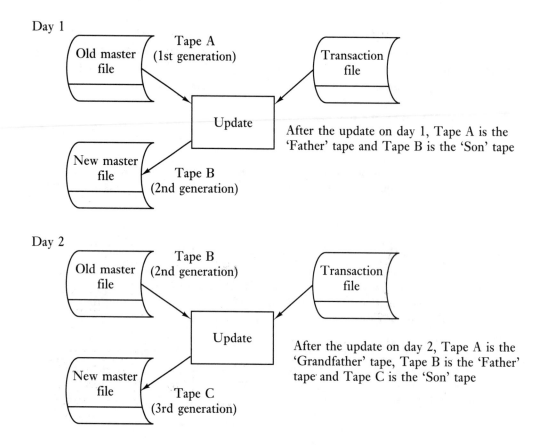

Figure 3.3: *Grandfather–father–son method of updating*

To update an indexed sequential or random file, updating by overlay (updating *in situ*) is used. Transactions do not have to be sorted as either of these files can be randomly accessed, and for each transaction the matching master record is read, updated and rewritten to the same place on the file.

Merging files

Sometimes it is necessary to merge two sequential files into one file. The process is similar to the sequential update described above, with a record being read from each file and the one with the lower key being written to a new file.

Hit rate

Hit rate measures the proportion of records being accessed during a particular run. It is calculated by dividing the number of records accessed by the total number of records on the file, and multiplying by 100 to express the result as a percentage.

For example, if 270 employee records out of 300 on the file are accessed on a particular payroll run, the hit rate is $270/300 \times 100 = 90\%$.

In general, if the hit rate is high, (say over 70%) whenever the file is processed, it is efficient to use a sequential file organisation, whereas if the hit rate is low, it is preferable to use a randomly organised file where records can be updated in any sequence. If the hit rate is sometimes high and sometimes low an indexed sequential file organisation is appropriate.

3.6 FILE BACKUP AND SECURITY

It is obviously essential to protect valuable master files from accidental or deliberate corruption, and from being read by unauthorised people. Methods used to protect files include:

1. Making regular backup copies of a file (say daily or weekly, depending on the frequency of updates). Note that with the grandfather–father–son method of updating, a backup copy of the 'old master' is automatically created, and so long as the corresponding transactions are preserved, the new master file can be recreated by repeating the update run. Several generations of the master file are usually preserved, along with the transaction files.

2. Having other backup copies (perhaps older generations) securely stored, for example in a fireproof safe off-site (i.e. in another building).

3. When master files are updated in real time, a copy of all transactions must be kept so that the master file can be brought up to date from a backup copy in the event of a disk failure or 'head crash' (see Section 5.6, Database Management, 'Maintaining the security and integrity of a multi-user database', page 102).

4. Data on the file may be *encrypted* to prevent unauthorised viewing.

Chapter summary

In Chapter 3, the difference between logical and physical file organisation, and the advantages and disadvantages of using fixed length records and variable length records, have been explained. The four major types of file organisation (serial, sequential, indexed-sequential and random) have been covered and methods described for accessing, adding and deleting records for each organisation.

Illustrative questions

1 A company records details of its business activities on a computer system. The company has a regular practice of file backup and it maintains transaction logs.
(a) Explain the meaning of the terms file backup and transaction log. (4)
(b) Explain how the company can recover its data following a system failure. (4)
(UCLES)

Suggested answer
(a) File backup means making a copy of a file for use if the original file becomes corrupted or is lost through fire, theft etc. A transaction log is a separate copy, stored on disk or tape, of each change to a data file.
(b) To recover the data, the backup copy of the file is copied back to the original medium to restore it to its state immediately before the last backup was taken, and then the transaction log is used to effect all subsequent data changes.

2 (a) Explain the difference between *fixed length records* and *variable length records* in a filing system.
(b) State *two* advantages of using fixed length records.
(c) Briefly describe an application which would use fixed length records and one which would use variable length records. (6)
(EDEXCEL)

Tutorial note
Fixed length records are very common and you can safely describe any data processing application such as stock control, customer records in a billing application, payroll etc. For variable length choose an application in which either the number of fields is variable, or one or more fields contain 'notes' in free text format.

Suggested answer
(a) A fixed length record has a predetermined number of bits or characters, with fields being padded out with blanks if necessary. In a variable length record the number of bits (or characters) is not predetermined.
(b) The size of the file can be calculated once the number of records is known. The layout of an input screen can be defined.
(c) A stock control application would use fixed length records for the stock file. An application such as patient records at a doctor's surgery, with records containing notes of a variable number of visits, would use variable length records.

3 (a) Describe the following types of file organisation and in each case give an example of its use.
   (i)   serial file;
   (ii) indexed sequential file;
   (iii) random file.
   (b) Explain why a multi-level index may be used in an indexed sequential file. Describe how a record is accessed when such a file is used.   (8)

(EDEXCEL)

Tutorial note
A common misunderstanding is that in a random file, the records are placed on the file in any random order because the order doesn't matter. This misses the point!

Suggested answer
(a) (i)   In a serial file, records are stored one after another in the order of entry. Suitable for sales transactions.
   (ii) An indexed sequential file has three areas; an index which typically holds for each block, an entry giving the highest key in the block; a home area, in which the records are stored in key sequence; an overflow area in which records are placed if there is no room for them in the block indicated by the index entry. Suitable for a stock control application in which updates or queries are made in real time.
   (iii) In a random file, a hashing algorithm is applied to the key field to determine the address where a particular record is stored. Suitable for a real-time transaction processing system such as an airline booking system.
(b)   A multi-level index is used when there are so many records that a single index would take too long to search. The top level index would be read first, typically indicating which disk cylinder to search on, then the next level of index (which might be the track index) and finally the block index would be searched to find the correct block, which is then read.

4 (a) Within the context of random access files:
   (i)   explain, with the aid of a simple example, what is meant by a hashing algorithm;   (4)
   (ii) state *two* desirable properties of a hashing function;   (2)
   (iii) outline the steps needed to insert a record into a random access file. These should include a method to overcome any difficulties which may occur as the space allocated for the file fills up.   (4)
   (b) An indexed sequential file consists of an index, home area and overflow areas.
   (i)   What would be contained in the index?   (2)
   (ii) Outline the steps needed to insert a record into this file. These should include a method of overcoming any difficulties which may occur as the space allocated for the file fills up.   (6)

(c) When would it be appropriate to use:
  (i)   a randomly organised file;
  (ii) an indexed sequential file? (2)

(AEB)

Tutorial note
In part (a)(i) you can take an actual example of a record key and apply a hashing algorithm to show where the record would be stored. Using the remainder method given in the suggested answer, if a file has space for 1000 records, a record with key 152638 would be stored at address 638.

Suggested answer
(a) (i) A hashing algorithm is a randomising formula or function for converting a record's key to an address where the record can be stored. For example, in a file with space for n records, the address can be calculated as

$$\text{address} = \text{record\_key mod } n$$

   (i.e. divide the record key by the number of spaces and take the remainder, to give an address between 0 and $n - 1$)

  (ii) A hashing function should be quick to calculate, and should minimise the number of collisions that occur. (It should also be capable of producing the complete range of addresses).

  (iii) To insert a record, its address is calculated using the hashing algorithm and then the relevant block is read into memory. If the block is empty, or contains a record which has been flagged as deleted, the record is written to the file. Otherwise, the next block is read and examined until an empty space is found.

(b) (i) The index will contain, for each block in the file, the block number and the highest record key in the block.

  (ii) to *insert* a record in an indexed sequential file, the index is read to determine which block the record should be written to. That block is then read into memory, and if there is space, the new record is inserted in the correct sequence in the block, which is then written back to the same place on the disk. If there is no room in the block, a tag is left in the block specifying a new location in overflow, where the record is written. (If there is no room for even a tag, then another record may be moved from the block to the overflow area to make room for both tags.)

(c) (i) A randomly organised file would be appropriate when fast access to a record is required, and where frequent insertion and deletion takes place – e.g. a real-time booking system.

  (ii) An indexed sequential file is appropriate when the file has to be processed sequentially on some occasions and randomly on other occasions, e.g. an application involving both batch and interactive processing.

5 A mail-order company has about 700 customers, each of whom is identified by a unique 5-digit code. Customer records are held in the company's computer system as a random disk file, each customer's data occupying one block. The blocks are numbered 000 to 999. When a new customer's data is added to the file, the customer code is hashed by taking the number formed from its middle three digits, and the corresponding block is accessed. If the block is empty, the data is stored there, but, if not, successive blocks are searched (with block 000 succeeding block 999) and the data stored in the first free block.

(a) The first customer records to be entered had the following code numbers: 63142, 13162, 73141, 23153, 63205. Show in which blocks each of the corresponding records will be stored. (3)

(b) Use diagrams and pseudocode to describe in detail how the system would search for a particular customer's record when a code is entered, or report that no record exists with the code. (6)

(c) When a record is deleted, a special marker must be stored in the block if occupied, rather than simply leaving it empty.

   (i) Explain the reason for this.

   (ii) Explain how such a block can be used for a new record.   (2)

(UCLES)

Tutorial note

It is important to understand that with a random file organisation, records may not necessarily be stored at their hash address if there is already a record at that address. Therefore when searching for a record, you first look in the hash address but if the record is not there the search continues until either an empty block is found or the correct record is located. In order for this algorithm to work, blocks cannot simply be left empty when records are deleted.

Suggested answer

(a)

Block no	Record code number	
314	63142	
315	73141	(overflowed from block 314)
316	13162	
317	23153	(overflowed from block 315)
318		
319		
320	63205	

(b) To search for a customer's code:

Procedure Search (reference parameters: RecordFound, HashAddress)
   Begin
      RecordFound := False
      RecordNotPresent := False
      Apply hashing algorithm to CustomerCode to find middle 3 digits giving HashAddress
      Repeat
         Read record at HashAddress
         If RecordCode = CustomerCode
           Then RecordFound
           Else
              If record empty or delete marker set
                Then RecordNotPresent
                Else HashAddress := (HashAddress + 1) Mod 1000
         EndIf
      Until RecordFound or RecordNotPresent
   EndProc

The procedure will pass back a True or False value for the parameter RecordFound, and a value for HashAddress giving the address of the customer record if found.

(c) (i) If the block is left empty, any records which originally caused a 'collision' and were stored at a different address (e.g. record 73141) would not be found by the search algorithm since the search would stop when the blank block was encountered.

   (ii) When a new record is to be added, the hash address is calculated and if *either* the block is empty, *or* a delete marker is set, the record is stored and the delete marker reset to indicate 'Not Deleted'.

SYSTEMS ENGINEERING

Units in this chapter

Chapter objectives

After working through the topics in this chapter, you should be able to:

- describe centralised and distributed processing systems;
- distinguish between batch, real-time and on-line systems;
- draw a diagram representing the stages in the system life cycle;
- describe the purpose of a feasibility study;
- identify the likely costs and benefits of a computer system;
- discuss methods of deriving the user and information requirements of a new system;
- specify and document the data flow and processing requirements;
- draw a systems flowchart for a specified system;
- design a suitable user interface for a given system;
- identify a suitable test strategy and design suitable test data;
- select a suitable method of implementing a new system;
- describe the documentation that will accompany a new software system;
- discuss the issues involved in a smooth changeover to a new system;
- evaluate solutions on the basis of effectiveness, costs, usability and maintainability.

4.1   TYPES OF SYSTEM

Centralised and distributed processing systems

Computer systems may be either **centralised** or **distributed**.

A **centralised** system is one in which all processing is carried out in one central location, often on a mainframe computer. There may be many terminals attached to the central computer, at geographically widespread locations, which are sending data for processing and receiving results, or accessing information held on a central database. Centralised systems were common in the 1970s before the widespread use of PCs, when organisations could get more computing power for their money by buying larger and larger computers.

This policy frequently led to a lack of responsiveness to the requirements of individual departments, and the trend reversed from centralisation to decentralisation through **distributed processing**.

In a **distributed** system, several processors are located in different places, linked by a communications network (see Fig 4.1). Distributed systems are often made up of local area networks in different branches of a company, with different software being used in different departments.

The advantages of a distributed system are

- The system can meet the specific needs of each local user as well as meeting the needs of the organisation as a whole.
- Data files can be held locally, reducing transmission costs and security risks.
- Processing is generally faster as each workstation or local area network can do its own processing.
- If the central computer goes down, individual users will still be able to perform many tasks using local processors.
- Particular PCs can be dedicated to particular applications such as word-processing or computer-aided design, allowing individual departments more control over what hardware and software to purchase.

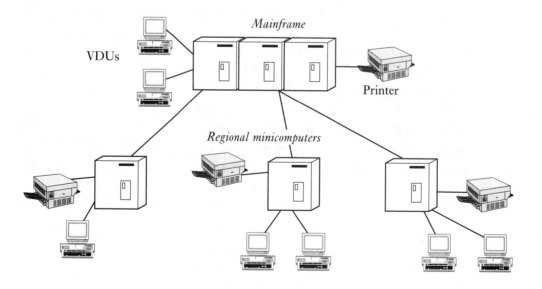

Figure 4.1: A distributed system

Processing methods

Computer systems may be broadly categorised as being one of

- batch;
- real–time;
- on–line.

Batch systems

Batch processing is appropriate in situations where there is a large volume of data coming in at regular intervals but where processing does not have to be done immediately. Examples of such systems are a mail-order company processing orders and payments, the DVLC processing requests for driving licences, the tax office processing income tax returns, an electricity company sending out bills and recording payments.

The key features of a batch processing system are:

1. The data is received in the form of input documents and manually sorted into batches of 50 or 100 documents. A batch header slip is filled in for each batch and attached to the front of the batch. The batch header may contain:

   (a) the batch number;

   (b) date;

   (c) number of documents in the batch;

   (d) control total, e.g. total of all invoices/orders/salaries;

   (e) hash total, e.g. a total of all customer numbers. A hash total is used solely to check that data entry is accurate; the computer will calculate the same hash total and compare it with that on the batch header, which is also keyed in. Any discrepancy will be reported.

2. The data is either keyed in or read directly using, for example, **optical character recognition** (OCR).

3. In the case of manually keyed data, the data is **verified** by keying it in a second time using a different data entry operator, with the computer automatically comparing the second version with the first and reporting any discrepancies.

4. The data is **validated** by means of a computer program which checks all possible fields for reasonableness using a variety of checks such as range checks (value within a specified range), presence checks (data item is not missing), check digits (see below) and comparing control totals and hash totals with those entered from the manually calculated batch header totals.

5. Invalid data is rekeyed and rechecked and finally the valid data is stored on a transaction file ready to be processed at a convenient time, perhaps overnight or at a time when the computer is not busy with interactive users.

Calculating check digits

Code numbers such as customer number, employee number or product number are often lengthy and prone to errors when being keyed in. One way of preventing these errors is to add to the end of a code number, an extra digit which has been calculated from the digits of the code number. In this way the code number with its extra check digit becomes self-checking.

The best-known method of calculating check digits is the modulo-11 system, which traps over 99% of all errors. The calculation of a check digit is shown below.

1. Each digit of the code number is assigned a weight. The right-hand (least significant) digit is given a weight of 2, the next digit to the left 3 and so on.

2. Each digit is multiplied by its weight and the products added together.

3. The sum of the products is divided by 11 and the remainder obtained.

4. The remainder is subtracted from 11 to give the check digit. The two exceptions are:

   - if the result is 11, the check digit is 0, not 11.
   - if the result is 10, the check digit is X, not 10.

EXAMPLE:

To calculate the check digit for the number 1349:

original code number	1	3	4	9
weights	5	4	3	2
multiply each digit by weight	5	12	12	18
add products together	47			
divide by 11	4 remainder 3			
subtract remainder from 11	$11 - 3 = 8$			

Check digit = 8. The complete code number is therefore 13498.

When the computer checks that this is a valid code number, it does not have to go through the whole calculation. It assigns weights of 1 to the rightmost digit (the check digit), 2 to the next and so on. After multiplying each digit by its weight and dividing by 11, the remainder must equal 0 if the check digit is valid.

EXAMPLE:

code number with check digit	1	3	4	9	8
weights	5	4	3	2	1
multiply each digit by weight	5	12	12	18	8
add products together	55				
divide by 11	5 remainder 0 so the number is a valid code number.				

Real-time systems

In a real-time system, the computer has to keep pace with some external operation, processing the received data more or less instantaneously and producing results immediately. Real-time systems generally fall into one of two categories:

1. process control;
2. information storage and retrieval.

In a process control system, the computer is dedicated to certain tasks, such as controlling the wing flaps on an airliner, the flight path of a guided missile or the temperature in a greenhouse. Sensors continuously monitor external readings or events, and activators cause an appropriate action to take place.

In an information retrieval system such as an airline reservation system, many different users in various travel agents around the country will require up-to-the-minute details of flight availability to be displayed within a few seconds, and have a reservation accepted within a similar time span.

On a smaller scale, any system which for example instantly updates a stock file when a sale is made, or a library database when a book is borrowed from a library, is also classified as a real-time system but to differentiate it from others is called a pseudo-real-time system.

On-line systems

An on-line system is one in which information is available to all users at their own terminals, although they may not be able to update the information. A cash-point machine may be on-line so that users' balances can be checked before cash is withdrawn, but the transaction may be recorded on a separate file rather than immediately updating the master file. The updating is done in batch mode late at night when the cash machine is closed.

4.2   THE SYSTEMS LIFE CYCLE

Commercial systems (payroll, accounts, stock control and so on) all share a common **life cycle** pattern. One method of doing things may work well for a period of time (maybe several years) and then, owing to expansion or changes in the nature of the business, the economic environment, the need to keep up with new technology or other factors, the system may start to deteriorate or seem inadequate. At this point investigations are made, requirements are analysed, a new system is proposed and the cycle starts all over again.

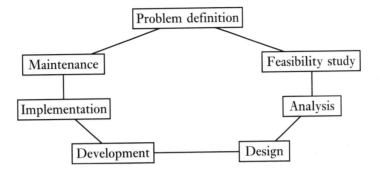

Figure 4.2: The systems life cycle

This is sometimes referred to as the **cascade** or **waterfall** model of systems development, because each stage must be finished before the next one can start.

Identification of problem areas for computerisation

Some manual systems have characteristics that make them obvious candidates for computerisation. These characteristics include

- large volumes of data all requiring similar processing (e.g. payroll, invoicing, mail-order processing);
- requirement for information to be available from several different locations (e.g. holiday booking, hospital patients database, customer accounts);
- requirement for very accurate calculations (e.g. engineering projects or process control);
- duplicated effort is involved (e.g. billing dental patients and then re-entering the same data to reclaim from the Dental Practitioners' Board);
- manual methods are too slow (e.g. numerical weather forecasting, simulation problems);
- data needs to be constantly up-to-date and accessible (e.g. customer bank accounts).

4.3   PROBLEM DEFINITION AND FEASIBILITY STUDY

The user or user department needs to have a clear idea of why computerisation of a particular function or area of business could be beneficial.

The first stage in the systems life cycle will be a formal request from a user or user department for a **feasibility study** to be conducted to examine the pros and cons of developing a new computer system. The *terms of reference* for the feasibility study may request the analyst to

- investigate and report on the existing system;
- specify objectives for the system (e.g. cost reductions, better service to customers, better management information, ability to handle increased volume of business);
- establish whether the objectives would be met by a new system;
- recommend the most suitable system to achieve the objectives;
- prepare a cost-benefit analysis;
- prepare a plan for implementing the new system within a set time scale.

The feasibility study, then, will address the above points.

Cost–benefit analysis

This is an important part of the feasibility study. The **costs** of a new system may include

- equipment costs (computers and peripherals);

- installation costs (building alterations, new wiring, air-conditioning etc.);
- development costs (systems analysis, design, programming or software package purchase, changeover costs);
- personnel costs (training, recruitment, salaries, redundancy payments);
- operating costs (consumables such as disks, tapes and stationery, maintenance, insurance and standby arrangements in case of system failure or sabotage).

The **benefits** of a new system may include

- savings in staff costs;
- savings in other operating costs such as consumables;
- extra sales revenue as a consequence of better marketing information;
- improved cash flow position because invoices are sent out faster, payments processed faster;
- better stock control and therefore less money tied up in superfluous stock;
- better customer service;
- improved staff morale as a result of working with a better system;
- better management information.

4.4   SYSTEMS ANALYSIS

Systems analysis is a detailed look at a current system and what a new system will be required to do. It will cover similar ground to the feasibility study but in more detail.

Methods of fact-finding

Methods of finding out about the current system include

- interviews;
- questionnaires;
- observation and inspection of records.

Interviews can be conducted with various levels of staff from clerical and manual staff up to top management. They are useful for gathering opinions as well as facts, and getting an insight into how things work and where problems lie, but are very time-consuming.

Questionnaires are most useful when a small amount of information is required from a large number of people, or when the organisation is spread over many separate sites. They enable the same questions to be put to everyone, thus ensuring consistency in fact-gathering. The questions have to be very carefully worded to obtain exactly the information required, and of course there is no way of ensuring that busy employees won't simply bin the questionnaire.

Observation and looking at documents, procedures manuals and so on is a good way of acquiring an in-depth knowledge of how things are currently done and where problems or inefficiencies occur.

Data flow diagrams

When a systems analyst looks at a system, a major task to be performed is to find out

- where the data originates;
- what processing is performed on it and by whom;
- who uses the data;
- what data is stored and where;
- what output is produced and who receives it.

One way of recording all this information is to use a **data flow diagram** (DFD).

There are only four symbols used in dataflow diagrams, and they should not be confused with any other type of flowcharting symbols.

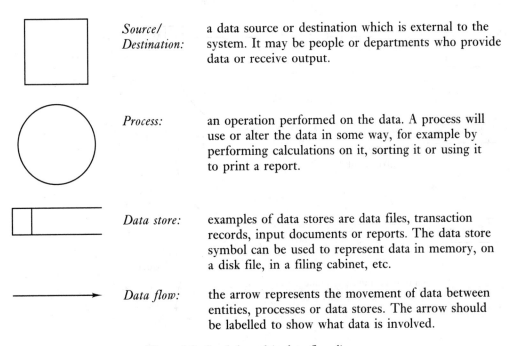

	Source/ Destination:	a data source or destination which is external to the system. It may be people or departments who provide data or receive output.
	Process:	an operation performed on the data. A process will use or alter the data in some way, for example by performing calculations on it, sorting it or using it to print a report.
	Data store:	examples of data stores are data files, transaction records, input documents or reports. The data store symbol can be used to represent data in memory, on a disk file, in a filing cabinet, etc.
	Data flow:	the arrow represents the movement of data between entities, processes or data stores. The arrow should be labelled to show what data is involved.

Figure 4.3: Symbols used in data flow diagrams

When drawing data flow diagrams, you should stick to the following conventions:

- Do not draw data flow lines directly between data stores and external entities: there should be a process box between them to show the operation performed (e.g. print a report).
- Label the data flow lines so that it is clear what data is being transferred.

Levelled DFDs

It is often impossible to represent a complete business system in a single diagram, so two or three levels of data flow diagrams may be used, each showing more detail.

EXAMPLE
The payroll system in a certain company may be described as follows:
At the end of each week, time sheets are collected and sent to the computer centre. There, the payroll data is entered via a key-to-disk system, verified and validated, producing a new file of valid transactions on disk and an error report. This file is used to update the employee master file, payslips are printed and funds are electronically transferred to employees' bank accounts.

Draw two levels of data flow diagram, the top level showing a single process, and the second level showing the detailed system as described above.

Top level diagram

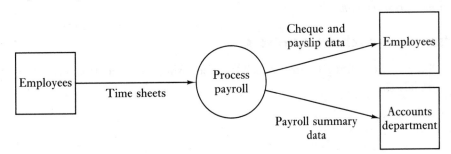
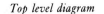

Second level diagram

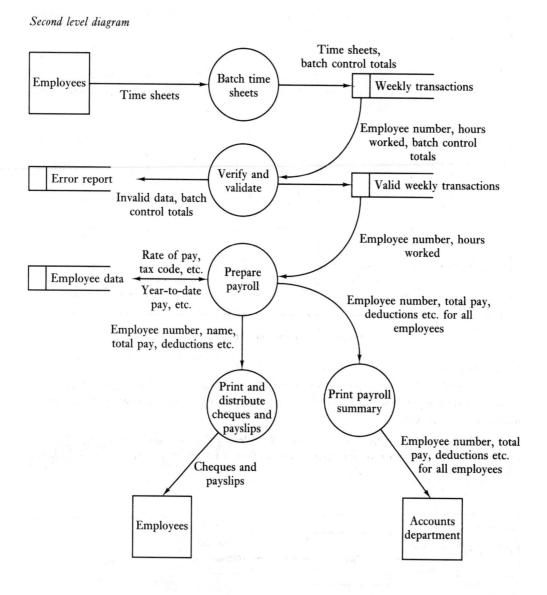

Systems flowcharts

A systems flowchart is another 'tool' used by a systems analyst which gives a complete overview of a system. It will show

- the tasks to be carried out in the new system;
- the devices that are to be used (keyboard, VDU, disk drives, printer etc.);
- the media used for input, storage and output;
- the files used by the system.

Systems flowcharts should not be confused with program flowcharts, which show the logic of a particular program within a system.

Systems flowchart symbols

The National Computing Centre (NCC) suggests using the symbols shown in Fig 4.4 in systems flowcharts.

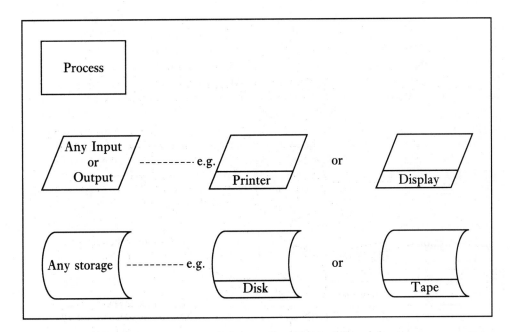

Figure 4.4: Systems flowchart symbols

EXAMPLE

A customer file is held on tape and receipts held on a transaction file are sorted and then used to update the master file, creating a new master file. Draw a systems flowchart to illustrate this process.

Notes: The system flowchart should show the files being used and the processes being carried out. The direction of the arrows on the flow lines indicates whether a file is being used for input, output or both.

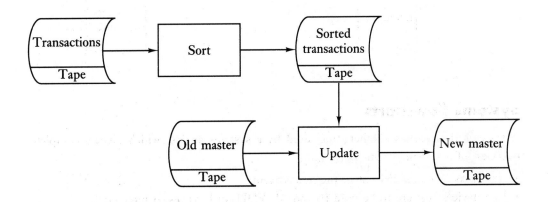

EXAMPLE

A transaction file is used to update an indexed sequential master file held on disk.

Notes: This differs from the first example in that no new file is created; on an indexed-sequential file the updates will be done *in situ*. Also, be careful to show the master file on disk, not tape, since it must be a direct access file if it is indexed.

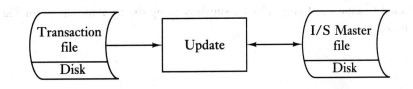

EXAMPLE

A stock master file stored in sequence order of a numeric key is updated by a transaction file using sequential file access. Transaction records, which represent additions and deletions to the stock levels, are collected in batches over a period of time and validated before being sorted into key order. Invalid data is corrected and entered into the next batch of transactions. The ordered transactions are used to update the master file. The update process produces a new master file and a file of all changes to records for audit purposes.

Draw a systems flowchart of the system described above.

(Note: Read the whole text through carefully first in order to work out what happens first; in this case, the second sentence is really the starting point of the whole process.)

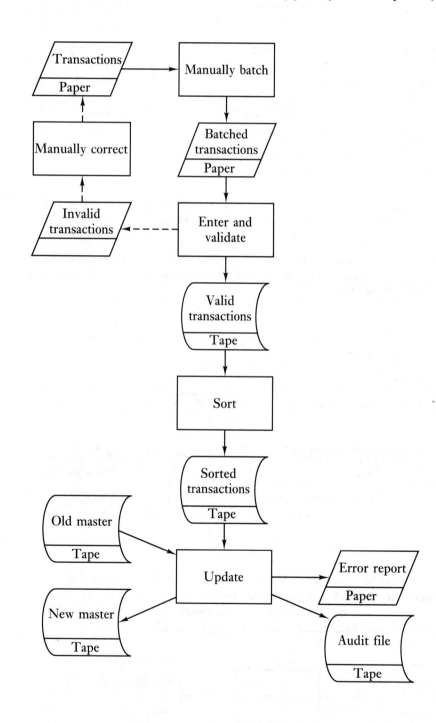

4.5 · SYSTEMS DESIGN

The systems designer will consider

- *output*: content, format, sequence, frequency, medium (e.g. screen or hard copy) etc;
- *input*: documents, screens and dialogues;
- *files*: contents, record layout, organisation and access methods;
- *processing*: the programs and procedures needed and their detailed design;
- *security*: how the data is to be kept secure from accidental corruption or deliberate tampering or hacking;
- *testing strategies*: how the system is to be thoroughly tested before going 'live';
- *hardware*: selection of an appropriate configuration.

User Interface

A good user interface design is an important aspect of a successful system. The design must take into consideration

- *who* is going to use the system – members of the public, experienced computer users, young children, etc.;
- *what tasks* the computer is performing; repetitive tasks, life-critical tasks such as flying a plane or dispensing radioactive doses to cancer patients, or variable tasks such as switching between a word-processor, spreadsheet and database;
- the *environment* in which the computer is used: hazardous, noisy, or comparatively calm and quiet;
- what is *technologically feasible*.

In particular, careful **screen design** can make a huge difference to the usability of a system. When designing an input screen, the following points should be borne in mind:

- The display should be given a title to identify it.
- It should not be too cluttered. Spaces and blanks are important.
- It should indicate the size and format of data entry in each field; i.e. don't just put

Date: _____

- Items should be put into a logical sequence to assist the user.
- Colour should be carefully used.
- Default values should be written in where possible.
- Help facilities should be provided where necessary.
- User should be able to go back and correct entries before they are accepted.

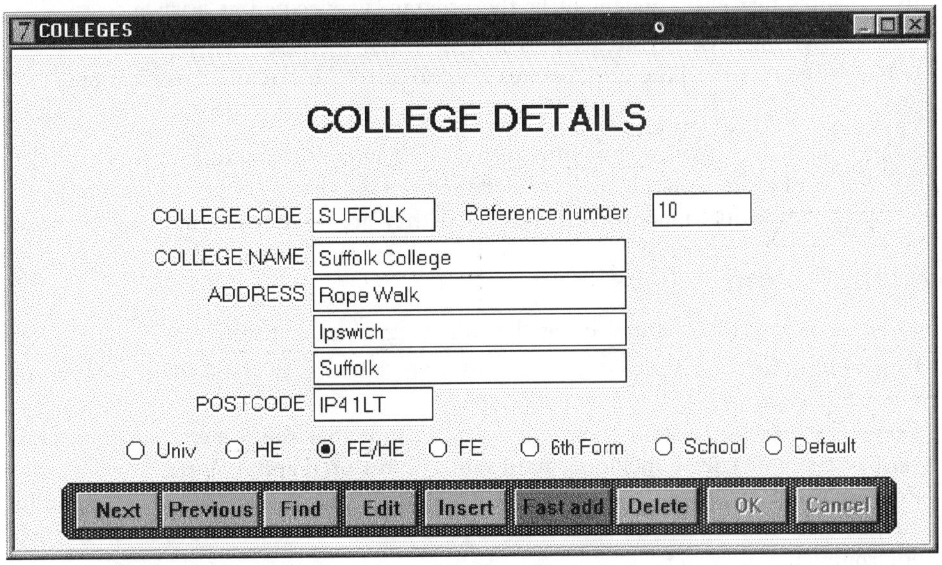

Figure 4.5: An input screen

Program design

This involves drawing structure charts and writing detailed program specifications.

Prototyping

Prototyping involves building a working model of a system in order to evaluate it, test it or have it approved before building the final product. When applied to computer systems, this could involve, for example, using special software to quickly design input screens, and running a program to input data. The user can then experience the 'look and feel' of the input process and suggest alterations before going any further.

Sometimes prototypes are simply discarded before the real system is started, and in other cases the prototype may be developed into a working system.

The prototyping approach is supported by a different life cycle model which spirals towards a final solution, and hence is known as the **spiral** model, contrasting with the traditional **waterfall** model.

Testing strategies

Obviously a system must be thoroughly tested before being installed to make sure that all errors are discovered and corrected before going 'live'. It is part of the designer's job to come up with a test strategy which will ensure that all parts of the system are properly tested.

Program testing

There are two possible strategies:

Bottom-up testing
1. Each individual module is tested as soon as it is written using pre-prepared test data. The data must include
   (a) normal data which the procedure is designed to handle;
   (b) extreme values which test the behaviour of the module at the upper and lower limits of acceptability;
   (c) exceptional or invalid data which the procedure should reject rather than attempting to process it.

2. Each complete program in the system is tested. Data should be chosen which
   (a) ensures that every route through the program is tested;
   (b) ensures that every statement in the program is executed at least once;
   (c) verifies the accuracy of the processing;
   (d) verifies that the program operates according to the original specifications.

Top-down testing
The skeleton of the complete system is tested, with individual modules being replaced by 'stubs' which may, for example, display a message to say that a certain procedure has been executed. As individual modules are completed they are included in subsequent tests.

System testing

The system as a whole is tested using the following types of test:
- **Functional testing**: the system is tested to make sure all parts of it work correctly using test data.
- **Recovery testing**: tests are carried out to ensure that the system can recover from various types of failure including hardware failures or power failures.
- **Performance testing**: this is carried out to ensure that the system performs satisfactorily with a realistic volume of data, in conditions which will prevail in the user environment.

4.6 DEVELOPMENT

This stage involves coding and testing programs according to the test plan. If a software package is being used it will probably involve tailoring the package, implementing screen designs and reports, writing macros, etc.

Once the system is complete, acceptance testing may take place.

Acceptance testing

Once the system is installed, acceptance testing may be carried out under the direction of the customer, who may provide the test plan. It has the following objectives:

- to confirm that the system delivered meets the original customer specifications;
- to find out whether any major changes in operating procedures will be needed;
- to test the system in the environment in which it will run, with realistic volumes of data.

4.7 IMPLEMENTATION

The implementation of a new computerised system will include

- hardware installation, with associated costs of rewiring, building modifications, new furniture etc.;
- file conversion, which can be a major part of the implementation. It often means converting old manual records into a medium usable by the computer, and this may involve hiring extra help to key in and verify data. Imagine keying in the details of 20,000 existing books for a new library system!
- staff training, which may be done by sending staff on special courses, bringing in an expert to teach small groups of staff, or allowing staff time for computer-aided training at their own desks.

Changeover options

Once the new system has been fully tested and accepted the changeover can be made. This can be done using any of the following strategies:

- *Direct changeover.* The user stops using the system one day and starts using the new system the next – usually over a weekend or during a slack period. This may be unavoidable when the new system is quite different from the old system, where the new system is a real-time system or where extra staff are not available to cope with the extra workload arising from parallel conversion. It is a risky option because normal operations could be quite seriously disrupted if the new system failed to function as expected for any reason.
- *Parallel conversion.* The old system continues alongside the new system for a few weeks or months, both processing current data. The advantage of this is that results from the new system can be checked against known results and if any difficulties occur, operations can continue under the old system while the errors or omissions are sorted out. The disadvantage of parallel running is the extra effort required to keep both systems running, which may put a strain on personnel.
- *Phased conversion.* This may be used with larger systems that can be broken down into individual modules that can be implemented separately at different times. For example in a supermarket the tills could be computerised first, being on-line to the stock master file to look up prices but not altering stock levels. When this aspect of the new system is known to be working well, the stock control system could be introduced so that items sold automatically reduce the quantity in stock.

- *Pilot conversion.* The new system is introduced into one department or branch of an organisation and run until it is proved to be working satisfactorily. This could be combined with parallel running in the relevant department.

4.8   DOCUMENTATION

Documentation for a system includes user manuals, a computer operations manual, systems specifications and program documentation.

User manual

This will typically contain

- an overview of the options available;
- guidance on the sequence of operations to follow;
- screen shots showing screen input 'forms';
- instructions on how to enter data;
- sample report layouts;
- error messages that may be displayed and what action to take.

Computer operations manual

This provides documentation of the procedures necessary to run the system. It may include

- system set-up procedures, including details for each application of the files required and stationery requirements;
- security procedures;
- recovery procedures in the event of system failure;
- a list of system messages that might appear on the operator's console and what action to take.

Systems specification

This is a complete description of the whole system showing data flows, system flowcharts, inputs, files, outputs and processing.

Program documentation

Each program within the system should have documentation which will include structure charts or pseudocode, full annotated listings and details of test data and results.

4.9   EVALUATION AND MAINTENANCE

Post-implementation review

Once the system is up and running a review needs to be performed to confirm that the new system is fulfilling expectations, and to identify any weaknesses or modifications that need to be made.

System maintenance

System maintenance involves

- updating the system to adapt it to changing circumstances, legislation or requirements;
- correcting any errors that come to light;
- documenting system updates and corrections.

Maintenance may be classified into three types:

- *perfective maintenance*: making improvements, possibly making the system easier to use or adding new facilities or reports;
- *adaptive maintenance*: making changes to take account of changes or expansion in the business or changes in legislation;
- *corrective maintenance*: correcting any errors that arise.

Chapter summary

Chapter 4 has outlined the difference between different types of computer system; centralised and distributed, batch, real-time and on-line. The stages in the system life cycle have been described and the symbols used in both systems flowcharts and data flow diagrams have been covered.

Illustrative questions

1 A company employs a software house to write a program for it. Before the program is written, an agreed *specification* is produced from the company's *problem description*.
   (a) State a difference between a specification and a problem description. (2)
   (b) After the program has been written, how would the specification be used by:
      (i) the company
      (ii) the software house? (2)
      (SQA)

Tutorial note
Don't try and rely on your memory to regurgitate the definition of 'specification'; use common sense and imagination instead!

Suggested answer
(a)   The specification describes how the problem will be solved, not what the problem is.
(b) (i)   The specification will be used by the company for acceptance testing, to ensure that the program performs as specified.
   (ii)   It will be used by the software house for system testing, and also kept for maintenance programming, should any changes need to be made to the program or bugs discovered.

2 User interfaces have gradually become more and more oriented to the needs of users over recent years.
   (a) Briefly describe *three* features of user interfaces which have been developed and explain how each has benefited the user. (3)
   (b) Describe two ways in which user interfaces need to be developed further to make computers more accessible and friendly to untrained users. (2)
      (EDEXCEL)

Tutorial note
User interfaces have been revolutionised since the bad old days of the DOS prompt. Your answer needs to cover aspects of interfaces such as Windows.

Suggested answer
(a) Icons which represent their meaning or a particular piece of software, the ability to use a pointer controlled by a mouse to select or execute a program, the use of on-line help accessible from a 'hot key' such as F1, and the use of 'undo' icons are all helpful to the user.

(b) The computer could be developed to accept voice input, or to give more helpful spoken or text messages when the user does something wrong.

3 Explain *without performing any calculation* the purpose of a check digit illustrating your answer with an example.   (4)

(NICCEA)

Tutorial note

A check digit is a validation technique; this question does not require you to perform a calculation but you should be able to calculate a modulo-11 check digit if asked.

Suggested answer

The purpose of a check digit is to detect errors occurring when data is entered into a computer system. The modulo-11 check digit system calculates the check digit from the code number using weights of 2,3,4 etc. and the calculated digit (0–9 or X) is appended to the end of the code number so that the whole code number is self-checking. A customer number, for example, might include a check digit.

4 Describe five main stages in the full life cycle of a computerised system.   (10)

(NEAB)

Tutorial note

A reasonable description of each stage is required. You won't get any marks for just naming five stages. Different stages from the ones in the suggested answer could be chosen, for example implementation and maintenance.

Suggested answer

Feasibility study: Pros and cons of developing a new system are investigated and a report written, which will cover a report on the existing system, the objectives of the new system, a cost-benefit analysis and a recommendation on how best to proceed.

Systems analysis: a more detailed investigation into the current system is made using interviews, questionnaires and/or observation, and data flows are investigated and documented.

Systems design: The detailed design of files, reports, screen inputs is decided upon and documented. The processing steps are identified and a testing strategy is designed.

Programming: Detailed program specifications are documented, structure charts or module charts drawn up and modules coded.

Testing: Each module is tested according to the test plan, then system tests are carried out and finally acceptance testing may take place in the user environment.

5 It is often necessary to process the same master file in both batch and interactive modes, at different times.

(a) Briefly describe an application in which this would be a requirement, and justify your answer.   (2)

(b) Describe a method of file organisation that would allow efficient processing of the master file in both modes. Indicate how the efficiency is achieved.   (3)

(EDEXCEL)

Tutorial note

Any system which allows enquiries to be made throughout the day, but where updating or processing takes place at set times of the day or week, can be used as a suitable example.

Suggested answer

(a) A payroll system may allow on-line queries of employee names, departments, pay-rates and so on and may allow updates to be made to certain fields. The payroll, however, will be carried out in batch mode in accordance with a weekly or monthly schedule.

(b) An indexed sequential file allows direct access to be made via the index to individual records, but also allows fast processing of the payroll by accessing the file sequentially without needing to use the index.

6 Student attendance is recorded daily on OMR forms. The forms are batched and the data is transferred onto a disk file, Weekly_Attendance. Once a week an update program is executed to transfer the attendance data to the indexed sequential file Student_Register and to produce a printed list of absences.
(a) What is the technique known as OMR? (1)
(b) Draw a system flowchart for the weekly update. (5)
(AEB)

Tutorial note
A common mistake is to draw a program flowchart instead of a system flowchart. Make sure you know the difference!

Suggested answer
(a) Optical mark recognition (OMR) is an optical technique used for transferring data encoded as marks made in pencil or pen on paper, to a computer.

(b)

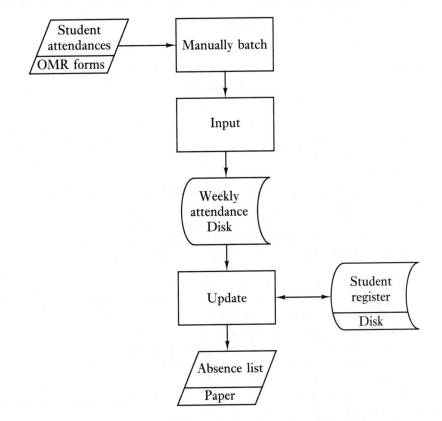

7 Explain clearly the difference between system documentation and user documentation. Outline the importance of documentation for software maintenance.
(6)
(NICCEA)

Tutorial note
You should be able to relate this question to work you have done on a practical computer project, which will contain both types of documentation, although the system documentation may be called 'technical documentation'.

Suggested answer
System documentation refers to all the documentation which was produced during the development of the software system. It includes system specifications, system flowcharts, DFDs, testing strategies.
  User documentation outlines the purpose of the software system and describes how to use it, and is written in non-technical language suitable for an end-user.
  Good documentation assists maintenance by describing the software system in a detailed and structured way making it easier for errors to be detected and corrected and for modifications to be made.

8 Suppose you work for a firm which provides software consultancy and development services. You receive an enquiry from a mail-order company which does not use computers, but thinks that maybe it should. Its business consists of producing and distributing catalogues, and providing a range of products in response to orders by post or telephone. The company thinks that it should computerise the stock control in its warehouse. You reply that you would be pleased to visit the mail-order company to discuss this and other potential computer applications.

    (a) (i) Summarise the other computer applications which might be appropriate. (4)

         (ii) List the main questions you will need to ask on your visit. (4)

    (b) Describe the specific information you will need to obtain from the company before you can develop a stock control system appropriate to its needs. (4)

                                                      (UCLES)

Tutorial note

The questions you would ask on a preliminary visit may relate to the stock control system, or they may be more wide-ranging. There should be no overlap between (a)(ii) and (b); (a)(ii) precedes the feasibility study, while (b) follows it. The questions asked on the first visit precede any decision to computerise.

Suggested answer

(a) (i) • *Word-processing* would be a useful application for dealing with day-to-day office correspondence, customer complaints, creating standard letters for mail shots.

        • A *customer mailing list* held on a database would be useful for marketing purposes, combined with the standard letter facility of a word processor.

        • *Customer accounts system* would be useful for automatic billing and recording of payments.

        • *Staff payroll system* would be useful for handling the payment of staff, P60 forms at end of year and so on.

     (ii) • What are the main objectives of a computerised system? Are there any particular problems with the current system that need to be addressed?

        • What is the current turnover, volume of data, number of customer accounts? Is this likely to increase substantially?

        • What is the maximum proposed expenditure on a new computer system?

(b) • How many different items are held in stock?

    • What information is held on each item of stock?

    • What paperwork is currently used to track the stock levels?

    • How does the stock reordering system work?

    • How many warehouse staff are involved in the stock control, and how do they operate?

9 A mail-order company uses a computer to manage its stock. Orders are received by post on the company's order forms but enquiries are also accepted by telephone and dealt with immediately. Orders are batched together, with a batch control sheet, for keying into the computer, validation and processing. The stock allocation program allocates stock to customers, updates the stock master file and produces a file of completed orders. If any particular item is out of stock that part of the order is transferred to a back-orders file. The printouts from the system include delivery notes and management reports.

    (a) State the purpose of the batch control sheet and describe how this is achieved.

                                                           (4)

    (b) State and justify a suitable medium for holding the stock master file. (2)

    (c) Draw a systems flowchart for the order processing system described above. (10)

    (d) Describe the management reports the system should produce. (3)

                                                               (NEAB)

Suggested answer

(a) The purpose is to check for missing forms, incorrect keying etc. Batch totals are calculated from the order forms, written on the batch header and keyed in as part of the data entry. The program compares these with values it calculates from the entered data.

(b) Magnetic disk would be suitable because direct access is required to individual records in order to answer telephone enquiries.

(c)

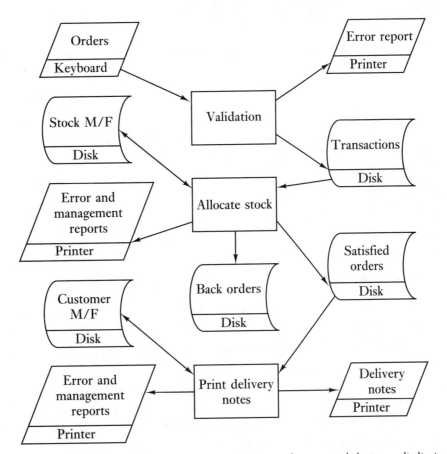

(d) The system should produce reports on customers who exceed their credit limits, the number and value of items which were out of stock, summary statistics on volumes and values of orders.

CHAPTER 5

DATABASES

Units in this chapter

Chapter objectives

After working through the topics in this chapter, you should be able to:

- distinguish a database from a traditional flat-file system;
- explain the advantages of a database over a flat-file system;
- define the terms **entity** and **attribute**;
- from given data requirements, produce a conceptual model and draw an entity relationship diagram;
- explain the concept of a relational database including the foreign key mechanism;
- show how data can be extracted from several tables;
- normalise a database;
- explain the concept of a multi-user database and the possible problems which arise;
- list the functions of a database administrator;
- explain the three-level architecture of a DBMS: external schema, conceptual schema and storage schema;
- explain the functions of a DBMS;
- explain the need for and general principles of database recovery.

5.1 THE EVOLUTION OF THE DATABASE MANAGEMENT SYSTEM (DBMS) APPROACH

Traditional file approach

In the early days of computerised data processing, an enterprise's data was duplicated in separate files for the use of individual departments. For example the personnel department would hold details on name, address, qualifications etc. of each employee, while the payroll department would hold details of name, address and salary of each employee. Each department had its own set of application programs to process the data in these files. This led to

- *duplicated data*, meaning wasted space;
- *inconsistency problems*, where for example an address was updated on one file but not on another;
- *the data was not shareable*; if one department needed data that was held by another, it was awkward to obtain it.

The database approach

In an attempt to solve the above problems, the data from the various departments was centralised in a common pool so that *all applications had access to the same set of data*. For example all the details about stock held by a garden centre would be held in a database which was accessible by all applications using the data. The sales department would update quantities in stock, the marketing department would use the data to produce a catalogue, the reorder system would use it to decide what stock to reorder.

Although this solved problems of duplication and inconsistency, it introduced two major new problems:

- *Unproductive maintenance*: if one department needed some change to the number or length of fields in a record on one of the common files, every department had to change its application programs to take this change into account, even if the field was not one used by that department. In other words, the programs were still dependent on the record structure, and all departments were affected by even minor changes in another department.
- *Problems of security*: even confidential or commercially sensitive data was accessible by every application, because the data was centrally held.

A **database**, therefore, is defined as a collection of non-redundant data shareable between different application systems.

The Database Management System (DBMS)

A DBMS is a layer of software which is inserted between the applications and the data, which attempts to solve the above problems. Two essential features of the DBMS are

- program–data independence, whereby the storage structure of the data is hidden from each application/user;
- restricted user access to the data – each user is given a limited view of the data according to need.

Advantages of the DBMS approach

1. *Data independence (program–data independence)*. Changes in the structure of the data do not affect programs which access the database, unlike a traditional flat-file system where the file structures are specified within the programs using them.

2. *Control over redundancy*. Each data item such as a name or an address is held once only. In a traditional file system, several different files may contain the same information, wasting space and making updating more time-consuming and error-prone.

3. *Data consistency*. Because the data is only held in one place, the situation cannot arise where for example an address has been changed on one file but not on another.

4. *Better security of data*. The database management system can control access rights to each individual item of data. Depending on a user's code and password, they may be allowed full update rights to some fields, read-only rights to other fields, and no access at all to certain fields.

5. *Better access to data*. Since all data is held centrally and access rights can be controlled, all employees can have the access that they need in order to do their jobs. It is also much easier to extract data from a database using queries than in a traditional file system, where a program would have to be specially written to obtain new or extra information from the files.

6. *Faster and cheaper development of new applications*. High-level database languages, screen design and report formatting facilities, etc., mean that new applications can be developed in a fraction of the time that it would take to write a set of programs to achieve the same end.

5.2 DATA MODELLING

The first stage in designing a database for an enterprise is to identify and state what data needs to be stored (the data requirements). For example, in a stock control application for a warehouse, a statement could be produced as follows:

> Each stock item has a stock number, a description, price, quantity in stock, reorder level and supplier. Each item has only one supplier.

From this statement of data requirements a **conceptual data model** is produced. The data model describes objects in terms of **entities** (representing things), **attributes** (representing properties of things) and **relationships** (representing the way things are related).

- An **entity** is a thing of interest to an organisation about which data is stored, for example, stock, supplier.

- An **attribute** is a property or characteristic of an entity, such as stock description, supplier name.

- A **relationship** is a link or association between entities. For example, there is a link between stock items and suppliers; namely one supplier may supply many stock items.

This **conceptual** or **logical** model is created without any regard to what type of database system will eventually be used to implement it. For example, the entity STOCK and its attributes are expressed as follows: STOCK (StockNumber, Description, Price, QuantityInStock, Reorder Level) where StockNumber is the entity identifier chosen because it uniquely identifies any occurrence of entity STOCK.

Types of relationship

Each relationship has a *name* (e.g. *supplies*) and a *degree*, which may be any of

- one-to-one;
- one-to-many;
- many-to-many.

In the warehouse example, the relationship between supplier and stock can be fully described by its name, *supplies*, and its *degree*, one-to-many.

Other examples:

- *One-to-one*. A vehicle has one tax disc, which belongs exclusively to that vehicle.
- *One-to-many*. A hospital ward is occupied by many patients, but a patient is assigned to only one ward.

- *Many-to-many*: A student may study several courses, each of which has many students enrolled on it.

Entity relationship diagrams

Diagrams are useful in providing a picture of the relationships, and by convention are drawn as shown in Fig. 5.1.

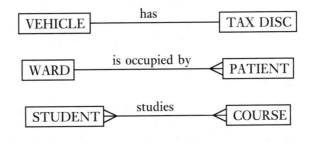

Figure 5.1: Entity relationship diagrams

The way in which these relationships are implemented will depend upon the particular type of database (e.g. relational, hierarchical, object-oriented, network) chosen. In this chapter we will only be looking at the relational database.

5.3   THE RELATIONAL DATABASE APPROACH

In a relational database, the data is held as a collection of tables. Each entity in the database will have its own table, as shown below. The relationships are implemented by having a common attribute to link the related tables – for example Supplier number is common to both STOCK and SUPPLIER.

STOCK

Stock number	Description	Price	Qty in stock	Reorder level	Supplier number
19893	Letter tray	6.05	21	15	A123
19898	Calendar holder	5.99	12	6	A123
43485	Date stamp	1.99	36	24	A123
13319	Tape cartridge (mini)	15.83	52	60	L227
13512	Tape cartridge (standard)	27.88	31	30	L227

SUPPLIER

Supplier number	Supplier name	Street	Town	Postcode
A123	Lowland Plastics	121 Hadleigh Ind Estate	Ipswich	IP9 8YU
L227	Crane Electronics	56 Crescent Street	Derby	DB6 5RT

The table is referred to as a *relation* in this approach.

The **attributes** of the relation STOCK are Stock number, Description, Price, Qty in stock, Reorder level and Supplier number. One attribute has a special role in identifying any particular row of the table. In the above case Stock number is an obvious identifier, but sometimes more than one attribute uniquely identifies a row and all such attributes are called **candidate keys**. If for example no two stock items were ever allowed to have identical descriptions, then Description and Stock number would both be candidate keys, and one would be chosen as the **primary key**. Generally speaking a numeric identifier which is short and not subject to being changed (because for example you found you had spelt a description wrong and wanted to change it) is preferable.

In some cases, the identifier may consist of more than one attribute. For example, two attributes Surname and First name may be needed to identify a member of a tennis club. (Again, it would be preferable to use a simple identifier like 'Membership number'.)

The attribute Supplier number in the STOCK table links the two tables together, and in this table it is known as a **foreign key**. It is the identifier or key field in the SUPPLIER table.

Database notation

It is convenient to have a standard notation when describing an entity/relation and its attributes. The notation which will be used follows the simple rules below:
*   Each table is shown with the table name in upper case, and in the singular (SUPPLIER not SUPPLIERS), followed by the attributes enclosed in brackets.
*   The key field (**identifier**) is underlined, and any foreign keys are shown in italics. The STOCK and SUPPLIER tables in the above example would be written as

STOCK   (Stock Number, Description, Price, Qty In Stock, Reorder level, *Supplier Number*)

SUPPLIER   (Supplier Number, Supplier Name, Street, Town, Postcode)

5.4   DATABASE DESIGN AND NORMALISATION

The first step in designing the relational database is to replace any many-to-many relationships in the conceptual entity relationship diagram with one-to-many relationships.

For example supposing we are designing a database to hold details of students and courses. The relationship is defined as follows:

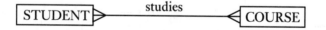

A new entity called Register is created as follows:

The next step is to create relations for each of these entities.

An alternative approach is to start from a single table containing all the data, and by a process called **normalisation**, arrive at the same set of tables. This process is demonstrated below.

Normalisation is a technique for deriving a satisfactory database model – that is, a database that is well designed in that it contains no redundant data, is not easily corrupted and will allow complex queries to be made which combine information held in several related tables. Normalisation can be carried out in three stages known as first, second and third normal form.

An unnormalised relation

A relation is **unnormalised** if it contains any attributes which are repeated within a single record. The STUDENT table below illustrates this.

STUDENT

Student number	Student name	Date of birth	Course number	Course name	Lecturer number	Lecturer name
12345	Heathcote,F	03-06-79	EC3211 EC1011 EC4521	Maths Yr 1 Computing Yr 1 Physics Yr 1	T223459 T345267 T318743	Peat,L Todd,M Chapman,H
22433	Head,J	06-04-79	AD6611 EC1011 BM7634	Art Yr 1 Computing Yr 1 French Yr 1	T886554 T345267 T165555	Lowry,B Todd,M Burke,D
128867	Harrison,E	07-04-79	EC1011 AD6611	Computing Yr 1 Art Yr 1	T345267 T886554	Todd,M Lowry,B

The STUDENT table can be described in standard notation as

> STUDENT (<u>Student number</u>, Student name, Date of birth, [Course number, Course name, Lecturer number, Lecturer name])

with repeating attributes shown in brackets [...].

First normal form (1NF)

A table is said to be in first normal form if it contains no repeating attributes or groups of attributes.

To convert this relation to first normal form, the entity COURSE needs to be given its own table, and each row in the STUDENT table needs to specify a course number. Since a student studies several courses, Student number is not enough to act as an identifier, as it does not uniquely identify a row in the table. The identifier consists of the two fields Student number and Course number.

> STUDENT   (<u>Student number</u>, Student name, Date of birth, *<u>Course number</u>*)

> COURSE   (<u>Course number</u>, Course name, Lecturer number, Lecturer name)

The data in the two tables can now be written as shown below.

STUDENT

Student number	Student name	Date of birth	Course number
12345	Heathcote,F	03-06-79	EC1011
12345	Heathcote,F	03-06-79	EC3211
12345	Heathcote,F	03-06-79	EC4521
22433	Head,J	06-04-79	AD6611
22433	Head,J	06-04-79	EC1011
22433	Head,J	06-04-79	BM7634
128867	Harrison,E	07-04-79	EC1011
128867	Harrison,E	07-04-79	AD6611

COURSE

Course number	Course name	Lecturer number	Lecturer name
EC1011	Computing Yr 1	T345267	Todd,M
EC3211	Maths Yr 1	T223459	Peat,L
EC4521	Physics Yr 1	T318743	Chapman,H
AD6611	Art Yr 1	T886554	Lowry,B
BM7634	French Yr 1	T165555	Burke,D

Second normal form (2NF)

A table is said to be in second normal form if it is in first normal form and no column that is not part of the primary key is dependent on only a portion of the primary key.

This is sometimes expressed by saying that *a table in second normal form contains no partial dependencies.*

This situation can only arise when the key identifier consists of more than one field, as in the STUDENT table above, where a particular row is identified by the Student number and the Course number. A student's name and date of birth, however, depend only on which student we are talking about, not on the particular student/course combination that a row in this table refers to. Therefore the table is not in second normal form.

To put it into second normal form, a new relation needs to be formed to act as the link between the relations STUDENT and COURSE.

The tables in second normal form are as follows:

STUDENT   (<u>Student number</u>, Student name, Date of birth)

REGISTER   (*<u>Student number</u>, <u>Course number</u>*)

COURSE   (<u>Course number</u>, Course name, Lecturer number, Lecturer name)

You can choose any convenient, meaningful name for the new relation. You will find that whenever two entities have a many-to-many relationship, you will always need to introduce a third table in order to put the tables into second normal form. Thus

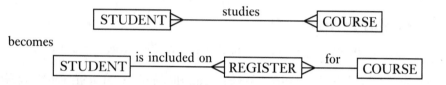

The two new relations now hold data as shown below.

STUDENT

Student number	Student name	Date of birth
12345	Heathcote,F	03-06-79
22433	Head,J	06-04-79
128867	Harrison,E	07-04-79

REGISTER

Student number	Course number
12345	EC1011
12345	EC3211
12345	EC4521
22433	AD6611
22433	EC1011
22433	BM7634
128867	EC1011
128867	AD6611

(The COURSE table is unchanged)

Notice that the relation REGISTER consists entirely of foreign keys, Student number being the key of the STUDENT table, and Course number being the key of the COURSE table.

Third normal form (3NF)

A table in third normal form contains no non-key dependencies. This is sometimes expressed rather neatly by saying that *in a table in third normal form, all attributes depend on 'the key, the whole key, and nothing but the key'.*

The COURSE table contains fields for Lecturer number and Lecturer name, but clearly Lecturer name depends only on Lecturer number and should not therefore be in this table. Once again a new relation has to be created, giving us a database in third normal form containing the four relations

STUDENT   (Student number, Student name, Date of birth)

REGISTER   (*Student number, Course number*)

COURSE   (Course number, Course name, *Lecturer number*)

LECTURER   (Lecturer number, Lecturer name)

The two modified tables COURSE and LECTURER contain data as shown below.

COURSE

Course number	Course name	Lecturer number
EC1011	Computing Yr 1	T345267
EC3211	Maths Yr 1	T223459
EC4521	Physics Yr 1	T318743
AD6611	Art Yr 1	T886554
BM7634	French Yr 1	T165555

LECTURER

Lecturer number	Lecturer name
T345267	Todd,M
T223459	Peat,L
T318743	Chapman,H
T886554	Lowry,B
T165555	Burke,D

The STUDENT and REGISTER tables are unchanged from second normal form.

5.5   MULTI-USER DATABASES

In any organisation using a database of a reasonable size, many people will have access to centrally stored data. A **multi-access database** is defined as one where many people may access the database *concurrently* (i.e. at the same time).

Problems of a multi-user database

Three major problems may occur in multi-user databases:
1. If two users simultaneously try to update the same record, one of the updates may be overwritten.
   Solution: The record should be 'locked' when the first user accesses it, so that no other user can update it until the first user has finished.
2. **Deadlock** may occur if two users both require access to a table or record currently in use, and locked, by the other user.
   Solution: Users and applications can be required to lock ALL required tables or records at the start of a transaction. Alternatively, either the user or the DBMS has to recognise when deadlock has occurred and abandon the operation, trying again in a few moments.
3. One user may be viewing a number of items on a screen, while another user is altering the same items in the database.
   Solution: The screen can be automatically 'refreshed' every few seconds or at the user's request.

Security of a multi-user database

Database security involves making sure that only authorised users have access to data in the database. It is achieved by giving each user a user ID and password which carries with it *privileges* granted by the Database Administrator. A particular user may have full access rights to some items, and read-only, update, and/or delete privileges or permissions to others. Passwords should be regularly changed and kept secret so that unauthorised users do not gain access to data illegally.

Performance factors

Sometimes users may find that some database operations are very slow. Suggestions for improving performance include the following:
- Educate users about the essential facts of multi-user operation so that they can schedule disk-intensive operations for quiet periods.
- Use the least restrictive locking mechanism possible; i.e. lock individual records rather than whole tables, or open a table in read-only mode if the operation does not perform updates.
- Index fields on which queries are made as this can speed up queries.
- Remove indexes on fields that do not require them as indexes have to be updated when records are updated, which can take extra time and space.
- Install more powerful hardware, e.g. processor, extra memory, upgraded cabling system.
- The Database Administrator can adjust buffer sizes.

5.6   DATABASE MANAGEMENT

The Database Administrator (DBA)

The tasks of the person assigned the role of DBA include:
1. design of the database;
2. implementing access privileges of all users;
3. monitoring of performance and fine-tuning the database to provide a satisfactory service;
4. keeping users informed of changes in the structure of the database that will affect them;
5. maintenance of the data dictionary;
6. providing training to users.

The three-level architecture of a 'database management system'

The word **schema** is used to mean a particular 'view' of the database, and there are three different levels of schema.
- The *external schema* is the individual user's view of the database. In a multi-user database, there are likely to be many different external schemas as each user will need to have access to different items of data. The DBA will be responsible for setting each user's access privileges.
- The *conceptual schema* is the overall view of the entire database as designed by the DBA and his/her team. The process of deciding upon entities, attributes and relationships, and normalising the database, is all part of designing the conceptual schema.
- The *internal* or *storage schema* is concerned with physical storage aspects such as file names, file organisation and access methods. This is generally transparent to both the developer and the end-user although in larger, more sophisticated mainframe databases the developer may have some control over the storage schema.

The functions of a database management system (DBMS)

The DBMS is the software which provides the interface between the application developer and the operating system. Its functions include the following:
1. organisation and storage of data in the database;
2. creation and maintenance of the data dictionary;
3. query processing;
4. maintaining the security and integrity of data in a multi-user database.

Each of these will now be discussed in turn.

Organisation and storage of data in the database

The DBMS has to organise and store the data in a manner that allows fast, efficient retrieval and updating of individual records. The way in which it does this is completely transparent to the application developer (programmer) and the end-user, except in the more sophisticated database systems where the developer may have some control over whether a particular table is organised as, say, a random (hash) file or an indexed file, and how the indexes are organised. This is the *internal schema* of the database.

Creation and maintenance of the data dictionary

When the requirements for a new database are being analysed, all the data items which need to be stored are identified, described in a systematic way, and stored for future reference in a table called the **data dictionary**. The data dictionary (the 'data about the data') is stored and managed by the DBMS. In some systems it is treated in the same way as any other table in the database; in others, it is held separately. It will contain such information as

- name and description of each data item;
- characteristics of each data item, such as length and data type;
- any restrictions on the value of certain data items;
- information on relationships between items in the database;
- control information such as who is allowed access to the data item, and what access right they have (read-only, read-write etc.);
- which programs access the data;
- statistical information showing, for example, frequency of access to tables or items.

Query processing

The DBMS will allow the user to query the database, typically by either writing a query in Structured Query Language (SQL) or by using Query by Example.

Using either of these methods the user may

- combine into one table information from two or more related tables;
- select which fields are to be shown in the 'Answer' table;
- specify criteria to search on;
- save the query so that it can be executed whenever required;
- save the results of the query (the 'Answer' table).

Figure 5.2 shows a **query by example** window in the MS Access database.

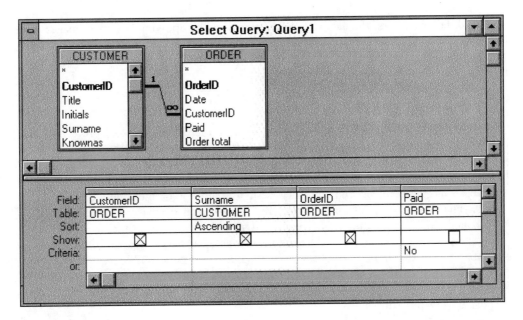

Figure 5.2

The query writes to an Answer table the Customer ID, Surname and Order ID of unpaid orders.

The DBMS automatically generates the equivalent query in SQL and stores the SQL code.

SQL

The basic retrieval facility in SQL is the Select statement, consisting of three clauses in the general form

    select ...
    from ...
    where...

For example, the above query could be coded

    select   ORDER.CustomerID, CUSTOMER.Surname, ORDER.OrderID
    from   CUSTOMER inner join ORDER on CUSTOMER.CustomerID=
                ORDER.CustomerID
    where   ORDER.Paid = No
    order by   CUSTOMER.Surname

Maintaining the security and integrity of data in a multi-user database

'Maintaining the integrity of the database' means ensuring that data is not accidentally or deliberately corrupted. Methods include
- extensive validation of input data;
- the use of *record-locking* and *access rights*.

Facilities must also be available to ensure that in the event of a system failure, no data is lost or corrupted, and that the database can quickly be restored to its state before the failure. Methods for doing this include

1. *Backing up the database.* Regular backups (perhaps daily) must be made and at least one copy kept in a separate location in a fireproof safe.
2. *Transaction logging.* A special file is created which contains information about each transaction. For example, if a user changes someone's address, a *before-image* and an *after-image* will be placed in the transaction log (i.e. copies of the record before and after the update).
3. *Checkpoints.* A checkpoint is a marker placed from time to time in the transaction log at a point in time when outstanding updates in temporary buffers are written permanently in the database.

If disk failure occurs, the database can be recovered by applying the after-images from the transaction log up to the latest checkpoint. Updates which were in the process of being written when failure occurred can be undone by applying the before-images to the affected records and re-entering the latest transactions.

Chapter summary

Chapter 5 has covered the major issues involved in the design, use and protection of databases. Entities, attributes and relationships have been defined and entity relationship diagrams used to give a graphical representation of one-to-one, one-to-many and many-to-many relationships. A standard notation for describing a relational database has been introduced, together with the concept of identifiers and foreign keys. The three stages in normalisation and their use in database design have been explained, and after reading this chapter you should be able to normalise a database.

You should also be able to describe the problems that may arise in multi-user databases, and the measures that are used to counteract these problems.

The role of the Database Administrator and the functions of the Database Management System have been discussed, together with the importance of backup and recovery procedures.

Illustrative questions

1 What is meant by program–data independence in the context of a database management system? (3)

(AEB)

Tutorial note
The point to get across here is that while traditional file systems are *program-oriented*, a database management system is *data-oriented*. The data structure is specified independently of the programs which use it, rather than being embedded within each program.

Suggested answer
A DBMS stores the description of the data organisation separately from the programs which access it. Hence changes in the data structure will not mean that programs have to be rewritten, as in a traditional file system.

2 State the purpose of a data dictionary and describe briefly *three* essentially different components you would expect to find in a data dictionary. (6)

(NICCEA)

Tutorial note
As applied to a DBMS, this question would be answered using the description of a data dictionary described in Section 5.6.

Suggested answer
The purpose of a data dictionary is to store information about the data held in a database in a well-organised and unambiguous form for use during the design, development and running of the database.
   The data dictionary will contain
- information about the entities and tables in the database;
- name, description and characteristics of each data item and any restriction on their value;
- information on relationships between objects in the database.

An alternative answer would be: Name, type, usage of each data item. For example:

Name	Type	Usage
Credit limit	Real	Used in order processing

3 In a multi-access application where the same data is shared by a number of different users it is important that users cannot change or view data without authority. Describe *one* way in which such a system can be designed to prevent this happening and comment on its effectiveness. (6)

(NICCEA)

Tutorial note
The question is not limited to databases but you can describe measures taken by a DBMS. Don't forget to comment on the effectiveness of the method – it's not sufficient just to say 'This is very effective', so think of possible justifications or alternatively weaknesses.

Suggested answer
A DBMS will maintain an access rights table which determines types of access granted to each user for each item in the database and makes use of external schemas to restrict users' views of data. The user is identified by user name/code and password. This is a very effective method of maintaining security provided that users are conscientious in keeping passwords secret and changing them at intervals.

4 The management of a company is concerned that its employees are becoming very casual regarding computer security. At the moment the company insists that its employees use passwords, but too many passwords are known by more than one person. Suggest a more effective method of security the company could consider, explaining how the proposed system would work and why it is more secure. Indicate how this method could still be breached. (4)

(NEAB)

Tutorial note

This question emphasises that passwords are sometimes not enough, and asks you to think of something that employees cannot bypass so easily. The best source of ideas for this type of question is newspaper articles, e.g. 'Innovations' in the *Sunday Times*, *Guardian* On Line section etc., so keep reading, and make a scrap book of relevant articles. For example the *Sunday Times* of 18 February 1996 carried an article about a £200 fingerprint scanner which can instantly verify a person's identity.

Suggested answer

A credit-card-shaped badge reader could be used, which the user would have to insert before logging on. The password would have to match the one on the badge, which would be held in encrypted form. This would be more secure because it would require the presence of the badge, which employees would be less inclined to lend. However, security could still be breached if an employee lent the badge to someone else and told them their password.

5 A company records details of its business activities on a computer system. The company has a regular practice of file backup and it maintains transaction logs.

(a) Explain the meaning of the terms **file backup** and **transaction log**. (4)

(b) Explain how the company can recover its data following a system failure. (4)

(UCLES)

Tutorial note

For two marks it is not enough to say, for example, that a 'file backup is a copy of a file', so think of something to add to that. Part (b) follows logically from part (a).

Suggested answer

(a) File backup means making a copy of a file for use if the original is destroyed or corrupted.

   A transaction log is a disk or tape file containing a copy of all transactions to a master file (or information about each change made to a data file, such as a before-image and after-image).

(b) Copy the backup file back to the original medium to restore the data to its state before the last backup was taken. Then use the transaction file to effect all subsequent data changes.

6 (a) Explain, with the aid of examples, how a database differs from a file. (3)

(b) Describe the functions carried out by a database management system and the facilities it offers to the user. (7)

(UCLES)

Tutorial note

It's important to get across the point that a database consists *of more than one* table and that the *relationships* between the tables are defined in a database. Give examples to support your explanation. In part (b), there is a subtle distinction between *functions* (what the DBMS does) and *facilities* (what it enables the user to do). There is an overlap because the function of the DBMS is to provide facilities for the user to do certain things!

Suggested answer

(a) A file is an organised collection of records, for example a payroll file used to produce pay-slips. A database consists of a number of related tables together with a definition of how they are related, e.g. a school database holding information about students, staff, courses etc.

(b) Functions provide facilities for setting up and managing the database, allow creation and maintenance of the data dictionary, control access to the data by means of passwords.

Facilities enable input screens and reports to be quickly and easily designed, enable queries to be made and stored, validation to be performed on input data, enable complete applications with menu structure to be implemented.

7 A large firm selling dental products does so through a series of representatives who visit dental surgeons throughout the country. If a visit is successful then the representative places an order with headquarters. In any event, the representative has to inform headquarters, at the end of the day, how many visits have been made, where and how much has been sold. This is done via a telephone link from the representative's home to the firm's computer. Each representative has a unique login code.

Headquarters has a list of all dentists in the country, and representatives are allocated to specific areas. It is, however, the representative who decides where to go each day within the designated area. Return visits are generally two months after the previous one.

To earn the basic wage, a representative has to visit an average of eleven dentists within the five-day working week. Commission of 0.5% is earned on all sales.

(i) Describe the hardware and software needed to link the representative to headquarters. (6)

The information on products, representatives and dentists is held in an appropriate file structure on the mainframe.

(ii) For each of products, representatives and dentists illustrate a typical record, noting any key fields and describing the data type in each field. (12)

(iii) Using a relational database, or otherwise, explain how the database could be interrogated to give a list of all dentists visited by a certain representative in one week, and also how the salary of an individual representative could be calculated at the end of each month. (12)

(UODLE)

Tutorial note
This question is designed to take about 45 minutes to answer so a fair amount of detail is expected in the answer. Parts (ii) and (iii) require a good understanding of setting up and using a database which you will most easily obtain from practical experience.

Suggested answer
(i) The representative will need a PC, laptop or hand-held computer with a modem to convert the digital signals from the computer to analogue for transmission over the telephone line. HQ will also need a modem to convert the signal back to digital, and probably a front-end processor to process the incoming transmissions. Communications software will be needed to dial up the remote computer, verify the login code and enable the file transfer to take place.

(ii) PRODUCT

Product number (key field)	6 alphanumeric characters	AX1234
Description	String (30)	Drill bit (diamond)
Selling price	Real	15.00

REPRESENTATIVE

Rep number (key field)	Integer	45623
Surname	String (15)	Pradesh
First Name	String (15)	Vini
Title	String (5)	Mr
Address 1	String (20)	3 Ewart Close
Address 2	String (20)	Oxford
Post code	String (8)	OX4 5ER
Telephone	String (15)	01865 - 123456

DENTIST

Dentist number (key field)	Integer	45623
Surname	String (15)	Newman
First Name	String (15)	Christopher
Title	String (5)	Mr
Address 1	String (20)	6 Bishops Hill
Address 2	String (20)	Oxford
Post code	String (8)	OX6 7TR
Telephone	String (15)	01865 - 654321
Rep number (foreign key)	Integer	45623

(iii) There would need to be two extra tables; a VISIT table defined as follows:
VISIT (<u>Date</u>, <u>Rep number</u>, <u>Dentist number</u>)
and a SALES table:
SALES (<u>Order number</u>, Date, Value, Dentist number, Rep number)
(There would also be an order details table but this is not needed for the specified queries)

To get a list of all dentists visited by a rep in one week, the VISIT and DENTIST tables would be queried setting date and rep number criteria as appropriate, e.g. Rep number = 46523, date >=1.8.96 and < 8.8.96. The dentist's name and details would be obtained from the DENTIST table using the common link Dentist number.

To calculate the salary of an individual rep, the SALES table would be queried, setting date and rep number appropriately, and adding a calculated field to add total sales and calculate 0.5%. The program would have to check that the rep had qualified for the basic wage, i.e., assuming that one month comprises four weeks, that the total number of visits during the month, divided by four was at least eleven.

8 The data requirements for a booking system are defined as follows.
An agency arranges booking of live bands for a number of clubs. Each band is registered with the agency and has its name (unique) recorded, together with the number of musicians, the type of music played and hiring fee. Each band is managed by a manager. A manager may manage several bands. Each manager is assigned an identification number and managers have their name, address and telephone number recorded. Each club is assigned an identification number and clubs have their name, address and telephone number recorded.

The agency records details of each booking made between a band and a club for a given date. A band will never have more than one booking on any particular date.

(a) In database modelling, what is:

    (i)   an attribute;   (1)

    (ii) a relationship?   (1)

(b) Four entities for the booking system are Manager, Club, Band and Booking.

    (i)   Suggest an identifier, with justification, for *each* of the entities Manager, Club and Band.   (3)

    (ii) Describe *four* relationships involving the entities Manager, Club, Band and Booking that can be inferred from the given data requirements.   (4)

(c) A relational database is to be used. Describe tables for the following entities underlining the primary key in each case:

    (i)   Manager;   (2)

    (ii) Band;   (4)

    (iii) Booking.   (5)

                                                                    (*AEB*)

Tutorial note
In part (a), if you find it difficult to define an attribute and a relationship, you will get the marks for giving correct examples.

In part (b) (ii) diagrams will do for describing relationships. In part (c), write the table definitions in standard notation – that is all the description that is required. Don't forget to put foreign keys in where necessary.

Suggested answer
(a) (i) An attribute is a property or characteristic of an entity (or, a column in a table).
    (ii) A relationship is an association or link between two entities (or give an example, e.g. 'A manager manages many bands' is a one-to-many relationship).
(b) (i) Manager – Identification number (because unique)

    Club – Identification number (unique)

    Band – Name (unique, registered with agency)

(ii)

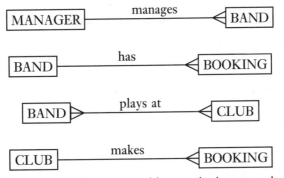

(c) (i)   MANAGER (<u>Manager ID</u>, name, address, telephone number)

    (ii) BAND (<u>Band name</u>, Number of musicians, Type of music, Hiring fee, *Manager ID*)

    (iii) BOOKING (*Band name, Date, Club ID*)

CHAPTER 6

DATA REPRESENTATION IN COMPUTERS

Units in this chapter

Chapter objectives

After working through the topics in this chapter, you should be able to:

- describe standard format for character representation in computers;
- translate a denary integer to binary and vice versa;
- show how a negative number can be held in two's complement form;
- perform integer addition and subtraction;
- translate a denary or binary integer to hexadecimal and vice versa;
- explain the use of BCD and its advantages;
- show how a real number can be held in floating point form;
- show how range and precision are affected by the chosen representation;
- explain why rounding errors and truncation errors occur;
- describe how bit patterns may also represent graphics and sound;
- explain the different interpretations that may be associated with a pattern of bits in computer memory dependent on its use and the computer architecture.

6.1 CHARACTER CODES AND THEIR REPRESENTATION

All types of data are represented in a computer's memory as patterns of binary digits. When you press an 'a' on the keyboard, for example, a particular pattern of 0s and 1s is stored in the keyboard buffer to represent that character. Computer memory is commonly divided up into groups of 8 bits known as **bytes,** with each byte able to store a single character. Over the years, different computer designers have used different sets of codes for representing characters, with American Standard Code for Information Interchange (**ASCII**) being commonly used on personal computers. Originally only 7 bits were used, enough to represent 128 different characters with the 8th bit being used as a **parity** bit, but the extended ASCII character set uses all 8 bits to represent 256 different characters. Other codes such as Extended Binary Coded Decimal Interchange Code (**EBCDIC**) are still in use on some mainframe computers.

The ASCII codes are shown below in Table 6.1.

Character	ASCII	Character	ASCII	Character	ASCII	Character	ASCII
space	00100000	8	00111000	P	01010000	h	01101000
!	00100001	9	00111001	Q	01010001	i	01101001
"	00100010	:	00111010	R	01010010	j	01101010
#	00100011	;	00111011	S	01010011	k	01101011
$	00100100	<	00111100	T	01010100	l	01101100
%	00100101	=	00111101	U	01010101	m	01101101
&	00100110	>	00111110	V	01010110	n	01101110
'	00100111	?	00111111	W	01010111	o	01101111
(	00101000	@	01000000	X	01011000	p	01110000
)	00101001	A	01000001	Y	01011001	q	01110001
*	00101010	B	01000010	Z	01011010	r	01110010
+	00101011	C	01000011	[	01011011	s	01110011
,	00101100	D	01000100	\	01011100	t	01110100
-	00101101	E	01000101	]	01011101	u	01110101
.	00101110	F	01000110	^	01011110	v	01110110
/	00101111	G	01000111	_	01011111	w	01110111
0	00110000	H	01001000	`	01100000	x	01111000
1	00110001	I	01001001	a	01100001	y	01111001
2	00110010	J	01001010	b	01100010	z	01111010
3	00110011	K	01001011	c	01100011	{	01111011
4	00110100	L	01001100	d	01100100	|	01111100
5	00110101	M	01001101	e	01100101	}	01111101
6	00110110	N	01001110	f	01100110	~	01111110
7	00110111	O	01001111	g	01100111	del	01111111

Table 6.1:   The ASCII character codes (excluding the extended character set)

6.2 REPRESENTATION OF INTEGERS

When the characters 15863 are pressed on the keyboard, the binary codes for 1, 5, 8, 6 and 3 are sent to the keyboard buffer. If these digits represent, say, a telephone number, they can be stored in this format in 5 consecutive bytes. If, on the other hand, the digits represent an integer (whole number) that is to be used in a calculation, they need to be converted to a **binary integer**.

Our ordinary number system is called the **denary** system and uses ten digits 0 to 9. In this system, the number **387** represents

$$3 \times 100 + 8 \times 10 + 7 \times 1$$

This is a base 10 number system and as we move from right to left, each digit is worth 10 times as much as the previous one.

Translating from binary to denary

In the binary system, only the two digits 0 and 1 are used, and as we move from right to left, each digit is worth twice as much as the previous one. Thus the binary number 01011101 can be set out under column headings as follows:

128	64	32	16	8	4	2	1
0	1	0	1	1	1	0	1

This represents $64 + 16 + 8 + 4 + 1 = 93$

Translating from denary to binary

To translate a denary number to binary, write down the column headings and starting from the left hand end, figure out the largest power of two that 'fits' into the given number. Put a 1 under the column heading, subtract this amount from the number, and continue in the same way. e.g. Translate the denary number 105 to binary.

	128	64	32	16	8	4	2	1
Write the column headings								
64 'fits'	0	1						
Subtract 64 from 105 leaving 41. 32 'fits'.	0	1	1					
Subtract 32 from 41 leaving 9, and so on	0	1	1	0	1	0	0	1

A programmer generally has some control over how many bytes are to be used to hold an integer value. In Turbo Pascal, for example, the following integer types are predefined:

Type	Range	Format	
Shortint	-128 .. 127	Signed	8-bit
Integer	-32768 .. 32767	Signed	16-bit
Longint	-2147483648 .. 2147483647	Signed	32-bit
Byte	0 .. 255	Unsigned	8-bit
Word	0 .. 65535	Unsigned	16-bit

Binary arithmetic

To add two binary numbers, remember that 'carry' occurs as soon as you add 1 and 1 to make two, which is written not as 2, but 10.

```
e.g.        0 1 1 0 1 0 1 1
       +    0 0 0 1 1 0 1 1
            ───────────────
            1 0 0 0 0 1 1 0
```

Representing negative numbers using sign and magnitude

There are two ways of representing negative numbers. In the *sign and magnitude* method, if the leftmost bit (the sign bit) is 1, the number is taken to be negative; if it is 0, the number is positive. Thus $00000011 = 3$,

$$10000011 = -3.$$

The problem with this method is that arithmetic is inconvenient; for example adding the representations of $+3$ and -3 does not result automatically in zero!

Representing negative numbers using two's complement

A better way of representing negative numbers is the two's complement method. To translate a negative denary number to binary using two's complement:
1. Find the binary value of the equivalent positive decimal number.
2. Change all the 1s to 0s and the 0s to 1s.
3. Add 1 to the result.

An even quicker way is to do the following:
1. Starting from the right, leave all the digits alone up to and including the first 1.
2. Change all the other digits from 0 to 1 and 1 to 0.
e.g. Two's complement of 01101011 is 10010101.
Tips:
1. Note that the sign bit is always 1 for a negative number.
2. The denary number −1 translates to 11111111 in an 8-bit byte.
3. To perform binary subtraction, first find the two's complement of the number to be subtracted, and then add the two numbers.

The hexadecimal number system

The hexadecimal number system uses 16 digits 0–9, A–F, with numbers being held in a base 16 format.

Thus the hexadecimal number 1B6 represents $1 \times 256 + 11 \times 16 + 6 \times 1 = 438$. The advantage of this system is that it is very easy to convert from binary to hexadecimal, and if a programmer wants to examine the contents of a portion of memory, for example, a hexadecimal memory 'dump' is very much easier to read than a string of binary digits.

To convert from binary to hexadecimal, divide the binary number into groups of 4 bits (starting from the right) and translate each group of 4 bits into a hexadecimal digit. For example,

$$0110\ 1111\ 1001\ 1100 = 6\ F\ 9\ C$$

The octal number system

In the octal (base 8) system only the 8 digits 0 to 7 are used. To convert a binary number to octal, divide the number into groups of 3 rather than groups of 4. This system was used on computers that had a 24-bit word divided into groups of 6 bits, instead of the now common 16-, 32- or 64-bit word divided into 8-bit bytes.

e.g. $001\ 101\ 111 = 157_8$
The subscript denotes the number base.

Binary coded decimal

In the binary coded decimal (BCD) system, each denary digit is represented by its own binary code, e.g. to translate the denary number 8319 to BCD translate each digit separately:

$$8\ 3\ 1\ 9 = 1000\ 0011\ 0001\ 1001$$

The advantage of BCD is the ease of conversion from BCD to denary and vice versa. Thus, when binary numbers have to be electronically decoded for a pocket calculator display, a number held in BCD format simply has to be split into groups of 4 bits and each group converted directly to the corresponding denary digit.

The disadvantage of BCD is that calculations are more complex than with pure binary numbers. For example, if we attempt to add the BCD representations of 1 and 19:

```
      0000    0001
 +    0001    1001
    - - - - - - - - -
      0001    1010
```

The first digit, 1, is wrong and 1010 does not exist in the BCD system because it represents denary 10, which is not a single digit.

The problem arises because only the first 10 out of 16 combinations of 4 digits are used to encode the denary digits '0' to '9'. Therefore, whenever the sum of two BCD digits is greater than 9, 6 has to be added to the result in order to skip over the six unused codes. Adding the binary representation of 6 to 1010:

```
      0001    1010
 +            0110
    - - - - - - - - -
      0010    0000    which represents the correct answer of 20.
```

6.3 FIXED POINT BINARY NUMBERS

A number with a decimal point is known (rather bafflingly) as a **real** number, as opposed to an integer which is a whole number. In denary, the number 15.24 represents

$$1 \times 10 \ + \ 5 \times 1 \ + \ 2 \times \tfrac{1}{10} \ + \ 4 \times \tfrac{1}{100}$$

In a similar way, the binary number 0011.1010 represents

$$1 \times 2 \ + \ 1 \times 1 \ + \ 1 \times \tfrac{1}{2} \ + \ 0 \times \tfrac{1}{4} \ + \ 1 \times \tfrac{1}{8}$$

Negative fractional fixed point numbers can be held using two's complement representation in the same way as integers.

The problem with this representation of fractional numbers is that wherever the binary point is placed, the **range** and **precision** of numbers is limited. Even with 8 digits on each side of the binary point, the smallest positive number that can be held is $\tfrac{1}{256}$ (00000000.00000001), and the largest positive number is just under 128 (01111111.11111111).

6.4 FLOATING POINT REPRESENTATION

A much better system of representing real numbers is to use floating point representation, in which the number is held in two parts, a **mantissa** and an **exponent**. This is the format used on a calculator display when the result of a calculation is too large or too small to be displayed in the ordinary format. For example, the display 1.45376   13 represents 1.45376×10^{13}, with 1.45376 being the mantissa and 13 the exponent.

Binary fractions can be held in the same way. In a 16-bit word, typically 10 bits may be used for the mantissa and 6 bits for the exponent, with the leftmost bit of each part being a sign bit, and the binary point assumed to be in the position shown below:

mantissa	exponent
0 . 1 0 1 1 0 0 0 0 0	0 0 0 0 1 1

This represents 0.101100000×2^3, i.e. 0101.1000 (moving the binary point 3 places to the right), which is 5.5.

If the sign bit of the exponent is negative, the binary point is moved left instead of right.

e.g.   0.110000000   111111   represents $0.110000000 \times 2^{-1}$ = 0.011000000 = 0.25 + 0.125 = 0.375

Normalisation

The *precision* of a number depends on the number of digits held in the mantissa. To achieve the maximum precision, the first digit after the binary point should be 1, not 0. To understand why, consider an equivalent situation in the denary system; using a 6 digit mantissa the number 1,234,567 can be held most precisely (but still sacrificing some precision) as $.123457 \times 10^7$. If it were held as $.012346 \times 10^8$, it would be less precise because fewer significant digits are stored.

A floating point binary number which has a 1 immediately following the point in the mantissa is said to be **normalised**; numbers are always stored in normalised form to maximise their precision.

If the number is negative, the sign bit will be 1 and in its normalised form there will be a 0 immediately following the point.

6.5 PROBLEMS WITH NUMERIC REPRESENTATIONS

Overflow and underflow

When the result of a computation is too large to be held in the bytes allocated, **overflow** occurs and the wrong answer may be stored. This can happen with both integers and floating point numbers. **Underflow** occurs when the result of a computation is smaller than the smallest number that can be represented; the system will generally set the result to zero if this occurs.

Truncation and rounding

Truncation or rounding down may occur where the precision is not adequate to represent all the digits in the number to be stored. If, for example, the mantissa is 0.11011101 but only 8 bits are allowed, it will be stored as 0.1101110. If the number is **rounded** instead of truncated, the mantissa will be stored as 0.1101111, since the digit after the last one to be represented is 1.

Note that many real numbers cannot be represented accurately in binary, however many bits are allowed. (The same is true in denary, for example $\frac{1}{3}$ cannot be represented exactly however many decimal places are allowed.)

6.6 REPRESENTATION OF GRAPHICS AND SOUND

A particular byte or group of bytes in memory may represent, among other things, a string of characters, an integer, a real number, a machine code instruction, a small part of a graphic or a sound of a particular frequency. A particular pattern of 0s and 1s can only be decoded by knowing what it is supposed to represent.

Chapter summary

Chapter 6 has described how integers and real numbers may be stored in a computer, and explained the translation of denary numbers to binary, hexadecimal and octal and vice versa. BCD format and its advantages have been explained. The format of floating point real numbers has been described, and how normalising them affects the range and precision of the number represented. A particular binary pattern may represent any one of many forms of information including graphics and sound.

Illustrative questions

1 The binary pattern 1011 1010 0011 can be interpreted in a number of different ways.

   (a) State its hexadecimal representation. (1)

   (b) State its value in denary if it represents a two's complement floating point number with an eight bit mantissa followed by a four bit exponent. (3)

   (AEB)

Tutorial note
The binary pattern 1010 is an easy one to recognise – it equals 10 in denary, or A in hexadecimal. (Denary is just another word for decimal, meaning our ordinary number system.) In part (b) convert mantissa to $-0.100\ 0110$ by finding its two's complement.

Suggested answer
(a) B A 3
(b) 1011 1010 0011
    First find the two's complement of the mantissa: 0100 0110
    Exponent = 3 (i.e. 0011)
    The number represents $-0.100\ 0110 \times 2^3 = -0100.0110 = -4.375$

2 State the binary results of each of the following:
    (i) $00001011_2 \times 8$
    (ii) $01101100_2 / 4$ (2)
                                                                   (NEAB)

Tutorial note
Remember that multiplying by 2 in binary is equivalent to multiplying by 10 in denary – add a zero to get the result.

Suggested answer
(i)   01011000
(ii)   00011011

3 (a) Explain the terms *integer* and *floating point number*.   (3)

    (b) Why are hexadecimal numbers often quoted in system error messages?   (2)
                                                                        (AEB)

Suggested answer
(a) An integer is a whole number.
    A floating point number has a fractional part (the mantissa) and a scale factor (the exponent).
(b) System error messages typically refer to memory addresses, which are held in binary format. However, binary is very difficult to read and hexadecimal is a convenient abbreviation.

4 A particular computer with a 16-bit word stores floating point numbers in the following form:

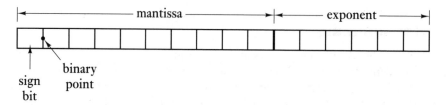

The 10-bit mantissa is stored in sign and magnitude representation.
The leftmost bit is the sign bit.
The binary point is immediately to the right of the sign bit.
The exponent occupies six bits and is represented as an integer in two's complement form.
A number is said to be normalised when the bit immediately to the right of the binary point has the value 1.

(i) State the value represented by the binary word
    0 1 1 0 1 0 1 1 0 0 0 0 0 0 1 1

(ii) The decimal number 0.2 corresponds to the recurring binary fraction
    0 . 0 0 1 1 0 0 1 1 0 0 1 1 ...

Show how this number would be stored as accurately as possible.   (5)
                                                                                           (EDEXCEL)

Suggested answer
(i) The value represents $0.110101100 \times 2^3 = 110.101100 = 6.6875$
(ii) The value needs to normalised, i.e. the first digit after the binary point should be 1. Therefore the exponent must be set to -2 to compensate for moving the binary point.
$2 = 000010$ Two's complement $= 111110$
Therefore the number is 0110011001 111110

5 State one advantage and one disadvantage of fixed point representation of numbers compared to floating point representation.   (4)
                                                                                (*NICCEA*)

Suggested answer
An advantage of fixed point arithmetic is that arithmetic is faster and less complex. A disadvantage of fixed point is that the range of numbers that can be represented is much less than in floating point format.

6 When instructing a computer to carry out calculations within a program a programmer has to be aware of the possibility of overflow and underflow.
   (a) Explain what is meant by overflow. Briefly describe *two* different types of calculations which can cause it.   (3)
   (b) Explain what is meant by underflow. Briefly describe *two* different types of calculations which can cause it.   (3)
                                                                                (*NEAB*)

Suggested answer
(a) Overflow – the result of a calculation is too big to fit into the register using the format specified. Caused by e.g. multiplying two large numbers or dividing a large number by a very small number.
(b) Underflow – the result of a calculation is too small to be stored in the register using the format specified. Caused by e.g. multiplying two very small numbers or dividing a small number by a large number.

7 The owner of a small shop selling electronic components has purchased a microcomputer to produce invoices for customers.
   The numeric data items included in these invoices are:

   • prices and totals of items purchased, e.g. £47.24

   • quantities of items purchased, e.g. 2.

   (a) Integers can be represented inside the microcomputer in locations of size 16 bits using:
       A : binary coded decimal;
       B : sign and magnitude;
       C : two's complement.
       (i) Show how the number 20 would be represented using method A.
       (ii) Show how the number –20 would be represented using methods B and C.
                                                                                (6)

   (b) Real numbers can be represented inside this computer in the following form:

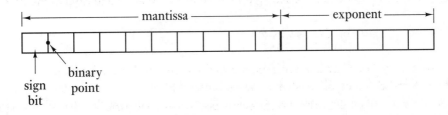

The 10-bit mantissa is stored in sign and magnitude representation.
The leftmost bit is the sign bit.

The binary point is immediately to the right of the sign bit.
The exponent occupies six bits and is represented as an integer in two's complement form.
Show how the number 20.5 can be represented using this system. (3)

(c) (i) Comment on the suitability of each of the methods A, B and C above to represent the numeric data items included in the invoice.
   (ii) Explain why real numbers are unlikely to be used to represent these data items.
(6)
(*EDEXCEL*)

Suggested answer

(a) BCD (20):   0000 0000 0010 0000
    Sign and magnitude (−20):   1000 0000 0001 0100
    two's complement (−20):   1111 1111 1110 1100

(b) 20.5 = 10100.1
    Point needs to be moved 5 places left to normalise the number. Make the exponent 5.
    0101001000 000101

(c) (i) Representing integers in BCD produces a range of numbers from 0 to 9999, or −999 to + 999 if the first four bits are used for the representation of a sign. Thus this method can only be used for bills up to £99.99 and quantities up to 9,999.

   Representing integers in sign and magnitude form produces a range of numbers from − 32,767 to + 32,767. Thus this method can only be used for bills up to £327.67 and quantities up to 32,767.

   Representing integers in two's complement form produces a range of numbers from −32,768 to + 32,767. Thus this method can only be used for bills up to £327.67 and quantities up to 32,767.
   The algorithms used to perform the arithmetic operations upon integers produce accurate results within the limits of the ranges of numbers which can be represented by the various methods.

   (ii) Real numbers are unlikely to be used to represent these data items because:
   • some denary numbers can only be represented in binary floating point form in an inaccurate truncated form;
   • the algorithms used to perform the arithmetic operations upon real numbers involve truncating the results.

8 A unique (different) numeric code, occupying a single byte, is generated for each key or valid key combination pressed on a computer's keyboard.
   (a) (i) How many bits make up one byte? (1)
       (ii) How many different numeric codes can be coded in a single byte? (1)

   In one coding system, the character digits 0 to 9 are assigned the decimal number codes 48 to 57 and the letters A to Z the decimal number codes 65 to 90. Table 1 is a hexadecimal dump of a part of an area of main memory used as a buffer for the keyboard.

Table 1

Memory location address	Contents
C063	37
C062	34
C061	5A

   (b) List the sequence of keys which were pressed to produce the Contents column of Table 1, assuming memory location $C063_{16}$ to contain the last of the codes generated. (3)
   (c) A decimal integer number is entered at the keyboard as a sequence of character digits. This sequence is then processed to convert a number's decimal number

codes representation into its equivalent decimal integer value using the following algorithm:

Table 2

```
Number ← 0
While more character digits
    Do
        Get next character digit from buffer
        and store in the variable CharacterDigitCode
        Number ← Number * 10 + CharacterDigitCode – 48₁₀
EndWhile
```

(i) Hand trace this algorithm for the keyboard sequence 527, showing the numeric contents of Number and CharacterDigitCode in decimal (denary) after each iteration. (6)

(ii) State one reason why this conversion is carried out. (1)

(d) The area of main memory reserved for buffering keyboard input is set up as a circular queue occupying locations $C000_{16}$ to $C063_{16}$.

(i) State *one* advantage of buffering keyboard input. (1)

(ii) State in decimal how many locations are allocated to the buffer. (1)

(iii) Explain the term *circular queue*. (2)

(iv) Assuming the circular queue for the keyboard already holds several characters:

(I) draw *two* diagrams to show the state of the keyboard buffer just before and just after further keyboard input; (2)

(II) draw a third diagram to show the effect on the buffer of the step *Get next character digit from buffer* from the algorithm in Table 2. (2)

(*AEB*)

Tutorial note

This question requires knowledge of two seemingly unrelated syllabus areas, namely number systems and queues, but is not as difficult as it may at first appear, so don't be put off! Read the whole question through carefully, apply common sense and keep a clear head.

When calculating the number of codes remember to include the zeroth code, 0000 0000. Part (b) is about converting the three values in the Contents column from hexadecimal to decimal. Part (c) requires an understanding of the difference between the external and internal form of an integer number. Externally, the number is created as a sequence of character codes, each occupying a byte. The code for '5' is generated first, followed by '2', and then '7', 3 bytes in all. This happens because the keyboard is designed to generate a byte of code each time a key is pressed. The internal form needs only 2 bytes using pure binary coding as follows: $0000\ 0000\ 0000\ 0000_2$ represents 0_{10}, $1111\ 1111\ 1111\ 1111_2$ represents $65,535_{10}$. The algorithm performs the conversion from the external form to the internal form. Subtracting 48 from the decimal code converts character '0' to integer value 0, etc.

In part (d) (ii), remember to include the zeroth location, i.e. $C000_{16}$. With 63_{16} other locations, this makes a total of $63_{16} + 1_{16} = 64_{16}$. Converting to decimal, this is 100_{10}.

It is important in part (d) (iv) to show clearly the front and rear pointer positions, with the rear moving when a character is added, and the front when a character is removed.

Suggested answer

(a) (i) 8

(ii) 256

(b) 48 49 50 51 52 53 54 55 56 57   65 66 67 68 69 70 71 72 ... 90

 0 1 2 3 4 5 6 7 8 9   A B C D E F G H   Z

$5A_{16}$ = 0101 1010 (or $5 \times 16 + 10$) = 90 34_{16} = $3 \times 16 + 4$ = 52 37_{16} = 55

Keys pressed = Z47

(c) (i) CharacterDigitCode   Number
    53   5
    50   52
    55   527

(ii) The conversion is carried out because it is easier to perform arithmetic on the integer form of a number. (Also less storage required.)

(d) (i) Buffering keyboard input means that the processor can be working on other tasks, and characters can be corrected before they are moved from the buffer area.

(ii) $(63_{16} + 1_{16}) = 100_{10}$

(iii) A circular queue is a first-in first-out data structure with wrap around – i.e. when the last space in the buffer queue is filled, the next data item will be placed in the first position in the queue.

(iv)

(I)

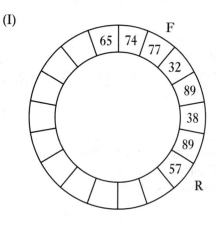
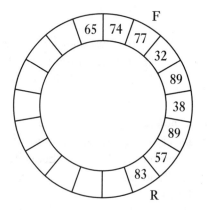

(II)

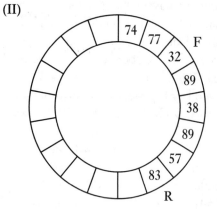

COMPUTER ARCHITECTURE

Units in this chapter

Chapter objectives

After working through the topics in this chapter, you should be able to:

- name the main internal components of a computer;
- explain the function of the control bus, the data bus and the address bus;
- explain why the width of the data bus affects the overall speed of the computer;
- explain the relationship between the width of the address bus and the maximum size of memory;
- explain the stored program concept and the von Neumann machine;
- name the major components of the processor;
- describe different types of main memory including RAM, ROM, PROM, EPROM and the use of cache memory;
- explain the role of the various registers within the processor;
- explain how the fetch–execute (FE) cycle is used to execute programs;
- define an interrupt in the context of the FE cycle;
- explain why interrupts are assigned priorities and explain how interrupts are handled;
- compare traditional von Neumann architecture to multiple processor architecture;
- explain the uses and benefits of parallel processing.

7.1   INTERNAL COMPONENTS OF A COMPUTER

A computer system consists of a set of independent components or subsystems which may be classified as **internal** or **external**. The internal subsystems are:

- processor;
- immediate access store (IAS) or main memory;
- I/O controllers – input only, output only, both input and output;
- buses.

The external subsystems are on the periphery of the computer system and are known, therefore, as peripherals or peripheral devices – for example, the keyboard, visual display unit, printer, magnetic disk drive and CD-ROM drive. The processor exchanges data with a peripheral device through a part of an I/O controller called an I/O port. Fig 7.1 illustrates the structure of a simple computer.

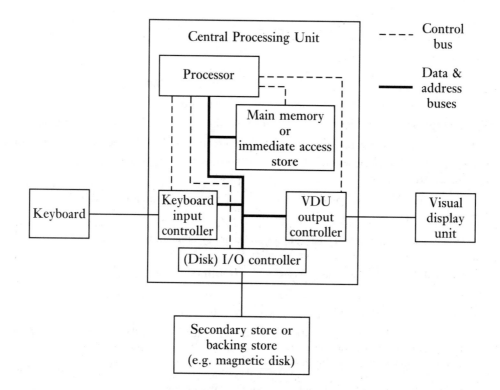

Figure 7.1   Block diagram of the structure of a simple computer

The bus subsystem

A **bus** is a set of parallel wires connecting two or more components of the computer; for example in Fig 7.1 control, data and address buses are shown connecting the processor, memory and I/O controllers. A key characteristic of a bus is that it is a *shared* transmission medium, so that only one component can successfully transmit at any one time.

A bus that connects together processor, main memory and I/O controllers is called a **system bus**.

A typical system bus contains from 50 to 100 separate lines. A line is a pathway for conveying a single bit. The number of lines is referred to as the *width* of the bus. Bus lines are classified into three functional groups: data, address and control lines. The sets of lines are collectively known as the *data*, *address* and *control* buses, respectively.

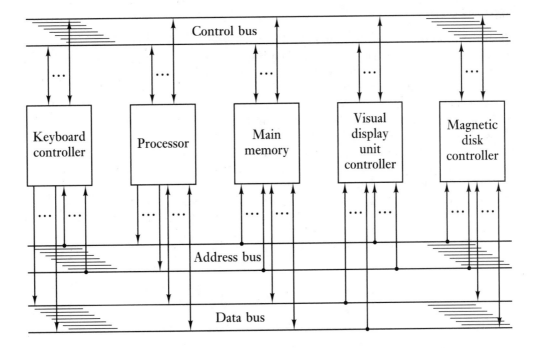

Figure 7.2   Internal components of a computer

Control bus

The control bus is a bi-directional bus, meaning that signals can be carried in both directions. The data and address buses are *shared* by all components of the system. Control lines must therefore be provided to ensure that *access to and use of the data and address buses* by the different components of the system does not lead to conflict. The purpose of the control bus is to transmit command, timing and specific status information between system components. Timing signals synchronise operations by indicating when information placed on the data, control and address buses is to be used. Command signals specify operations to be performed. Specific status signals indicate the state of a data transfer request, or the status of a request by a component to gain control of the system bus.

Typical control lines include:

- *Memory write*: causes data on the data bus to be written into the addressed location.
- *Memory read:* causes data from the addressed location to be placed on the data bus.
- *I/O write*: causes data on the data bus to be output to the addressed I/O port.
- *I/O read*: causes data from the addressed I/O port to be placed on the data bus.
- *Transfer ACK*: signals that data have been accepted from or placed on the data bus.
- *Bus request*: signal from a component requesting control of the system bus.
- *Bus grant*: signal to a requesting component that it has been granted control of the system bus.
- *Interrupt request*: signal indicating that an interrupt is pending.
- *Interrupt ACK*: used to acknowledge that the pending interrupt has been recognised.
- *Clock:* is used to synchronise operations.
- *Reset:* initialises all components.

Data bus

A typical data bus consists of 8, 16 or 32 separate lines. It provides a bi-directional path for moving data and instructions between system components. *The width of the data bus is a key factor in determining overall system performance.* For example, if the data bus is 16 bits wide, and each instruction is 32 bits long, then the processor must access the main memory twice during each instruction cycle.

Address bus

When the processor wishes to read a word (say 8, 16 or 32 bits) of data from memory, it first puts the address of the desired word on the address bus. *The width of the address bus determines the maximum possible memory capacity of the system.* For example, if the address bus consisted of only 8 lines, then the maximum address it could transmit would be (in binary) 11111111 or 255 – giving a maximum memory capacity of 256 (including address 0). A more realistic minimum bus width would be 20 lines, giving a memory capacity of 2^{20}, i.e. 1Mb.

The address bus is also used to address I/O ports during input/output operations.

No. of address lines, m	Maximum no. of addressable cells	Maximum no. of addressable cells expressed as a power of two, 2^m
1	2	2^1
2	4	2^2
3	8	2^3
4	16	2^4
8	256	2^8
16	65,536	2^{16}
20	1,048,576	2^{20}
24	16,777,216	2^{24}

Table 7.1:   Relationship between number of address lines m and maximum number of addressable memory cells

The stored program concept and the von Neumann machine

The *stored-program* concept was proposed by John von Neumann and Alan Turing in separate publications in 1945. Essentially, they proposed that both the program and the data on which it performed processing should be stored in memory together.

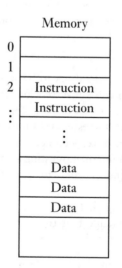

Figure 7.3:   Main memory or immediate access store

In 1946, von Neumann and his colleagues began the design of the first stored-program computer, referred to as the IAS (immediate access store) computer. Fig 7.4 shows the general structure of the IAS computer. It consists of

- a main memory which stores both data and instructions;
- an arithmetic and logic unit (ALU) which performs calculations on binary data;

- a control unit which interprets the instructions in memory and causes them to be executed;
- input and output (I/O) equipment operated by the control unit.

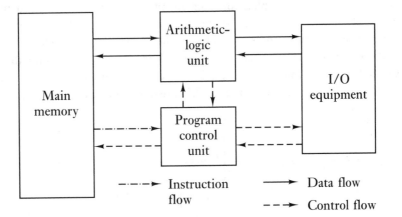

Figure 7.4: Structure of IAS computer

With rare exceptions, all of today's computers have this same general structure and function and are all referred to as von Neumann machines. The operation of a von Neumann machine is based upon the *fetch–execute cycle*. This cycle executes a single machine instruction and is therefore, sometimes, referred to as an *instruction cycle*. A computer operates by repetitively performing an *instruction cycle*.

Main memory

There are several different types of main memory:

- **Random access memory (RAM)**. This type of memory can be both read from and written to, and any location can be accessed independently – this is the ordinary memory used for storing programs and data. It loses its contents when the power is switched off.
- **Read-only memory (ROM)**. This type of memory is non-volatile, i.e. it retains its contents when the power is switched off. It is typically used for the **bootstrap loader** (the program which makes something appear on your screen when you switch on the computer), and for character pattern memory (which determines the combination of pixels which make up each character on the screen in text mode).
  There are several other types of read-only memory including:
  1. **PROM**: Programmable read-only memories have their contents created electrically by blowing fused links, selectively. The contents once set up cannot be erased.
  2. **EPROM**: Erasable programmable read-only memories have their contents created electrically and erased optically by shining ultraviolet light through a window on the top of each integrated circuit. The erasure covers a block of locations simultaneously. The contents of EPROM can only be altered by removing the chip and using a special device.
  3. **EEPROM**: Electrically erasable programmable read-only memories have their contents set up and erased electrically. Erasure works at the level of individual locations. A write operation takes considerably longer than a read operation. EEPROM combines the advantage of non-volatility with the flexibility of being updateable in place, using ordinary bus control, address and data lines. The set-up configuration of a PC is held in this type of memory and can be altered by a user through the keyboard.

• **Processor cache memory**. This is a small amount (say 256K) of fast but expensive memory placed between the processor and main memory. When the processor attempts to read a word of main memory, a check is made first to determine if the word is in the cache. If it is, a copy of the word is transferred to the processor. If not, a block of main memory, consisting of a fixed number of words, is transferred into the cache and then a copy of the reference word is transferred to the processor. The cache memory approach relies for its effectiveness on the fact that when a block of data is copied into the cache to service a single memory reference, it is likely that subsequent references will be to other words in the block. Figure 7.5 illustrates the relationship.

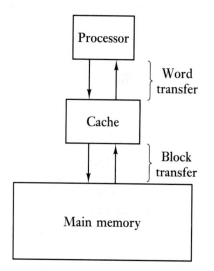

Figure 7.5: Cache, processor and main memory

I/O Controllers

Peripheral devices cannot be connected directly to the processor. Each peripheral operates in a different way and it would not be sensible to design processors to directly control every possible peripheral. Otherwise, the invention of a new type of peripheral would require the processor to be redesigned. Instead, the processor controls and communicates with a peripheral device through an *I/O or device controller*. I/O controllers are available which can operate both input and output transfers of bits, e.g. floppy disk controller. Other controllers operate in one direction only, either as input controllers, e.g. keyboard controllers or as output controllers, e.g. VDU controllers.

The controller is a board of electronics consisting of three parts:

• an interface that allows connection of the controller to the system or I/O bus;
• a set of data, command and status registers;
• an interface that enables connection of the controller to the cable connecting the device to the computer.

An interface is a standardised form of connection defining such things as signals, number of connecting pins/sockets and voltage levels that appear at the interface. An example is an RS232 interface which enables serial transmission of data between a computer and a serially connected printer. The printer also contains an RS232 interface so that both ends of the connection are compatible with each other.

7.2 STRUCTURE AND ROLE OF THE PROCESSOR

The processor consists of the following components:

- **program control unit**, which fetches instructions from memory, decodes and executes them one at a time;
- **system clock**, which generates a continuous sequence of clock pulses to step the control unit through its operation;
- **arithmetic-logic unit (ALU)** which performs arithmetic and logical operations on the data. It can perform, for example, addition and subtraction, fixed and floating point arithmetic, boolean logic operations such as AND, OR, XOR and a range of shift operations.

Registers

Registers are very fast memory locations internal to the processor. A processor will contain several different types of register:

- **general-purpose registers** available to the programmer and referenced in assembly language programs;
- **stack pointer** which points to a stack holding return addresses and is accessed when an interrupt or break in sequential program execution occurs;
- **flags** – registers which hold condition codes to indicate the outcome of operations – for example an arithmetic operation may produce a positive, negative, zero or overflow result, and a flag is set accordingly. These condition codes may subsequently be tested as part of a conditional branch operation.
- **program status word (PSW)**, also known as the **status register**, which combines condition codes with status information. For example, it may contain bits used to indicate the following conditions:
  — *Sign:* Set when the result of the last arithmetic operation is negative.
  — *Zero:* Set when the result is zero.
  — *Carry:* Set if an operation resulted in a carry (addition) into or borrow (subtraction) out of a high-order bit. Used for multi-word arithmetic operations.
  — *Equal:* Set if a logical compare result is equality. (Alternatively the zero flag may be used).
  — *Overflow:* Used to indicate arithmetic overflow.
  — *Interrupt enable/disable:* Used to enable or disable interrupts.
  — *Supervisor:* Indicates whether the processor is executing in supervisor or user mode. Certain privileged instructions can be executed only in supervisor mode, e.g. disabling interrupts, and certain areas of memory can be accessed only in supervisor mode.
  The last two flags indicate the operating status of the processor.

Registers involved in the fetch–execute cycle

The following special-purpose registers are used in the execution of each instruction:

- **Memory buffer register (MBR):** Contains a word to be stored in memory, or is used to receive a word from memory.
- **Memory address register (MAR):** Specifies the memory address to be used when a word is transferred between memory and the MBR.
- **Instruction register (IR):** Contains the last instruction to be decoded and executed or the current instruction being decoded and executed.
- **Program counter (PC):** Contains the address of the next instruction to be fetched from memory.
- **Accumulator (AC):** Employed to hold operands and results of ALU operations, temporarily.

The fetch–execute cycle

The instruction cycle can be broken down into a series of steps, synchronised by the system clock and controlled by the control unit. The steps are as follows:

(Fetch phase)

1. The address of the next instruction to be executed (held in the PC) is copied to the MAR.
2. The instruction held at that address is placed in the MBR.
3. Simultaneously, the contents of the PC are incremented by 1 to get ready for the next instruction.
4. The contents of the MBR are copied to the IR. (This frees up the MBR for the *execute* phase).

(Execute phase)

5. The instruction held in the IR is decoded.
6. The instruction is executed. (The sequence of micro-operations in the execute phase depends on the particular instruction being executed.)

   In *register transfer notation*, the fetch–execute cycle is described as follows:

$$MAR \longleftarrow [PC]$$

$$MBR \longleftarrow [Memory]; \quad PC \longleftarrow [PC] + 1$$

$$IR \longleftarrow [MBR]$$

$$[IR]_{opcode\ part} \text{ decoded and executed}$$

where [ ] means *contents of* and $\longleftarrow$ means *assign*.

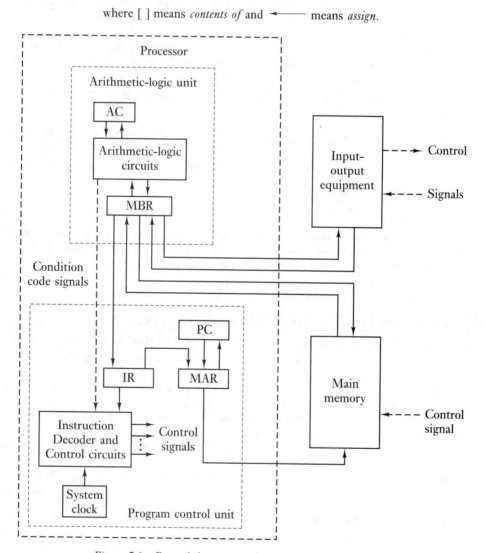

Figure 7.6   Expanded structure of a von Neumann machine

7.3 INTERRUPTS

Interrupt mechanism

Almost all computers provide a mechanism by which a program currently executing on the processor may be interrupted by a module (such as an I/O controller) seeking the attention of the processor. The module generates a signal called an interrupt signal which is sent along a control line to the processor. Thus an interrupt may be defined as follows:

An interrupt is a signal from some device/source seeking the attention of the processor.

If interrupts are enabled then, on receipt of an interrupt, the currently executing program is suspended in an orderly fashion and control is passed to an **interrupt service routine**. The currently executing program is suspended in such a way that its execution can be resumed without error after the servicing of the interrupting device has been carried out.

The most common classes of interrupts are given in Table 7.2.

Program	Generated by some condition that occurs as a result of an instruction execution, such as arithmetic overflow, division by zero, attempt to execute an illegal machine instruction, attempt to execute a privileged instruction in user mode and reference outside a user's allowed memory space.
Timer	Generated by a timer within the processor. This allows the operating system to perform certain functions at regular intervals of time.
I/O	Generated by an I/O controller, to signal normal completion of an operation or to signal a variety of error conditions.
Hardware failure	Generated by a failure such as power failure or memory parity error.

Table 7.2   Common classes of interrupts

Priority of interrupts

Some of the sources of interrupt are for conditions which warrant immediate attention, e.g. power failure, others for conditions that may be ignored temporarily, e.g. printer requests the sending of the next line of characters for printing. It is necessary to assign a *priority* to each interrupt so that when two or more interrupts occur simultaneously or an interrupt occurs while another interrupt is being serviced, the processor can compare interrupt priorities to determine whether to allow an interrupt. If an interrupt is already being serviced when another interrupt occurs then interrupts of equal or lower priority must await the completion of the current one. Only an interrupt of a higher priority is allowed to interrupt the servicing of another. In the case of two or more interrupts occurring simultaneously the interrupts are serviced in order of priority.

Examples of interrupt priorities are given in Table 7.3 below; one is highest priority, four is lowest.

Class of interrupt	Source of interrupt	Priority
Hardware failure:	Power failure	1
	Memory parity	1
Program:	Arithmetic overflow	2
	Division by zero	2
	Attempt to execute	2
	an illegal machine instruction	
	Reference outside a user's	
	allowed memory space	2
Timer	Real-time clock	3
I/O	Keyboard key pressed	4
	Printer ready to accept	
	next block/line of characters	4

Table 7.3 Examples of interrupt priorities

The interrupt handler

What happens when, for example, a key on the keyboard is pressed, thus generating an interrupt? A small program called an **interrupt service routine (ISR)** or **interrupt handler** is executed to transfer the character value of the key pressed into main memory. *A different ISR is provided for each different source of interrupt.* A typical sequence of actions when an interrupt occurs would be:

1. The processor must complete the current fetch–execute cycle for the user program if begun.

2. The contents of the program counter, which points to the next instruction of the user program to be executed, must be stored away safely so it can be restored after servicing the interrupt.

3. The contents of other registers used by the user program are stored away safely for later restoration.

4. The source of the interrupt is identified.

5. Interrupts of a lower priority are disabled.

6. The program counter is loaded with the start address of the relevant interrupt service routine.

7. The interrupt service routine is executed.

8. The saved values belonging to the user program for registers other than the program counter are restored to the processor's registers.

9. Interrupts are re-enabled.

10. The program counter is restored to point to the next instruction to be fetched and executed in user program.

7.4 PARALLEL PROCESSING

In the **von Neumann machine**, instructions are fetched and executed one at a time in a serial manner, leading to its being labelled a **serial machine**. Over the years, the speed of individual components has been increased dramatically, to the point where the speed of light (approximately 300,000,000 metres per second) is the limiting factor. To bring about further increases in speed of operation, a change in the principle of operation was required.

Pipelining (SISD)

The first change became known as *instruction pipelining* because the execution of an instruction was overlapped with the fetching of the next instruction. The second change became known as *arithmetic operation pipelining* because the operation of the ALU was overlapped with the fetching of the next operand.

The von Neumann machine and its pipelined versions are classified as a *single instruction stream single data stream (SISD) computer.*

Vector (array) processing (SIMD)

In order to gain an even greater speed of operation a degree of parallelism was introduced, using one of two basic approaches. In the first, the processor architecture consists of:
- one control unit;
- several arithmetic and logic units, each with its own set of registers.

This architecture enables a single instruction to be decoded and executed at a time. However, the multiple ALUs permit this single instruction to be applied simultaneously to an array of data. For example, the assignment operation in the following block of code would be carried out one array cell at a time in a serial machine but simultaneously in a parallel machine:

```
For i := 1 To 10
   Do ResultsArray[i] := 6;
```

This type of parallel machine is known as a *vector* or *array processor*. It is classified as a *single instruction stream multiple data stream (SIMD) computer*.

Applications which can make use of array processing include
- numerical weather forecasting, which involves thousands of calculations on arrays of data;
- manipulating and processing graphical or photographic images (for example, pictures transmitted live from a satellite, or virtual reality images) which consist of two-dimensional arrays of pixels.

Multiple processor architecture (MIMD)

The second approach to parallelism allows a multiple instruction stream as well as a multiple data stream. This requires the processor to contain
- several control units;
- several ALUs.

This type of parallel computer is classified as a *multiple instruction stream multiple data stream computer* or *MIMD*.

The human brain is a wonderful example of a parallel processor: with no difficulty at all you can walk down the street, chew gum, hum a song, notice that it's raining and open an umbrella, think about the film you saw last night and be aware that you are getting a blister on your right heel. Much current research in the field of **artificial intelligence** is focused on **neural networks**, which mimic the functioning of a human brain, using a network of thousands of parallel processors. Some parallel-processing supercomputers used for this purpose contain more than 65,000 processors.

Chapter summary

Chapter 7 has explained the nature and function of each of the main internal components of a computer. The bus subsystem, the different types of memory, I/O controllers and registers have all been described, together with the roles of various registers used in the fetch–execute cycle. The interrupt mechanism has been described and the reasons for giving priority to certain types of interrupt explained. The architecture of the von Neumann machine has been compared with more recent developments in parallel processing.

Illustrative questions

1 Name *two* registers involved in the fetch–execute cycle. (2)

(AEB)

Tutorial note

The question means those registers defined in the von Neumann machine that are essential to the action of fetching and decoding instructions from main memory. Any register that might subsequently be used when an instruction is carried out is excluded.

Suggested answer
Any two registers from the following list are acceptable answers.
Program counter (PC)/sequence control register (SCR), memory address register (MAR), memory buffer register (MBR)/memory data register (MDR), current instruction register (CIR)/instruction register (IR).

2 A microprocessor *data bus* has 16 lines and its *address bus* has 20 lines.
   (a) What is the maximum memory capacity that can be connected to the microprocessor?   (2)
   (b) Name the *two* registers directly involved in the reading of data from this memory and state their lengths.   (2)
                                                                            (AEB)

Tutorial note
(a) The key to answering this question is to realise that the number of memory locations is determined by the number of lines in the address bus and the number of different bit patterns that can exist on these lines. This is simply $2^{no\ of\ address\ lines}$. The number of lines in the data bus determines the size of the memory word that can be transferred in one memory access. The word size is 16 bits or 2 bytes in this case.
(b) There are only two registers. The memory address register holds the address placed on the address lines and the memory buffer register (also known as the memory data register) holds the memory word transferred over the data bus. Their lengths must reflect the size of the bus they are connected to.

Suggested answer
(a) The maximum memory capacity is 2^{20} 16-bit words or 2^{21} bytes.
(b) Memory address register of length 20 bits.
    Memory buffer register of length 16 bits.

3 Briefly explain the *stored program concept*.   (2)
                                                                            (AEB)

Tutorial note
The **stored program concept** applies to the von Neumann machine in which program instructions stored in main memory are fetched in sequence, decoded and executed. The key is to realise that the instructions must be resident in main memory before they can be executed.

Suggested answer
This concept places a program of instructions in main memory from where they are fetched in sequence, decoded and executed.

4 Describe the function of *three* of the flags contained within the status register of a microcomputer.   (3)
                                                                            (AEB)

Tutorial note
The marks here are given for the description of the *function* of each flag mentioned. Any three of the flags mentioned in paragraph 7.2 can be described.

Suggested answer
The zero flag indicating a zero result.
The negative flag indicating a negative result.
The overflow flag indicating that overflow has taken place.

5 Two models of microcomputer have identical specifications except that one has a 25 MHz clock while the other has a 33 MHz clock. State the purpose of a microprocessor clock and outline the way in which these different clocks will influence the microcomputers' performances.   (3)
                                                                            (NICCEA)

Suggested answer
The microcomputer clock generates a sequence of electronic pulses at a fixed interval. The production of this pulse is used to set in motion an electronic activity within the computer, e.g. a fetch operation. The 25 MHz generates 25 million pulses every second

while the 33 MHz generates 33 million pulses every second. All other things being equal, the 33 MHz model will perform faster than the 25 MHz model.

6 Briefly explain the operation and purpose of RAM cache and of disk cache. (6)
(NEAB)

Suggested answer
RAM cache is part of main store, a small amount of very fast memory between the processor and the rest of main store. Sections of program and/or data are copied there when first accessed, in the knowledge that the next thing to be accessed is likely to be in the same block and will therefore already be in the cache memory, the use of which can greatly reduce processing time.
Disk cache works on a similar principle, being a section of memory (a buffer) used to hold data that has been read from disk storage.

7 (a) Describe the fetch–execute cycle. Explain the use of internal registers in the fetch process. (5)
(b) Describe what happens when a peripheral device interrupts the processor. (3)
(c) Explain why interrupts are allocated different levels of priority. (3)
(d) Explain what happens when:
(i) The CPU is servicing a keyboard interrupt and an interrupt arrives from the line printer;
(ii) The CPU is servicing an interrupt from the line printer and an interrupt arrives from the keyboard. (4)
(EDEXCEL)

Tutorial note
Marks in part (a) are given for identifying the registers used in the cycle, describing how they are used and for a mention of interrupts occurring. The rest of the question is about interrupts which should remind you to mention this aspect of the processor's operation – it's always a good idea to read right through a question before starting to answer it!

Look back to Section 7.3 for a complete description of interrupt handling. In part (d), you must decide which you think would have a higher priority – a keyboard interrupt or a printer interrupt. Should the computer ignore a keyboard input if it is busy printing?

Suggested answer
(a) *Fetch:* Contents of PC copied to MAR. Instruction at that address copied to MBR and then to CIR. PC incremented. *Execute:* Instruction in CIR decoded and executed. A check is made for interrupts.
(b) Contents of PC and other registers are stored. Source of interrupt is identified and interrupts of a lower priority are disabled. The PC is loaded with the address of the correct interrupt service routine (ISR).
(c) Some interrupts have greater urgency than others – for example a power failure has to be dealt with before a keyboard interrupt. A priority is assigned to each interrupt so that interrupts of a lower priority can be disabled while another interrupt is being serviced. Only an interrupt of a higher priority can interrupt the servicing of another.
(d) (i) The interrupt is recognised but it is of lower priority than a keyboard interrupt so the information is stored until the keyboard interrupt has been dealt with.
(ii) The state of the registers is stored, the new interrupt is serviced, then the first interrupt is serviced.

8 A microprocessor has an 8-bit data bus, a 16-bit address bus and a control bus. Some of the lines on the control bus are: clock, reset, non-maskable interrupt, maskable interrupt, memory read and memory write.
(a) What is the function of the clock line? (1)
(b) With reference to the flow of data between the processor and memory, what is the function of:
(i) data bus
(ii) address bus
(iii) control bus? (3)
(c) At one stage in the execution of a program, the value $3F_{hex}$ has to be stored in the memory location with address $204B_{hex}$. Describe how the processor uses the data, address and control buses to perform this operation. (3)
(d) The reset and maskable interrupt lines can interrupt a running process. Describe *two* differences between these methods of interrupting a running process. (2)
(SQA)

Tutorial note
Section 7.1 describes the functions of the various buses in the CPU.

Suggested answer
(a) The clock line is used to synchronise operations.
(b) (i) The data bus is used to carry data between the MBR, a register within the processor, and memory.
   (ii) The address bus is used to carry the address of a memory word between the MAR (a register in the processor) and memory. The data in that word can then be transmitted along the data bus.
   (iii) The control bus transmits command, timing and specific status information between system components, and ensures that signals travelling along the shared buses do not get mixed up.
(c) $204B_{hex}$ is placed on the address bus, then $3F_{hex}$ is placed on the data bus. Finally, a memory write signal is placed on the control bus.
(d) Reset: the process is not resumable; maskable interrupt: the process is resumable. Reset: register contents/state of machine lost; Maskable interrupt: register contents/state of machine saved.

ASSEMBLY LANGUAGE

Units in this chapter

Chapter objectives

After working through the topics in this chapter, you should be able to:

- explain the format of machine code instructions and the use of operation codes and addresses;

- explain the relationship between operation code length and instruction repertoire;

- describe the types of instruction (arithmetic, logical, branch etc.) in a typical instruction set;

- distinguish between machine code language and assembly code language;

- explain the format of an assembly language statement;

- write simple algorithms in assembly language to perform jumps and iteration;

- write simple algorithms involving masks, shifts, comparisons or arithmetic operations;

- describe the use of addressing modes for locating addresses in memory;

- describe the use of macros, directives and forward referencing.

8.1   MACHINE CODE INSTRUCTIONS

Instruction set

For a digital computer, the language of instruction is machine code; instructions consisting of sequences of binary digits which a machine can recognise and interpret. Digital computers are designed to carry out a limited number of simple operations such as addition and storage, but by combining together sequences of these basic operations quite complicated tasks can be performed. The set of bit patterns (strings of bits) that represent these operations for a given machine is known as the machine's **instruction set**.

A machine code instruction consists of two main parts:

- an **opcode** or operation code that specifies which operation is to be performed;
- zero or more operands; these specify the data upon which the operation is to be performed.

15 14 13 12 11 10 9 8	7 6 5 4 3 2 1 0
Operation code	Operand

Figure 8.1:   A possible machine code format

Figure 8.1 shows a machine code instruction with 8 bits allowed for the opcode and 8 bits allowed for a single operand. The operand field of a machine instruction is often referred to as an address field because it can contain the address of a memory word. A typical instruction using just one operand is

Load into the accumulator *(the operation)* **the contents of address X** *(the operand)*

In the above example, the accumulator is a special register in which all calculations are carried out. Other processors use 8 or 16 registers and the particular register being used has to be specified. (See Section 8.7, one-and-a-half-address instructions).

Some instructions may use more than one operand, or need more than 8 bits to hold a single operand, so there are many possible formats for machine code instructions.

The number of bits allowed for the **opcode** determines the maximum possible number of operations in the machine's instruction set. With 8 bits, 2^8 (256) different operations are possible.

8.2   ASSEMBLY LANGUAGE INSTRUCTIONS

The use of mnemonics

It is difficult for the programmer to deal with the binary representation of machine instructions, so opcodes are represented symbolically by abbreviations called **mnemonics**, that indicate the operation. Common examples include

ADD	Add
SUB	Subtract
LOAD	Load data from memory
STORE	Store data to memory

Types of instruction

Processors are designed with a set of machine instructions that allows the user to formulate a range of data-processing tasks. With this in mind it is possible to categorise instruction types as follows:

- *data processing*: Arithmetic, logic and shift instructions;
- *CPU data transfers*: Memory instructions;
- *I/O transfers*: I/O instructions;
- *control*: test and branch instructions.

8.3 ARITHMETIC INSTRUCTIONS

Arithmetic instructions include those for adding, subtracting, multiplying and dividing. Machines typically do not support direct addition of the contents of two memory locations, as all arithmetic must take place in a **register**. For example, suppose the high-level language statement

$$X := X + Y$$

is to be coded in assembly language. This operation could be accomplished with three instructions:

1. Load a register with the contents of memory location X.
2. Add the contents of memory location Y to the register.
3. Store the contents of the register in memory location X.

Symbolically this is described by

LOAD R,X
ADD R,Y
STORE R,X

where **R** is the symbolic name for the register.

The result of an arithmetic operation may be tested by examining bits in the **status register**. The status register typically includes 4 bits referred to as N, Z, V and C which are set to 1 or 0 depending on the result of the previous operation.

- If the result is negative, N = 1.
- If the result is zero, Z = 1.
- If overflow occurred, V = 1.
- If carry occurred, C = 1.

The carry bit indicates that an extra bit has been set as the result was too large to fit into the register; it is up to the programmer to test for this and handle the situation appropriately.

The overflow bit is set if the sign of the result has been accidentally changed, as in the example below:

```
    0100 0000    (64)
  + 0100 0001    (65)
    1000 0001    (−127)
```

Again, this situation can be tested for and appropriate action taken.

8.4 SHIFT INSTRUCTIONS

There are generally three different types of shift instruction which all operate by shifting bits left or right within a register.

Arithmetic shift instructions

Arithmetic shifts preserve the arithmetic meaning of the bit pattern that is being shifted. Essentially, they achieve this by preserving the sign of the number that the bit pattern represents. There are two types of arithmetic shift:

1. Arithmetic left shift
Typical assembly code instructions:

ASL R   ;arithmetic shift left contents of register R

The sign bit is left unchanged while the bit pattern is shifted one bit place to the left. The least significant bit is replaced by a zero. In the first example below, when the bit pattern represents a two's complement integer, −17, a single arithmetic left shift operation is carried out as shown in Fig 8.2 to produce −34, representing a multiplication by two.

In the second example in Fig 8.2, the sign bit is preserved, but the shift results in a number too large to be held in the register so the overflow flag will be set.

-128	64	32	16	8	4	2	1
1	1	1	0	1	1	1	1

-128	64	32	16	8	4	2	1
1	1	0	1	1	1	1	0

(a) Before arithmetic left shift is applied.   (b) After arithmetic left shift is applied.

-128	64	32	16	8	4	2	1
0	1	1	0	0	1	1	1

-128	64	32	16	8	4	2	1
0	1	0	0	1	1	1	0

(a) Before arithmetic left shift is applied.   (b) After arithmetic left shift is applied.

Figure 8.2:   Arithmetic left shift

2. Arithmetic right shift
Typical assembly code instruction:

ASR R   ;shift right arithmetic contents of register R

The sign bit is left unchanged while the bit pattern is shifted one bit place to the right. The least significant bit is transferred into the carry bit of the status register. For example, when the bit pattern represents a two's complement integer number, 103, a single arithmetic right shift operation is carried out as shown in Fig 8.3 to produce 51 with remainder 1, representing integer division by two.

-128	64	32	16	8	4	2	1
0	1	1	0	0	1	1	1

-128	64	32	16	8	4	2	1	Carry flag
0	0	1	1	0	0	1	1	1

(a) Before arithmetic right shift is applied.   (b) After arithmetic right shift is applied.

Figure 8.3:   Arithmetic right shift

An arithmetic left or right shift corresponds to multiplication or division by two, respectively, provided there is no overflow or underflow.

Logical Shifts

With logical shifts no arithmetic meaning is attached to the bit pattern and any sign bit is not preserved during the shift operation. There are two types of logical shift operation:

1. Logical left shift
Typical assembly code instruction:

LSL R   ;shift left logical contents of register R

With a logical left shift the bit pattern is moved one bit place to the left with the least significant bit position being replaced by a zero. Fig 8.4 illustrates this.

1	0	1	1	0	1	0	0

0	1	1	0	1	0	0	0

(a) Before logical left shift is applied.   (b) After logical left shift is applied.

Figure 8.4:   Logical left shift

2. Logical right shift
Typical assembly code instruction:

LSR R   ;shift right logical contents of register R

With a logical right shift the bit pattern is moved one bit place to the right with the most significant bit position being replaced by a zero. Fig 8.5 illustrates this.

(a) Before logical right shift is applied.   (b) After logical right shift is applied.

Figure 8.5: Logical right shift

Cyclic shift or rotation

Cyclic shift, or rotate, operations preserve all of the bits being operated upon. There are two types:

1. Cyclic left shift or rotate left
Typical assembly code instruction:

    ROL R   ;rotate left 1 bit position contents of register R

In this shift the bits are moved one bit place to the left. The bit value shifted out of the most significant bit position is placed in the least significant bit position.

2. Cyclic right shift or rotate right
Typical assembly code instruction:

    ROR R   ;rotate right 1 bit contents of register R

In this shift the bits are moved one bit place to the right. The bit value shifted out of the least significant bit position is placed in the most significant bit position.

One possible use of a cyclic shift is to test individual bits by bringing each bit successively into the most significant bit position. The machine automatically uses this bit position as a sign bit whose setting is indicated by the sign flag (N) of the status register.

8.5   LOGICAL INSTRUCTIONS

The instructions **OR, NOT, AND** and **XOR** (exclusive OR) have the following effects:

		OR	NOT	AND	XOR
Inputs	(A)	1010	1010	1010	1010
	(B)	1100		1100	1100
Result		1110	0101	1000	0110

The OR function can be used to set particular bits to 1 without affecting the other bits.
EXAMPLE
The current contents of register R are unknown. Write an assembly code instruction to set bits 0, 2, 4 and 5 of the register to 1 (bit 0 being the least significant bit). The status of the other bits is to be left unchanged.
Answer: OR R, #000110101b
(The 'b' indicates a binary rather than a decimal value. # denotes an 'immediate' or actual value rather than the contents of an address.)

The NOT function can be used to invert all the bits in a register, which is the same thing as finding the one's complement of a number. To find the two's complement, 1 is added. In the example below, the accumulator register is implied in the instructions LDA, ADD and STA.

EXAMPLE

Find the two's complement of the number held in X

Answer:
```
LDA X       ;load X into the accumulator
NOT A       ;invert all bits in the accumulator
ADD #1      ;add the number 1
STA X       ;store back in X
```

The AND function can be used as a **mask** to let certain bits through while 'blocking' other bits. For example in order to convert the ASCII code for a numeric digit to a pure binary digit, the most significant 4 bits need to be set to zero. (The ASCII code for 3 is 00110011, and the pure binary code for 3 is 00000011.)

EXAMPLE

Convert the ASCII character in Register R to a binary number

Answer:
```
AND R, #00001111b      ;apply a binary mask to R
```

Sometimes the mask is expressed in hexadecimal, with a symbol such as & being used to indicate this.

```
AND R, #&0F       ;apply a hexadecimal mask 0F to R
```

The XOR function can be used to check if two different registers have identical contents.

EXAMPLE

Write assembly code instructions to branch to a label LAB1 if R0 = R1.

```
XOR R0,R1    ;exclusive OR the contents of the two registers R0 and R1
BZ LAB1      ;branch to LAB1 if the result is zero

......

.....
LAB1:   (some instruction)
```

8.6   COMPARE AND BRANCH INSTRUCTIONS

The instruction 'BZ LAB1' tests the status register to see what the result of the last operation was. Typical conditional branch instructions include

```
BZ      (branch if zero)
BNZ     (branch if not zero)
```

Branch instructions such as JUMP LAB2 cause an unconditional branch to the instruction labelled LAB2.

Compare instructions may be used to compare the contents of two registers. If the contents of the registers are equal, the zero flag in the status register is set to 1 and can be tested. An alternative solution to the problem 'Write assembly code instructions to branch to a label LAB1 if R0=R1' would be

```
CMP R0, R1
BZ LAB1
```

8.7   INSTRUCTION FORMATS

One of the traditional ways of describing processor architecture is in terms of the number of addresses contained in each instruction.

1. *Two-address instructions*: use two address fields, one of which doubles as an operand and a result. For example, ADD X,Y carries out the calculation X + Y and stores the result in X.

2. *One-address instructions*: use a single address field. For this to work, a second address must be implicit. For example, in the BBC microcomputer the implied address can be the accumulator register. The accumulator carries one of the operands and is used to store the result. An example of this type is ADC &81 which adds the contents of memory location &81 to the contents of the accumulator register storing the result back in the accumulator.

3. *Zero-address instructions*: use no address fields because the addresses of the operands are implied. e.g. CLC is a mnemonic for a machine instruction which CLears the Carry bit in the status register.

4. *One-and-a-half-address instructions*: some processors have a number of general purpose registers which can be used in computations. In this case the first address field can signify the register to be used and the second, a memory address. However, since the number of bits to signify the register to be used is considerably less than would be necessary to signify a main memory address, these instructions are sometimes called one-and-a-half-address instructions.

      e.g.   ADD R,X   ;add the contents of memory location X to register R

The number of address fields per instruction is a basic design decision. Having fewer address fields per instruction results in more primitive instructions, which requires a less complex processor. It also results in instructions of shorter length. On the other hand, programs contain more instructions in total, which in general results in longer execution times and longer, more complex programs. With one-address instructions, the processor offers only one general-purpose register, the **accumulator**. With multiple-address instructions, it is common to have several general-purpose registers. This allows some operations to be performed solely with registers. Since register references are faster than memory references, this speeds up execution.

Complex instruction set computer (CISC) architecture

CISC architecture is characterised by a large instruction set, many addressing modes and various high-level language statements implemented in hardware. For example, the VAX 11/780 minicomputer has 25 different ADD instructions and a CASE machine instruction.

Reduced instruction set computer (RISC) architecture

RISC architecture is based upon a small, simplified instruction set and therefore a simplified control unit. For example, a RISC instruction set may include only one or two ADD instructions. With such an instruction set heavy use is made of registers, of which there are usually many more than is the case with CISC architectures. Frequently accessed operands are held in registers. Therefore, most operations are register-to-register operations with only simple LOAD and STORE operations accessing memory. The reliance on register-to-register operations is a major feature of RISC architectures. CISC architectures rely heavily upon memory-to-memory and memory/register operations, as well as register-to-register operations.

In RISC architecture every machine instruction requires only one machine cycle for its operation. For example, to fetch two operands from registers, perform an ALU operation, and store the result in a register takes the time for one machine cycle (i.e. clock cycle). In fact this basic operation is used to define a machine cycle for a RISC machine.

8.8 ADDRESSING MODES

Addressing modes are concerned with how machine instructions specify the address of an operand. The most commonly employed addressing techniques are

- immediate;
- direct or absolute;
- indirect;
- register;
- indexed;
- base register;
- relative.

Immediate

The simplest form of addressing is immediate addressing. An operand field contains, instead of an address, the data required by the operation. For example,

    ADD R,#36 ;add the number 36 to Register R

would add the value 36 to the contents of register R storing the result in R.

Direct or absolute addressing

The operand is the address of the data to be used in the operation.

    LOAD R,&FCC0 ;load contents of location &FCC0 into register R
            ;(& indicates hexadecimal)

Indirect addressing

The address field refers to the address of a location in main memory, which in turn contains an address for the location holding the operand. For example,

    LOAD R,(&F4) ;load into R the contents of memory location whose address
           ;is in location &F4

The parentheses surrounding &F4 indicate indirect addressing.

Register addressing

Register addressing is similar to direct addressing: the only difference is that the address field refers to a register rather than a memory address.

Typically an address field that references registers will have 3 or 4 bits, so that a total of 8 or 16 general purpose registers can be referenced. For example,

    ADD R1,R2 ;add contents of R2 to R1, storing result in R1.

Indexed addressing

The operand address is calculated by adding to a base address the value held in an index register. This is very similar to using an array subscript in a high-level language. For example, to put zero in memory locations A to A+6, you could write assembly code something like:

      LOAD I,#0   ;load zero into the index register
   Loop: Load A(I), #0 ;load zero into location (A + I)
      ADD I, #1   ;add 1 to the index register
      CMP I, #7   ;compare I with 7
      BNZ Loop   ;branch if not equal to Loop, otherwise continue.

Base register addressing

This is similar to indexed addressing, but this time the base address is held in the register, and the address field contains a displacement or offset. The following example alters a value held in a memory location &F056. (Assume B, the base register, contains &F000.)

      LOAD R, B:&56 ;loads register R with contents of address formed by
             ;adding contents of B (the base register) and &56
      ADD R, #3   ;add 3 to contents of register R
      STO R, B:&56 ;store contents of R at address &F056

Relative addressing

This type of addressing is often used in branch instructions to specify where the next instruction is located relative to the current instruction whose address is held in the PC. For example,

        BRA &2C   ;branch to address &2C bytes from current address in
                             ;the PC

These relative jumps allow relocatable machine code to be produced which can be loaded anywhere in main memory without needing to modify any address fields. Otherwise, a jump to an absolute address, for example, will only work if the machine code is run at the same address at which it was assembled.

8.9 THE ASSEMBLY PROCESS

Assembler directives

Assembling a program means translating it into machine code. A complete assembly code program will contain, as well as basic instructions such as ADD, LOAD and so on, **directives**, which are instructions to the assembler program, and which do not get translated into machine code. Directives may include instructions as to where in memory the program is to be loaded, or instructions to name and reserve memory locations (similar to **var** statements to declare variables in Pascal). For example:

        ORG   &1400
    W   DS   3

reserves three words of memory called W, W+1 and W+2 at hexadecimal addresses 1400, 1401, 1402.

Macro instructions

A **macro** instruction is a single instruction representing a group of instructions. It is different from a subroutine call statement because when the assembler translates the macro instruction, it actually replaces it with the group of instructions that it represents. A call statement is just that – it instructs the computer to look somewhere else for the subroutine instructions. A macro is an example of an *open subroutine*, as opposed to a *closed subroutine* which is entered by means of a CALL statement or equivalent instruction.

Two-pass assemblers

Some assembly languages allow what is known as **forward referencing**; in other words the program may contain instructions such as

        JMP LAB1   ;jump to the instruction labelled LAB1
        ...
        ...
LAB1: (instruction)

As the assembler goes through the program it can't translate the instruction JMP LAB1 until it knows where LAB1 is, further down the program. Therefore on the first pass it puts all such labels in a **symbol table** and assigns them memory addresses, and on the second pass puts these memory addresses in the appropriate Jump instructions and translates the whole program into machine code.

Chapter summary

Chapter 8 has introduced the basic concepts of machine code and assembly language programming. Different types of instruction including arithmetic, shift, logical, compare and branch instructions have been described and examples given of their use. Instruction formats and addressing modes have been explained and the basics of the assembly process covered.

Illustrative questions

1 An 8-bit word holds the binary pattern
        10110010
(i)   State the contents of the word after a logical left shift of 2 bits.
(ii) State the contents of the word after a cyclic left shift of 3 bits.
(iii) Interpreting the word as a number in two's complement form, state the contents
of the word after an arithmetic right shift of 2 bits.   (3)
                                                (EDEXCEL)

Tutorial note
Be careful to notice that parts (i) and (ii) involve *left* shifts, and part (iii) a *right* shift. The
sign bit is preserved in an arithmetic shift so 1s are moved in.

Suggested answer
(i)   11001000
(ii) 10010101 (or if the instruction follows (i), 01000110)
(iii) 11101100

2 A process can begin only if bits 0, 2, 4 and 7 of an 8 bit accumulator are set to 1.
The status of the other bits has no effect on the process. Write the key assembly
language instructions to check whether the process can take place.   (3)
                                                 (AEB)

Tutorial note
A mask is required which isolates the bits which are important. These bits can then be
tested to see if they are set to 1. Whenever a mask is required the logical AND operator
will be involved. The mask required is 10010101. A one appears in each bit position
that needs to be tested. This bit pattern reflects the fact that it is traditional to label the
rightmost bit, bit 0 and the leftmost bit, bit 7. Bit 1 is then the nearest neighbour to the
rightmost bit, bit 2 the next nearest, and so on. If the accumulator's contents are ANDed
with this mask then a zero will result in every bit position where the mask is zero and a
zero or one in every position where the mask is one, depending upon whether the
corresponding accumulator bit is zero or one, respectively. The result can then be
compared with the mask pattern again and only if there is an exact match can the
process begin.

Suggested answer
       AND A, #10010101b   ;AND contents of accumulator A and given binary
                                     ;number storing result in A
       CMP A, #10010101b   ;compare contents of A with given binary number
       BEQ process   ;branch if equal to code for process

       (b indicates binary number)
       (# indicates immediate addressing, i.e. operand is datum)

3 Write the *sequence* of key assembly language instructions, with annotation, which
corresponds to the following block of high-level language code:
       For K   ←   1 To 10
          Do N   ← N + 1
       EndFor
                                                   (5)
                                             (AEB)

Tutorial note
Any sensible set of mnemonics is acceptable. The set doesn't have to match any existing
assembly language. The requirement for annotation is to ensure that the examiner can
check that the correct operation is being performed. At the assembly language level
controlling a program loop involves using a machine register as a loop counter. This

register will be referenced in the assembly language program by a symbolic address. Choosing K as this register's symbolic address, an assembly language instruction is needed which will increment the contents of K by one each time. When ten iterations of the loop have been performed the program should stop looping. In assembly language, the loop's terminating condition must be checked for after each loop execution by using a compare instruction followed by a conditional branch instruction. The assembly language program must label the first instruction in the block of instructions which are to be repeated so that the branch can work. A memory location with symbolic address LocN is chosen for the variable N.

Suggested answer
The following is just one of several possible solutions:

```
        LOAD K, #0           ;initialise loop counter with zero
.loop
        INC K                ;increment loop counter by 1
        ADD LocN, #1         ;add 1 to contents of N's location
        CMP K, #10           ;test loop counter is equal to 10
        BNE Loop             ;branch to loop label if not zero
```

means immediate addressing, i.e. the operand is the datum, not the address of the datum.

Another acceptable solution relies upon the fact that in the case of an optimising compiler, code optimisation could produce the result

```
        ADD LocN, #10        ;add 10 to contents of location N
```

4 In a particular computer, characters are represented by 8-bit patterns. The codes for capital letters are from 01000001 for A to 01011010 for Z and the codes for lower case letters are from 01100001 for a to 01111010 for z. Give an 8-bit mask and the appropriate logical instruction which will
(i)   change any capital letter into its lower case equivalent;   (2)
(ii) change any lower case letter into its capital equivalent.   (2)
                                                                        (NEAB)

Tutorial note
Several different masks will do the trick here. Note first that only bit 5 needs to be changed (bit 0 being the rightmost bit). So a mask of 00100000 seems a good bet. Now do you need OR, XOR or AND?

Suggested answer
(i)   XOR 00100000
(ii) same!   (Alternatively, AND 11011111)

5 Describe how a typical two-pass assembler will cope with the problem posed by forward referencing in an assembly language program.   (4)
                                                                        (NISEAC)

Tutorial note
Refer to Section 8.9 if you are not sure what is meant by *forward referencing*; it simply means that an instruction in a program (for example a Jump instruction) may refer to a label attached to a statement further on in the program whose address is not yet known to the assembler.

Suggested answer
On the first pass, any forward reference will be placed in the symbol table without any address. By the end of the first pass the reference will have been allocated an address. On the second pass, the symbolic reference in the instruction will be replaced by the appropriate address read from the symbol table.

6 Explain what is meant by relocatable code and state *one* advantage of relocatable code.   (4)
                                                                        (NICCEA)

Tutorial note
The key to understanding relocation is the need to modify the address fields of those instructions which reference main memory locations. When relocatable code is produced by a compiler, these references are made relative to the beginning of the code module which is assigned the logical address zero. When this module is loaded into main memory the first instruction in the module will no longer have as its location address, the value zero. Instead, it will have a non-zero value.

Suggested answer
Relocatable code contains no absolute memory addresses, only addresses relative to the start of the program. Jumps within the program are relative to the current instruction (as in BRA &2C) or to instructions at relative, not absolute, addresses. The advantage of relocatable code is that it can be loaded anywhere in main memory – useful in a multiprogramming computer where the program may be swapped in and out of memory and occupy different memory blocks on different occasions.

7 A certain computer system uses a word-length of 24 bits. Each machine-code instruction consists of an 8-bit operation code followed by a 16-bit operand. Here is a short segment of assembly code, together with the corresponding machine code (in hexadecimal notation).

LABEL	OPERATION	OPERAND	COMMENT	MACHINE CODE
START	LDA	FIRST	Load accumulator	32 20 2A
	JSR	PRINT	Jump to subroutine to print accumulator	13 10 88
	ADD	#2	Add 2 to accumulator	07 00 02
	STA	FIRST	Store accumulator	33 20 2A
	SUB	LAST	Subtract from accumulator	08 20 2B
	BNP	START	Branch if accumulator <= 0	22 FF FB
	STOP			

(a) (i) What is the operation code for LOAD ACCUMULATOR?
   (ii) At what address is the number FIRST stored?
   (iii) The ADD instruction quoted above has an **immediate** operand. What does this mean?
   (iv) What mode of addressing does the BNP instruction use?
   (v) If FIRST and LAST initially contain the numbers 4 and 12, what will be printed when the program segment is run?   (6)
(b) Describe the machine instruction cycle as it applies to the BNP instruction above.   (4)
                     (*UCLES*)

Tutorial note
Remember that an 8-bit binary number can be represented by two hexadecimal digits. Each machine code instruction is therefore coded in hexadecimal by 6 hexadecimal digits, the first two representing the operation code and the last four the operand.
In part (b), you are describing the fetch–execute cycle.

Suggested answer
(a) (i) Op code for LDA is 32 (hex)
   (ii) FIRST is stored at address 202A (hex)
   (iii) The actual number 2 is added to the accumulator, rather than the contents of address 2.
   (iv) The BNP instruction uses direct addressing.
   (v) 4 6 8 10 12
(b) Address of BNP instruction is held in PC at the start of the cycle. This address is copied to the MAR. The BNP instruction is copied to the MBR, and thence to the CIR, whilst the PC is incremented. The instruction is decoded and the address of START (FFFB) is placed in the PC if the accumulator contents are less than or equal to zero.

8 The following is a pseudo-assembly language program:

> Store zero in the R register;
> Set base to 1000;
> LOOP: Read a character from the keyboard into the accumulator;
> Copy the contents of the accumulator to the storage location with an address equal to (base + the contents of the R register);
> Compare the contents of the accumulator with the ASCII code for carriage return;
> Jump to END if equal;
> Add 1 to the contents of the R register;
> Jump to LOOP;
> END:

(a) Describe the result when the characters T R A P followed by carriage return are input as data to this program. (2)

(b) Append statements to this program to output the characters P A R T when the data described in (a) has been input. (6)

(c) Identify the data structure used within this program. Justify your answer. (3)

(d) Explain the purpose of the R register within:
 (i) the architecture of the computer;
 (ii) the program. (4)

(EDEXCEL)

Tutorial note
To answer part (c), think of all the data structures you have covered to get an insight into what the examiner is asking.

Suggested answer
(a) The characters TRAP<cr> are copied to locations 1000–<1004, and the program then jumps to END because the accumulator contains <cr>. (<cr> denotes carriage return.)

(b)
> Store 3 in the R register;
> Set base to 1000;
> OUTPUT: Copy to accumulator contents of storage location (base + contents of the R register);
> Output contents of accumulator;
> Subtract 1 from R;
> Branch to FINISH if negative;
> Jump to OUTPUT;
> FINISH:

(c) The data structure used is an array of characters forming a stack. It is a stack because the last character inserted is the first one to be removed.

(d) (i) The R register is an index register.
 (ii) In the program R is used in the calculation of the operand address by adding its contents to a base address.

9 A microprocessor with a 16-bit memory word uses a *bitmapped* screen occupying memory locations 50000_{16} to $6FFFF_{16}$. By allocating four bits to each screen *pixel*, each memory location controls the colour of four *pixels*. For example, the pattern 0000_2 represents black, while 0001_2 represents red.

Locations 50000_{16} to $500FF_{16}$ correspond to the bottom row of pixels on the screen.

(a) Explain the term pixel. (2)

(b) For the given screen memory, what is the maximum possible number of colours that a pixel may be set to? (1)

(c) Showing *all* working, express your answers to the following in *denary*.
 (i) What is the total number of locations reserved for the screen memory? (2)

(ii) How many pixels are there in the bottom row of the screen?   (2)

(d) A fragment of an assembly language program is shown below. (The effect of each mnemonic is explained in Table 1) The program makes use of the A register and the X register. These registers are 16 bits wide.

Label	Function	Operands	Comment
	LOAD	A, #0	\ Loads A register with zero
	LOAD	X, #8	
LOOP:	SUB	X, #1	
	STORE	X(&50000), A	
	BNE	X, LOOP	
	HALT		

Table 1

Function	Operands	Description
LOAD	register, #N	load specified register with the value N
SUB	register, #N	subtract the value N from the specified register
STORE	X(n), register	store contents of specified register in location n indexed by contents of index register, X
BNE	register, n	branch to location n if contents of specified register do not equal zero
HALT		stop executing instructions
&		denotes a hexadecimal address, e.g. &50000 = 50000_{16}
\		introduces a comment

(i) Trace the action of this routine, showing after each iteration the contents of the index register, X and all memory locations encompassed by the program.   (8)

(ii) Describe, in words, the function of this fragment of program.   (3)

(e) Give two advantages of allocating main memory for the bitmapped screen. (2)

(AEB)

Tutorial note

For part (b), the maximum possible number of colours is given by the number of different bit patterns that can be produced by 4 bits, i.e. 2^4.

Part (d) is about indexed addressing. For an explanation, see section 8.8.

Suggested answer

(a) A pixel is the smallest addressable area on screen.

(b) 16.

(c) (i) $(458751_{10} - 327680_{10} + 1) = 131072$

Alternatively, work it out as: $(6FFFF_{16} - 50000_{16}) + 1 = 20000_{16}$
$$= 2 * 65536_{10} = 131072_{10} \ (= 128K)$$

(ii) No. of locations on bottom row = $(500FF_{16} - 50000_{16}) + 1 = 100_{16} = 256_{10}$
No. of pixels on bottom row = $4_{10} * 256_{10} = 1024_{10}$

(d) (i) See below.

It	X	50007	50006	50005	50004	50003	50002	50001	50000
1	7	0							
2	6	0	0						
3	5	0	0	0					
4	4	0	0	0	0				
5	3	0	0	0	0	0			
6	2	0	0	0	0	0	0		
7	1	0	0	0	0	0	0	0	
8	0	0	0	0	0	0	0	0	0

(ii) The program sets the bottom row to black.

(e) (Any two points)
No need to have separate I/O instructions for screen output
No need to have a separate bus for I/O
Can draw picture off screen
Faster updating of/access to screen.

CHAPTER 9

DATA COMMUNICATION AND NETWORKING

Units in this chapter

Chapter objectives

After working through the topics in this chapter, you should be able to:

- describe the transmission of analogue and digital data;
- describe the use of modems, multiplexors and types of line including ISDN;
- describe the use of simplex, half-duplex and full-duplex transmission;
- explain circuit switching and packet switching;
- explain error detection methods;
- explain the use of data compression and data encryption;
- describe the benefits of local area networks;
- describe ring, star and bus topologies and advantages of each;
- describe applications of wide area networks and on-line services available to the public.

9.1 PRINCIPLE OF ELECTRONIC DATA COMMUNICATION

Data communication involves sending and receiving data from one computer or data processing device to another. Applications using for example e-mail, supermarket EPOS (electronic point-of-sale) terminals, cash dispensers, facsimile, and video conferencing are all examples of this.

When the devices are close together, for example in the same building, they can be linked by means of cables. However, when devices are separated by more than a few hundred yards, data has to be sent over a communications link (e.g. telephone line) and extra equipment such as a modem is required.

Communications links

In the UK, British Telecom, Mercury and other telecom operators provide services and data links. Telephone lines may be either

- public lines, on which the cost of sending data depends on the length of time taken;
- private or leased lines, for which there is a fixed annual fee and the line can be used as often as needed for no extra cost.

Communications media

Communication may take place over a combination of different media:

- twisted pair (copper cable), used in much of the telephone network;
- coaxial cable – high quality, well-insulated cable that can transmit data at higher speeds;
- fibre optic cable through which pulses of light, rather than electricity, are sent in digital form;
- communications satellite, using one of the hundreds of satellites now in geosynchronous orbit about 22,000 miles above the Earth (geosynchronous orbit means that they are rotating at the same speed as the Earth and are therefore stationary relative to Earth);
- microwave – similar to radio waves. Microwave stations cannot be much more than 30 miles apart because of the Earth's curvature as microwaves travel in straight lines. Mobile telephones use microwave radio links.

The amount of data that can be sent over a line depends partly on the **bandwidth**, which is the range of frequencies that the line can carry. The greater the bandwidth, the greater the rate at which data can be sent, as several messages can be transmitted simultaneously.

A network that is capable of sending voice, video and computer data is called an *integrated services digital network* (ISDN), and this requires a high bandwidth.

Modems

Telephone lines were originally designed for speech, which is transmitted in analogue or wave form. In order for digital data to be sent over a telephone line, it must first be converted to analogue form and then converted back to digital at the other end. This is achieved by means of a modem (MOdulator DEModulator) at either end of the line.

Figure 9.1: A modem converts digital signals to analogue and vice versa.

Multiplexors

A multiplexor combines more than one input signal into a single stream of data that can be transmitted over a single communications channel. This means, for example, that a local area network of 48 PCs could all communicate with a mainframe at some geographically remote head office via a single leased line attached to a multiplexor. At the mainframe end, there is likely to be a **front-end processor** which will handle the communications, leaving the main processor free for other tasks.

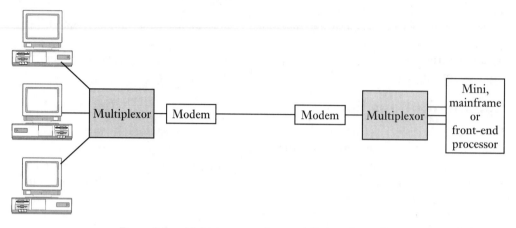

Figure 9.2:   Multiplexors, modems and front-end processor

9.2   COMMUNICATION METHODS

Simplex, half-duplex and full-duplex transmission

There are three possible modes of transmission:

- Simplex – transmission can take place only in one direction. This type of transmission could be used for example when the sending device such as a temperature sensor never requires a response from the computer.
- Half-duplex – transmission can take place in both directions but not simultaneously. This type of transmission is often used between a central computer and terminals.
- Full-duplex – transmission can take place in both directions simultaneously. It is suitable for interactive computer applications.

Synchronous and asynchronous transmission

With **asynchronous** transmission, one character at a time is sent, with each character being preceded by a start bit and followed by a stop bit. A parity bit is also usually included as a check against incorrect transmission. This type of transmission is usually used by PCs, and is fast and economical for relatively small amounts of data.

In **synchronous** transmission mode, timing signals (usually the computer's internal clock) control the rate of transmission and there is no need for start and stop bits to accompany each character. Mainframe computers usually use synchronous transmission. It is less error-prone than asynchronous transmission.

Data transfer checks

The following checks may be made during data transmission:

- **parity checks** – an extra bit is transmitted with each character to make the number of bits set to 1 even (for even parity) or odd (for odd parity).
- **checksum** may be sent with each block of data transmitted. All the elements in the

block (e.g. words or bytes) are added together (ignoring overflow) to produce a single element known as the checksum, and this is stored and transmitted with the block, and checked on receipt.

Circuit switching

The public telephone system is an example of a switched network using circuit-switched paths. When a caller dials a number, the path between the two telephones is set up by operating switches in all of the exchanges involved in the path, and the circuit is set up and held for the duration of the call. This permits two people on the phone to have a conversation with no waiting at either end for the message to arrive. However, because switches are used to connect and disconnect the circuits, electrical interference is produced, and although this is not a serious problem for speech, it may produce corrupt or lost data if the path is being used to transmit computer data.

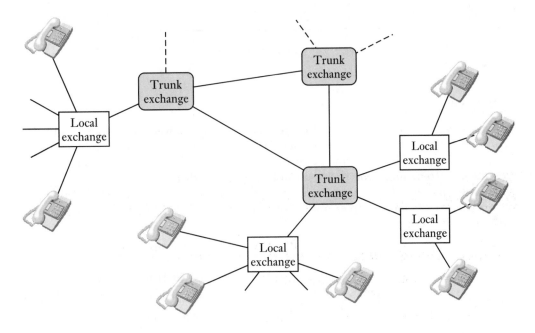

Figure 9.3:   A telephone network

Packet switching

In a packet switching system (PSS) data is divided into **packets** – fixed length blocks of data of say 128 bytes. As well as the data, each packet also carries

- the source and destination address;
- a packet sequence number so that the whole message can be correctly reassembled;
- a checksum (longitudinal parity check) for the purpose of error checking.

The PSS takes the form of a computer network in which each computer redirects packets it receives to the next computer along an appropriate route to its destination.

Advantages of packet switching

- More efficient use of lines is possible.
- Cost depends only on the number of packets sent not on distance, so all data is transmitted at local call rates.
- It is less likely to be affected by network failure because of the multiple routes available to transmit data packets.
- Security is better; data is less likely to be intercepted because the packets may be sent along different routes or be interleaved with other unrelated packets.

CHAPTER 9 DATA COMMUNICATION AND NETWORKING

Data compression

Data compression is frequently used when transmitting large quantities of data, thereby reducing the number of blocks transmitted and hence the cost. It basically works by replacing repeated bytes by one copy of the byte plus a count of the repetitions.

Data encryption

Data encryption is used for security purposes when transmitting or storing confidential data. The data to be transmitted is encoded using a mathematical algorithm or substitution of letters, so that even if it is intercepted it cannot be read. Other uses of encryption include the encryption of personal identification numbers (PINs) stored on cash cards, and passwords stored on disk.

> *The answer is 1743* → ENCRYPTION → *Vj2 1ptx2s 3t *agdc* → DECRYPTION → *The answer is 1743*
>
> *(Plaintext)*   *(Ciphertext)*   *(Plaintext)*

Figure 9.4: Encryption and decryption

Protocol

In order to allow equipment from different suppliers to be networked, a strict set of rules (**protocols**) has been devised covering standards for physical connections, cabling, mode of transmission, speed, data format, error detection and correction. Any equipment which uses the same communication protocol can be linked together.

It is also possible to link equipment using a special translation device called a protocol converter to link, for example, a PC to a mainframe. This overcomes problems of incompatibility such as

- different types of transmission: the PC may use asynchronous transmission, and the mainframe synchronous transmission;
- different character representations: PCs commonly use ASCII to represent characters, whereas many mainframes use a different code such as Extended Binary Coded Decimal Interchange Code (EBCDIC).

The ISO standard

The International Standards Organisation (ISO) Open Systems Interconnection (OSI) model is used to define the ways in which different computer networks may be connected to each other. This manages the often complex data communications between different systems. The model breaks the task into seven different subtasks, known as

1. the physical layer (the wiring and electrical signals on the wires);
2. the data link layer, which provides for the transfer of data, error detection and synchronisation;
3. network link layer, which specifies how the information is to be transmitted in the form of a frame consisting of address fields, a control field, a date field and an error control field;
4. the transport layer, which deals with the routing and multiplexing of the signals;
5. the session layer, which undertakes the management of communications sessions between two different systems;
6. the presentation layer, which deals with how the information is presented, e.g. ASCII or EBCDIC;
7. the application layer, which defines the interface through which the users' applications or programs gain access to the communications services. Typical facilities would be file transfer and message handling.

Bridges and gateways/routers

A **bridge** is a connection between two local area networks. Wide area networks may be connected through a system of **routers/gateways**, a gateway being a computer which acts as a point of connection between different networks.

9.3   LOCAL AREA NETWORKS

A local area network (LAN) is a collection of computers connected together by cables, and confined to one building or site. It offers several advantages over a collection of stand-alone computers:

- sharing of resources such as disk storage, printers, scanner etc.;
- sharing of information held on disk drives accessible by all users;
- sharing of software;
- ability to communicate with other users on the network.

Network topologies

The topology of a network is its physical layout – the way in which the computers and other units are connected. There are three basic layouts: star, bus and ring.

Star network

Each node in a star network is connected to a central computer which controls the network. Network signals travel from the server to the station along each individual station's cable. A polling system is commonly used; the file server polls each station in turn to see if it has a signal to send. The server then handles signals as they are received.

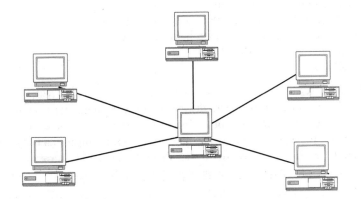

Figure 9.5:   A star network

Advantages of a star network configuration
- If one cable fails, the others are not affected.
- Performance is consistent even when the network is being heavily used.
- Variable transmission rates are possible between the file server and each workstation.
- The passing of messages from one workstation to another or from the file server to a workstation is more secure since each station has its own cable to the server.
- It is easy to add new stations without disrupting the network.

Disadvantages of a star network
- It is costly to install because of the length of cable required.

A variation of the star topology is the **distributed star** topology. A number of stations are linked to connection boxes which are then linked together to form a 'string of stars'.

Bus network

In a bus network, all the devices share a single cable. Information can be transmitted in either direction between any computers on the network. This means that when two computers want to use the line at the same time, there has to be some method of deciding who gets the line first. **Ethernet** networks use a system known as 'Carrier sense multiple access with collision detection' (CSMA-CD). Before a station begins to transmit, it checks that the channel is not busy; if it is, it has to wait before transmission can begin. Once it begins transmission, it listens for other nodes also beginning transmission. If the transmitted message collides with another, both stations abort and wait a random period of time before trying again.

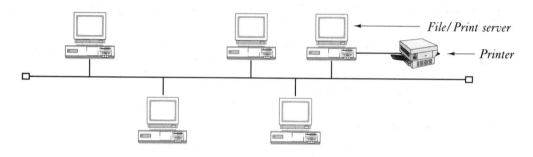

Figure 9.6:   A bus network

Advantages of a bus network configuration
- It is easy and inexpensive to install as it requires the least amount of cable.
- It is easy to add more stations without disrupting the network.

Disadvantages of a bus network configuration
- The whole network goes down if the main cable fails at any point.
- Cable failure is difficult to isolate.
- Network performance degrades under a heavy load.

Ring network

In a ring network, a series of computers is connected together and each computer may communicate with any other on the network typically using a 'token ring' system. Using this system, a 'message token' in the form of a unique character sequence is passed from node to node (always in the same direction), and each node has a designated time at which it can 'grab' the token and either read the message or add a new message together with the addresses of the receiving node and sending node and some control information.

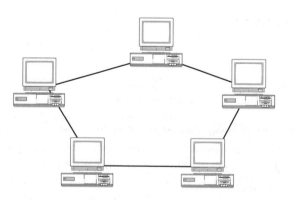

Figure 9.7:   Ring network

Advantages of a ring network configuration
- There is no dependence on a central file server.
- Transmission of messages around the ring is relatively simple, with messages travelling in one direction only.
- Very high transmission rates are possible.

Disadvantage of a ring network configuration
- If one node in the ring breaks down, transmission between any of the devices in the ring is disrupted.

9.4 WIDE AREA NETWORKS

A wide area network is a collection of computers spread over a wide geographical area, possibly spanning several continents. Communication may be by ordinary telephone line, satellite or microwave link. More and more organisations and private homes are being offered the facility of an ISDN line, an optic fibre line which enables high-speed transmission of multimedia material including video and photographic images.

9.5 APPLICATIONS OF NETWORKING

Electronic mail

Using electronic mail, data and messages can be sent to other subscribers anywhere in the world. It has the following advantages over ordinary mail:
- *Speed*: being electronic, the data can be sent to any destination in a few seconds. There may be a delay of up to a few hours if the network is particularly busy.
- *Economy*: it is much cheaper to send a large volume of data via e-mail than to post bulky documents. Data may be **compressed** before it is sent to save on transmission charges.
- *Convenience*: transmissions can be made without having to move from your office chair.
- *Security:* access can be restricted by the use of passwords.
  In addition, e-mail offers various facilities for inter-office communication such as
- the ability to send the same message simultaneously to a group of colleagues;
- the ability to prioritise mail so that urgent messages are sent immediately, less urgent communications wait until after 6pm when the cheap rate starts;
- the facility to attach and send a reply to a message;
- the facility to keep an 'address-book' of addressees.

Video conferencing

Video conferencing, whereby several people at remote locations can hold a 'meeting' and see each other as well as hear each other is also possible with an ISDN line. Strategically-placed video cameras capture the images which are transmitted and appear on the screen of a remote PC, or in some cases, on video screens in a conference room.

Electronic funds transfer (EFT and EFTPOS)

In EFT a computer system is used to transfer funds from one account to another – for example to pay employees' salaries directly into bank accounts or pay for goods ordered over the phone. In EFTPOS (electronic funds transfer at point of sale) goods are paid for at the till by presenting a payment card, and funds are automatically transferred from the customer's account to the store's account.

Distributed processing

Organisations with several branches in different locations frequently have a central mainframe computer together with a number of linked local area networks forming a wide area network (see Section 4.1).

The Internet and intranets

The Internet is a collection of interconnected computer networks which span the globe, linked by telecommunication systems. Some of these networks act as **service providers** and members of the public may join these networks in return for a monthly subscription, thereby gaining access to vast amounts of information on every conceivable topic as well as electronic mail facilities and access to the **World Wide Web**, a collection of pages stored on computers throughout the world.

An intranet provides the facilities and technology of the Internet on a private network.

Chapter summary

Various types of transmission links such as telephone lines, satellite and microwave have been described, and the role of modems and multiplexors explained. Types of transmission – simplex, half-duplex and full-duplex – have been described and the use of parity checks and checksums outlined, as well as the need for standard protocols for linking networks and individual computers on a network. The benefits to the user of networking include sharing programs, data and resources. Various topologies for local area networks such as ring, star and bus may be used. Wide area networks span a wide geographical area and may be used for internal communications, electronic mail, conferencing and distributed processing.

Illustrative questions

1 Distinguish clearly between half-duplex and full-duplex in the context of data transmission.

(4)

(NICCEA)

Suggested answer
Half-duplex mode supports communications in both directions but not at the same time. It is suitable for data transmission between a computer and dumb terminals.

Full-duplex mode allows communication in both directions at the same time and is suitable for interactive systems.

2 A local area network (LAN) is a collection of computers and peripherals linked by cables for the use of a single organisation or company. Most LANs are confined to a single office block or commercial site.

State three advantages of a LAN compared with the use of a collection of stand-alone microcomputers.

(3)

(AEB)

Suggested answer
Advantages of a LAN:
• sharing hardware resources such as printers and disk storage;
• sharing software;
• ability to communicate via e-mail
(could also specify sharing of data held on a company database).

3 List four advantages of the use of e-mail compared to the use of the ordinary postal system. *(New question)*

Tutorial note
Even when the question says 'list', it is not sufficient to give one word answers such as 'speed, cost, convenience'. You must give a short explanation of each advantage.

Suggested answer
- *Speed*: the data can be sent to any destination in a few hours (or even a few seconds if the network is not busy).
- *Economy*: it is much cheaper to transmit a large volume of data to another country than to post it.
- *Convenience*: transmissions can be made from an office computer without having to look up an address (addresses can be stored in an electronic 'address book').
- The same message can be sent simultaneously to several people.

4 Teleworking, that is remote access to office networks from home, is becoming increasingly popular. Briefly explain the implications of this way of working.   (5)
(NEAB)

In your answer you may consider the effects on the employee, the employer or society in general.

Suggested answer
The employee will have more flexible working hours and may be able to combine his/her job with looking after children at home. There will be fewer journeys to work, thus saving petrol and pollution and making the roads less crowded. Employers may be able to have less office space thus saving on rent, heating, lighting etc. On the negative side, employees may feel isolated, have no one to turn to for help and not have the opportunity to enjoy the social side of office life. There will be more demand for ISDN lines able to transmit large volumes of data and graphic images at high speed.

5 (a) What is a *local area network* (LAN)?   (2)
   (b) Messages are transmitted over LANs in *data packets*. State three components of a data packet other than the message data.   (3)
   (AEB)

Suggested answer
(a) A LAN is a method of linking computers occupying a small geographical area such as a single building or site.
(b) A data packet will contain in addition to the message data: destination address, source address, packet number (also number of packets in message, checksum, parity bit).

6 A newspaper has a multi-access system which supports 200 terminals. As the number of users increases, there is a gradual degradation of performance which rapidly worsens as the number of users approaches 150.
   (a) Explain the gradual degradation of performance.   (2)
   (b) Explain the rapid worsening of performance and suggest how this could be remedied.   (4)
   (EDEXCEL)

Suggested answer
(a) If this is a bus network, all stations share the same communication link and so as the number of users increases, each person's transmission has to compete with many others for the use of the line. A high bandwidth line may be used enabling data streams to be transmitted at a higher bit rate.
(b) When the number of users approaches 150 there will be many clashes as users try to send information simultaneously and a large proportion of time will be spent by the network software attempting to re-send the information, detecting a collision, waiting and trying again.

This could be remedied by increasing the bandwidth of the cable, or by using compression techniques to compress data so that it is transmitted more quickly. Or, each station could download the software/data it needs to a local hard disk so that thereafter there would be less network traffic.

7 A bank has set up a wide area network (WAN) so that branches can pass data to each other.
   (a) Distinguish between serial and parallel transmission in a network. State *one* advantage and *one* disadvantage of serial transmission. (4)
   (b) Describe *three* security aspects of a network which must be addressed. (3)
   (c) Noise on the line can distort a data signal and result in bits being incorrectly received. Name and describe a technique to detect such errors. (2)
   (d) Explain how a number of terminals can share a communication line. (3)
   (e) Explain the role of a protocol in data transmission. (3)
   (EDEXCEL)

Suggested answer
(a) Using serial transmission, single bits are transmitted one after the other, whereas in parallel transmission, typically 8, 16 or 32 bits can be transmitted simultaneously. The advantage of serial transmission is that almost all computers (Apple, IBM, Archimedes) have a serial data communications port called the RS232 port, and so different types of computer can be linked in a single network. The disadvantage is that the rate of transmission is slow.
(b) Need to guard against: unauthorised users logging on to the network, unauthorised users accessing confidential data and outsiders tapping the line to gain access to data. Data held on the network must be protected from catastrophes such as fire and flood.
(c) **Parity checking** may be used. For even parity, an extra bit is added to the code for each character to make the total number of bits set to 1 an even number. (You could alternatively discuss the **checksum** method).
(d) A number of terminals can share a communications line by using a multiplexor. Using frequency division multiplexing, different carrier frequencies are allocated to different signals over a broadband line so that several terminals linked to the multiplexor at one end of the line can transmit simultaneously. A demultiplexor at the other end of the line separates the signals.
(e) A protocol is a set of rules used to define the ways in which different computer networks may be connected to each other. Without a common standard it would be impossible to establish a global communications network as each computer manufacturer would have their own way of doing things. The standard open systems interconnection (OSI) protocol defines the interface, methods of representing character and graphical data, size of packets sent, error detection methods and so on.

8 A new secondary school has a limited budget available for purchasing and installing computers for student use. A main decision is whether to have a school-wide network or to use stand-alone computers. Related to this decision is the specification of each computer and the provision for file storage and printing.
   (a) Outline the main requirements of the computing facilities provided for student use in a secondary school. (4)
   (b) In the light of your answer to part (a), discuss the advantages and disadvantages of opting for a school-wide network rather than for stand-alone computers. (6)
   (UCLES)

Tutorial note
There are several different angles you could choose in your answer; for example you could concentrate more on hardware than in the suggested answer, as appropriate hardware with sufficient memory, high-resolution monitors, large-capacity disk storage will be needed for some applications. Also on the software side, facilities for preventing students deliberately or accidentally deleting software or introducing viruses.

Suggested answer

(a) The main requirements are that:

- many students must be able to simultaneously access software such as word-processing, spreadsheets, graphics packages etc.
- students need access to suitable printers for the type of work, e.g. dot-matrix for program listings, laser printers for graphics or high quality documentation.
- student work needs to be kept secure so that it cannot be accessed by other students, either by being saved on individual floppy disks or by saving it centrally and having a secure password system.
- facilities for accessing reference material on CD-ROMs and access to the Internet for various projects needs to be made available.

(b) *Advantages*: Only one copy of each software package needs to be held, making control and upgrading easier. Printers, CD-ROM drives etc., can be shared. A central filestore for students' work is easier to back up than individual hard drives attached to stand-alone machines.

Disadvantages: more specialised expertise is needed to support and maintain a network. Failure in the network results in all computers being unusable. Networked computers may run slower than stand-alone computers.

9 A college currently uses two separate local area networks, one for administration and one for teaching. Both networks use a bus topology.

   (a) The administration network consists of 12 workstations and a dedicated file server. One of the workstations also acts as a printer server.

      (i) Explain the function of the printer server and the file server.

      (ii) State *two* possible disadvantages of using a workstation as a printer server. (4)

   (b) Ring and Star are common topologies for local area networks.

      Describe these topologies, using *clearly labelled diagrams* to illustrate your answer. (3)

   (c) The college wishes to connect the two networks so that teaching staff can have access to student records. This connection can be made using a bridge.

      (i) When would it be necessary to use a gateway, rather than a bridge, to connect two networks?

      (ii) State *two* functions provided by a gateway that would not be provided by a bridge. (3)

                                          (SQA)

Suggested answer

(a) (i) The printer server allows all the networked machines to have access to a common printer. Printing jobs sent to the printer are queued, the output is spooled to a disk drive and printed when the printer becomes free. The file server is used to store applications such as word-processing, spreadsheet and database software, and also to store users' data files.

    (ii) The disadvantages of using a workstation as a printer server are: if the user is running a program that requires a lot of processing, users' requests to print will not be handled immediately. The disk space may not be sufficient to handle both the spool queue and work that the user saves on the local hard disk.

(b) Ring network: (see Figure 9.7)

    Star network: (see Figure 9.5)

(c) (i) It would be necessary to use a gateway rather than a bridge when the networks are to be connected over long distances.

    (ii) A gateway provides access to external systems such as local area networks at a different site or a global wide area network. A gateway can give access to a packet switching network and use a router to work out the most cost effective route to send a message.

CHAPTER 10

SYSTEM SOFTWARE

Units in this chapter

Chapter objectives

After working through the topics in this chapter, you should be able to:

- define the role of an operating system;
- define the common types of operating system: batch, interactive, multi-access, multi-tasking, multiprocessing, real-time and, time-sharing;
- describe a structure for an operating system based upon separate but interacting modules;
- define the concept of a process, explain the need for process scheduling in a multiprogramming environment;
- define the round-robin scheduling algorithm;
- describe techniques of memory management including paging, segmentation, virtual memory and relocation;
- describe the role of the file manager in managing data residing on secondary storage;
- describe I/O management in terms of device drivers and second-level interrupt handlers;
- describe JCL, command-line and graphical user interface types.

10.1 ROLE OF AN OPERATING SYSTEM

Without its software, a computer is basically a useless collection of metal, silicon and plastic. With its software, a computer becomes a powerful information-processing tool.

Computer software can be divided into two categories:
1. the system programs, which manage the operation of the computer itself;
2. the application programs, which solve problems for their users.

The most fundamental of all the system programs is the operating system.

The operating system role is to
- hide the complexities of the hardware from the user;
- manage the hardware resources in order to provide for an orderly and controlled allocation of the processors, memories and I/O devices among the various programs competing for them.

10.2 TYPES OF OPERATING SYSTEM

Single-user single-process

The most basic type of operating system exists to allow the machine to be operated by only one user at a time with at most one application program loaded into main memory.

Multiprogramming

Multiprogramming is defined as the *apparent simultaneous execution of two or more programs*.

All executing application programs get held up at some stage because hardware devices such as disk drives, printers, etc., cannot respond as quickly as processors can work. Operating systems were therefore developed to allow several application programs to occupy main memory at the same time so that when one became halted temporarily another could take its place. A multiprogramming operating system balances the sharing of the processor among the application programs in order to achieve a good service to all.

Batch

The technique of multiprogramming was developed when computers were operated in batch-processing mode. In batch-processing mode, *processing is carried out from beginning to end without user interaction*.

Jobs prepared in this way have all their processing requirements defined in advance. By using multiprogramming, a batch of several jobs can be loaded so that when executed over the same time period the processor is kept as busy as possible by switching between the jobs as and when necessary. This increases *throughput*, i.e. the total number of jobs completed per unit time, and reduces the *turnaround time*, i.e. time between job submission and job completion.

Interactive

With this type of processing the user interacts directly with the system to supply commands and data as the application program undergoes execution and receives the results of processing immediately. An operating system which allows such interaction is said to support *interactive processing*. Such an operating system allows the user and the computer to be in *direct two-way communication*.

Multi-access

By applying the concept of multiprogramming to interactive processing it is possible to develop a multi-access (user) operating system. A **multi-access** (multi-user) operating system is defined as one that *allows two or more users to communicate with the computer at any one time*, with each user interacting with the computer via a terminal (which must have, at the minimum, a keyboard and VDU). The system operates in such a way as to give the impression to the user that he/she has sole access to the computer even though many users may actually be interacting with the computer, simultaneously. This effect is produced by allowing each user to share the computer's processor, main memory and file store. Each application program resident in main memory is then executed a bit at a time by rotating the use of the processor between them. The trick of giving a user the impression of having sole access is achieved by choosing, for each turn, the right length of processor time. Too long and some users will notice delays. Too short and all users will find that processing is noticeably slowed.

Multi-tasking

The multiprogramming concept applied to a **multi-tasking** operating system allows the concurrent execution (over the same time period) of two or more **related** tasks between which communication is possible and the execution of a group of cooperating tasks to achieve some common goal. Multi-tasking may be applied to both single and multi-user operating systems.

Time-sharing

In a time-sharing operating system processes are allowed to run concurrently but unlike multiprogramming only one process is allowed to be resident in main memory at any one time. This requires that processes are swapped in and out. Time-sharing was applied to interactive systems where users operating keyboards were relatively unaffected by this swapping in and out.

Multi-access and batch

Some operating systems provide both multi-access and batch processing opportunities. In such systems batch-processing jobs are run at times of low interactive demand, e.g. during the night when few users are active on the system. In this way expensive mainframe computers are kept productive 24 hours a day.

Interactive users on the system are also able to benefit from the advantages of batch processing by handing over responsibility for printing their work to the system to manage as a batch job. Users' application programs which contain print statements are then not held up by the need to wait until a printer is free or to wait while a line of data is printed. The work to be printed is sent immediately to a disk file. These disk files are scheduled for printing by the system during periods when the load on the processor is low. The technique is known as **spooling** and the disk files are called **spool files**. The part of the operating system which manages the printing of the spooled files is called the **spooler**.

Real-time

In this mode of operation, the computer responds immediately to an external stimulus, processing the input generated quickly enough to have an immediate influence on the stimulus.

Real-time operating systems are characterised by four requirements:

1. They have to support application programs which are non-sequential in nature, i.e. programs which do not have a START–PROCESS–END structure.
2. They have to deal with a number of events which happen in parallel and at unpredictable moments in time.
3. They have to carry out processing and produce a response within a specified interval of time.

4. Some systems are safety-critical, meaning they must be fail-safe and guarantee a response within a specified time interval.

Examples of real-time operating systems are:

- Airline reservation system: up to a 1000 messages per second can arrive from any one of 11,000–12,000 terminals, situated all over the world. The response time must be less than 3 seconds.
- Process control system: up to 1000 signals per second can arrive from sensors attached to the system being controlled. The response time must be less than one thousandth of a second.

Client–server system

An environment in which cooperation and intercommunication between the various elements of a network is conducted on the basis of some computers 'serving' others is referred to as a **client–server system**.

Most network operating systems operate a client–server system. In a client–server system, application programs reside on a network server connected to the LAN. The server is a powerful high specification PC, minicomputer or mainframe computer. Also connected to the LAN are a number of client computers. The clients are each loaded with an operating system which allows work to be carried out at the client computer, e.g. DOS, but in addition they contain an extension which intercepts requests to run application programs or to access files or other services which can only be met by the server. In a manner completely transparent to the user of the client system, the requests are redirected to and satisfied by the server. In this way, server files and application programs resident on the server are available to the client user exactly as if they were resident on that user's system. The client extended operating system can itself be downloaded from the server.

The client–server approach is also used when printing work from an application running on a client computer. The work to be printed is sent over the network to a print server to which are connected one or more printers. The server is responsible for carrying out the printing of clients' work.

Distributed computer systems

With the development of the personal computer (PC), the need arose for stand-alone PCs to be able to share expensive peripheral devices such as printers. This led, in the early 1980s, to PCs being organised in local-area networks (LANs) using interconnection technologies such as Ethernet. Allowing PCs access to the file system of another PC located somewhere else on the network became a requirement as well, especially as the cost of hard disk drives was still relatively high.

The file server and print server networks are examples of **distributed computer systems**. A distributed system is one *in which system resources, e.g. processors, disk storage and printers, exist in separate nodes of a network with transparent access to these resources by users being possible.* For example, computer A can run a program on computer B, using a file located elsewhere on the network without the user being aware of where execution is taking place or where the files are physically located.

Multiprocessing

An operating system running on a machine that contains more than one processor for executing programs is known as a **multiprocessing** operating system if it spreads the execution of programs over several processors.

10.3 OPERATING SYSTEM IMPLEMENTATION

An operating system consists of the programs which make the hardware usable. The hardware is a collection of resources.

Managing resources

One purpose of an operating system is to manage the hardware so that a satisfactory performance is achieved as judged by criteria such as the number of jobs completed per unit time or the response time to interactive users.

The operating system programs may be classified according to the resource which they manage. The key *resources* an operating system manages and the corresponding *operating system programs* are:

* processors – processor scheduling;
* storage – memory management;
* input/output devices – I/O management;
* data – file management.

Another purpose of an operating system is to hide from the user all the details of how the hardware works so that the user is presented with a machine which is much easier to use – a so-called 'virtual machine'. These details are progressively hidden by placing layer upon layer of software on top of the hardware.

Modules of an operating system

The layer immediately next to the hardware is called the **nucleus** or **kernel**. This layer is machine-specific because it requires an intimate knowledge of a machine's registers and the way the machine handles interrupts. The nucleus contains the **first level interrupt handler**, the **despatcher** which switches a processor from executing one process to executing another by changing the contents of the program counter and other registers (this is called a **context switch**), and the **inter-process communication handler** which via hardware signals enables communication between executing processes.

The nucleus insulates the other layers or modules of the operating system from directly interfacing with the hardware. This makes it possible for the other layers to be written in a high-level language, which is useful because if it is required to install the operating system on another machine with a similar architecture but a different instruction set, then it is only necessary to rewrite the nucleus. The other layers or modules are:

* memory management module;
* I/O management module;
* file management module;
* scheduling module;
* user interface module.

10.4 PROCESS MANAGEMENT AND SCHEDULING

The concept of a process is central to the study of operating systems. It is defined as an *instance of a program in execution*. It is necessary to distinguish between a program and its execution in this way for three reasons:

1. There may be several copies of a program in main memory at any time, e.g. each user has their own copy.
2. One program loaded into main memory may be under execution more than once simultaneously, e.g. when users share a single copy of a compiler.
3. When a program is loaded into main memory ready for execution, its form changes, e.g. the program contains relocation information which is abandoned after it has been used to relocate the program in main memory.

States of a process

A process may be, at any instant in time, in one of three possible states:

* RUNNING – the process is using the processor.
* RUNNABLE – the process could make use of the processor if it were free.

- SUSPENDED – the process is waiting to be granted the use of an I/O device such as a disk, or for the completion of an I/O transfer.

Three queues of processes are maintained by the operating system, one for each possible state. In the case of the state RUNNING this will consist of just one process in a single processor system.

Processes move constantly between these three queues – for example, if a running process uses up its time-slice, it will be moved to the RUNNABLE queue and the operating system will move the next process in the RUNNABLE queue to the RUNNING queue. If this process then needs some I/O, it will move to the SUSPENDED queue and so on.

Process control block

Whenever a new process is created the operating system creates a data structure, called a **Process control block** (PCB) which is used to hold information about the process and its state of execution. Included in the PCB is an identification number, called the **Process ID**.

As soon as a process is stopped from executing so that the operating system or another process can execute, its current state must be saved so that when eventually this process is chosen for execution again it can be resumed at the correct point in its code and with the correct values installed in all the registers. This information is held in the PCB, typical contents of which are shown in Fig 10.1.

Process ID	6
User ID	MGREGORY
Priority	100
Account No	12345
No. of processor units consumed	1000
Status	SUSPENDED
Link in RUNNABLE queue	
Link in SUSPENDED queue	
Resource waiting for	Disk
Resource status	Free
Status of program counter, stack pointer, other registers	(various)

Figure 10.1: Process control block (PCB)

Scheduling

A **scheduler** is an operating system module that selects the next job to be admitted into the system and the next process to execute. The next job to be admitted and the next process to execute are chosen so as to achieve as many as possible of the following objectives:
- maximise system throughput;
- be fair to all users;
- provide acceptable response-time to interactive users and an acceptable turn-around time for batch users;
- degrade performance gracefully. If the system becomes overloaded, it should not collapse, but avoid further loading (e.g. by inhibiting any new jobs or users) and/or temporarily reduce the level of service (e.g. response time);
- ensure the hardware resources are kept as busy as possible;
- avoid deadlock.

The job of scheduling is often divided into three tasks managed by three sub-modules known as the
- long-term scheduler;
- medium-term scheduler;
- short-term scheduler.

The **long-term scheduler**, when present, is applied to a queue of batch jobs which are waiting to be admitted to the system. Batch jobs are admitted at times when the system resources are lightly loaded or when there is an unbalanced mix of I/O-bound and processor-bound processes (I/O-bound uses I/O time, predominantly, whilst processor-bound uses processor time, predominantly). If the processor is involved in too much processing-intensive work it is unlikely that the I/O devices are being kept busy or serviced frequently enough to give a good response time for interactive use. The long-term scheduler may also be involved in admitting interactive users to the system when they log-on. This scheduler may use a *first-come first-served* or a *shortest job first* algorithm to choose the next job to be admitted (see below).

The **medium-term scheduler** is used to select suspended processes to remove temporarily to secondary storage in order to make more room available in main memory for processes which are runnable. Suspended processes are SWAPPED OUT or ROLLED OUT of main memory only to be returned when their suspension is lifted.

The **short-term scheduler** is responsible for selecting the next RUNNABLE process to execute. This scheduler may use a *round-robin* scheduling algorithm.

Scheduling algorithms

There are a number of selection policies that the scheduler could use in picking the next process. The main ones are:
- shortest job first;
- shortest remaining time;
- round robin.

The first two are self-explanatory. The third is explained below.

Round-robin scheduling

In the round robin scheme, a process is selected for running from the RUNNABLE queue in FIFO sequence. However, if the process runs beyond a certain fixed length of time, called the time slice, it is interrupted and returned to the end of the RUNNABLE queue. In other words each active process is given a time slice in rotation. The timing required by this scheme is obtained by using a hardware timer which generates an interrupt at preset intervals.

Deadlock

The scheduler is also responsible for detecting deadlock and removing it when its scheduling policies do not achieve its avoidance. Deadlock occurs when two processes each has the resource which the other needs in order to execute. Since both processes do not have all the resources they need to execute they are in a permanent state of suspension.

Multi-threading

A thread is an independent instance of execution within a process. Using this mechanism, several independent threads may be scheduled to execute in a single process. Thus only one copy of a particular program (e.g. a compiler) need be resident in memory, simultaneously servicing several users in different stages of compilation. In a multi-processing system (e.g. some file servers), each thread is allocated its own processor.

10.5   MEMORY MANAGEMENT

The memory manager is primarily concerned with the allocation of the physical main memory to processes. No process may exist until a certain amount of main memory is allocated to it.

The objectives of memory management are

- to support the allocation of main memory to a process or to several processes that are to be executed concurrently;
- to protect processes from each other when executing concurrently;
- to allow processes executing concurrently to have shared access to common areas of memory;
- to make the addressing of memory space as transparent as possible to the programmer.

A process to be executed is loaded into main memory by a program called a **loader,** which may be one of two basic types:

- an **absolute loader,** which loads the program into a single fixed area of memory. All address references in the program are fixed at translation time (when the program is assembled or compiled) and it will only work properly when loaded into one specific position in main memory.
- a **relocating loader** which can load the program anywhere in main memory because the program has been translated in such a way that all addresses are relative to the start of the program. The start address of the program can be held in a special register called the **base register**.

For an object program to be relocatable it must have been prepared with a translator which has been designed for the purpose.

There are two basic forms in which a relocatable object program can be prepared. For the first form, **static relocation**, once the object program has been loaded into main memory relocatability is lost and the process cannot be moved again. For the second form, **dynamic relocation**, relocatability is retained and a process may be moved to a different memory area during its execution (essential in a multiprogramming set-up where programs are constantly being swapped in and out of memory). This is made possible by not replacing any logical address references with physical addresses. The logical to physical mapping is done at run time using **base register addressing**, as shown in Fig 10.2.

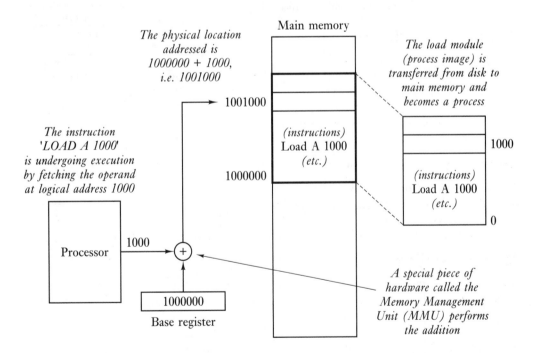

Figure 10.2:   Logical to physical address mapping using base register addressing

Another register called the **limit register** holds the highest addressable location of the process, and this enables the memory manager to protect other programs' memory space being accidentally addressed by program error. Imagine the ensuing chaos if a variable of your program was changed by another program that happened to be running at the same time!

Segmentation and paging

The memory manager maintains a map of the free and occupied areas of main memory so that it is able to allocate main memory space to processes. It is greatly assisted in this if memory is partitioned into fixed size blocks. There are two different approaches to partitioning. In the first, **segmentation,** the partition is called a segment and its size is fairly large, e.g. 64 kilobytes. In the second, **paging,** the partition is called a page frame and its size is relatively small, e.g. 1 kilobyte.

In segmentation, segments are formed at translation time by grouping together logically related items, e.g. one segment for code, another for data. The programmer is aware of segment size and attempts to design code and define data which does not exceed this size.

In paging, a translator splits an object program into fixed size pages of the same dimension as main memory page frames. The splitting is done without regard to the logical structure of the program and is totally transparent to the programmer.

A paged memory is preferred to a segmented one because it makes better use of main memory. In segmented memory a segment may be far from being full, e.g. a 2.5 K code segment loaded into a 64 K main memory segment will waste 61.5 K of storage whereas loaded into paged memory with page size 1 K it will waste only 0.5 K.

In both paged and segmented memory it is not necessary to allocate free memory contiguously to a process, i.e. to use consecutive pages or segments. A page of a process may be fitted into any free page frame of main memory. Similarly, a segment of a process may be fitted into any free memory segment.

Virtual memory

In early multiprogramming systems each executing application program had to be fully loaded into main memory. The number of application programs that could be executed concurrently, i.e. over the same time interval, was therefore limited by the amount of available main memory. In order to overcome this limitation a technique called **virtual**

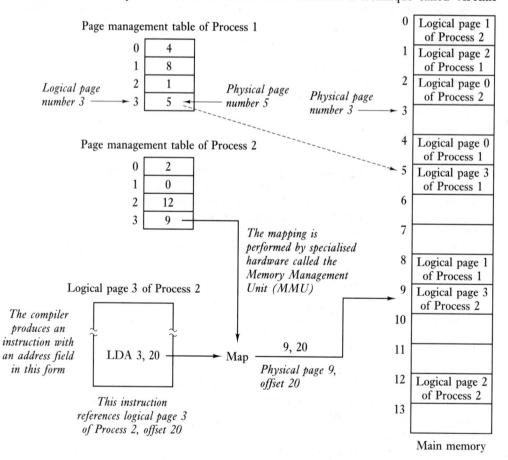

Figure 10.3   Logical to physical page mapping

memory was invented which allows partially loaded application programs to be executed. By dividing both main memory and programs into fixed size pages only those pages of a program which are currently required by the execution need be resident in main memory. Program pages are loaded when in demand and unloaded when not.

Each process has a corresponding **page management table** (PMT) which indicates whether a particular page of the process is loaded or not, and maps each page of the process with a corresponding memory page number. For a paged memory, a specific memory location is addressed using an address with the form (p,d), where p is the logical number of the page containing the location and d is the displacement or offset of the location from the start of the page. Fig 10.3 illustrates this.

10.6 FILE MANAGEMENT

The file management part of an operating system is charged with managing the data that resides on secondary storage, e.g. magnetic disk. It performs four main functions:
- keeps track of all files in the system;
- controls sharing and enforces protection of files;
- manages disk space and its allocation and de-allocation;
- maps logical file addresses to physical disk addresses.

The file manager allows users to organise their work into logical units of storage called files, such as a document file consisting of word-processed text. (As always, the term *logical* means 'as perceived by the user'.) Physically, a file is split into smaller units called blocks before being stored on secondary storage, because the disk is formatted into fixed-size blocks of say 512 bytes. It is the job of the file manager to provide the logical to physical mapping, and to maintain on the disk a map of free blocks so that it can allocate storage to new files.

A user references a particular unit of work symbolically by its logical name or file name, e.g. Book.Doc. The part following the period, e.g. *Doc*, is called the **file extension**.

Multi-level directory systems

A directory is a logical grouping of files. By maintaining several directories the file manager can permit the same file name to be used in separate directories to refer to independent copies of the same file or completely different files.

The contents of a directory – a list of file names and their associated information – are stored in a special file called a directory file which is assigned a file name which distinguishes it from non-directory files. By allowing directory file names to appear alongside non-directory file names in a directory, the file manager is able to link separate directories hierarchically as shown in Fig. 10.4. The directory at the top of the structure is given the special name **ROOT** because the hierarchical structure resembles an upside-down tree. The directories below the root directory are known as **subdirectories**.

Each file name can be uniquely identified by its full **pathname**, e.g. file Penny.Xls in subdirectory Sally has the full pathname:

>**\Sally\Penny.Xls**

To locate the referenced file Penny.Xls, the pathname is interpreted as follows:
\ means select the root of the tree and scan the directory, searching for a match with Sally. The next \ means select the root of the subtree, Sally, and scan the subdirectory, searching for a match with Penny.Xls.

Each entry in a directory refers to a file name and the following set of information:
- file type: e.g. directory file, system file, hidden file, batch, executable, text;
- information indicating the location of the file on secondary storage: e.g. disk address of the first block in the file;
- **access rights**: who can access the file and how it can be accessed: e.g. read–only, read–write, write–only, delete permission;
- file size in bytes;
- date information: e.g. date of creation, date of last access, date of last amendment, purge date.

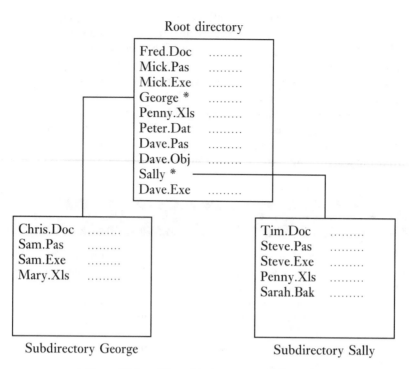

Root directory

Fred.Doc	....
Mick.Pas	....
Mick.Exe	....
George *	....
Penny.Xls	....
Peter.Dat	....
Dave.Pas	....
Dave.Obj	....
Sally *	
Dave.Exe	....

Chris.Doc	....
Sam.Pas	....
Sam.Exe	....
Mary.Xls	....

Tim.Doc	....
Steve.Pas	....
Steve.Exe	....
Penny.Xls	....
Sarah.Bak	....

Subdirectory George　　　　　　　　　　　Subdirectory Sally

Figure 10.4:　Hierarchical structure of directories

Using the access rights the file manager is able to control who can share a particular file, and protect that file against unauthorised alteration.

10.7　INPUT/OUTPUT MANAGEMENT

The input/output manager is the part of the operating system charged with the management of I/O devices. It provides an interface between other modules of the operating system and I/O devices, e.g. file manager. It provides a means by which files and devices can be treated in a uniform manner and manipulated by a set of high-level commands, such as Readln (StringVariable). At the device end, the I/O system must supply the device-specific control signals to each particular type of device, possibly many times in the course of execution of a single high-level command. It does this using software called a **device driver**. Each different type of device will need a corresponding device driver. The I/O system will maintain buffers into which data is transferred to and from devices and to and from application programs or the user interface. For example, the keyboard is usually buffered with a circular buffer to allow typing ahead and correction of a command line. The second level interrupt handlers for each device type are located in this module. When, for instance, a key is pressed on the keyboard it is a keyboard interrupt handler which actually transfers the typed character into the circular buffer.

10.8　USER INTERFACE

The user interface is that part of a computer system through which a human user and the computer communicate. User interfaces may be classified as
* job control language (JCL);
* command-line;
* graphical user interface or GUI.

Job control language

In a job control language interface a user has no direct interaction with the computer system. Instead a user prepares a series of instructions off-line using a JCL to describe to the system the requirements of his/her task. Eventually, when a user's job is executed, the execution is guided by the JCL-prepared description and the results made available at a later time via some off-line medium, e.g. line printer paper.

Typically, job control statements will specify
- who owns the job;
- job priority;
- the maximum processor time to allow the job;
- maximum lines to be printed;
- names of data files used;
- what action to take if one of the programs in the job fails to execute correctly.

Command-line interface

In a command-line user interface, an interactive terminal allows the system to prompt and the user to type a command to initiate program execution or to perform housekeeping tasks, e.g.

   C:\>Del *.bak

will cause all files in the current directory with the extension .bak to be deleted. The command prompt is the > character and the C:\ is the pathname for the current directory. The user interface module contains a **command-line interpreter** (CLI) which performs the actual task of identifying and executing the command.

Graphical user interface

A graphical user interface (GUI) provides a different means of interacting with the system using windows, icons (pictures) and a mouse to control the operating system. Icons represent programs, groups of programs, directories, devices and files. Figure 10.5 illustrates a typical GUI. Instead of typing a command or file name, selection is achieved by moving a pointer with a mouse and operating (clicking) a mouse button.

GUIs are easier for the novice to use because they are more intuitive. The screen is arranged as a metaphor of a desktop with graphical symbols to represent familiar objects. Only valid options are available and there is a consistency of layout and command representation in applications which can be launched into execution through operation of the GUI. Comprehensive on-line help is available. Disadvantages of a GUI over a command-line interface are:

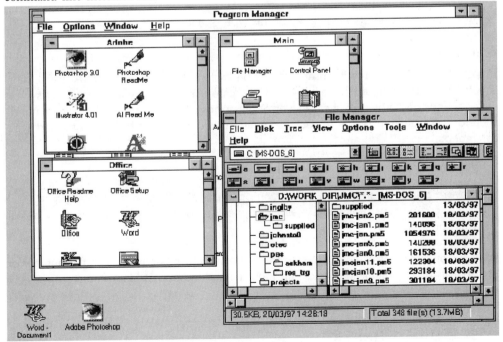

Figure 10.5:   Graphical user interface

- they use more immediate access store and secondary store;
- they require a more powerful processor and a better graphics display;
- they are slower when executing a command because much more interpretation takes place;
- they can be irritating to use for simple tasks because a greater number of operations is required.

Chapter summary

Chapter 10 has covered the major types of operating system: batch, interactive, real-time, multi-access, multi-tasking and distributed. The functions of an operating system have been defined in terms of providing a virtual machine and managing hardware resources. The concept of a process has been introduced and the reasons for scheduling of processes explained. The structure of an operating system is described as a collection of modules: the system nucleus, the memory manager, the I/O manager, the scheduler, the file manager, the user interface. Each of these modules are described in terms of their function and content. In memory management, relocation, paging, segmentation and virtual memory are described. In I/O management, the concept of a device driver is introduced and the purpose of the second level interrupt handler explained. The round-robin scheduling algorithm is described. Three types of user interface are introduced: batch, command-line and graphical. File management is explained in terms of the concept of a file and the need to map files onto the physical areas of the secondary storage device.

Illustrative questions

1 Many machines now offer a *graphical user interface* such as Windows.
  (i) Describe *two* features of such interfaces which are likely to be helpful to a non-technically minded user.   (2)
  (ii) Describe *three* disadvantages of this type of interface.   (3)
                                                                                        (AEB)

Tutorial note
The question only requires the user to describe features which are useful. A justification is not required. Command-driven interfaces require users to remember the exact syntax of commands and provide rather terse error messages when a user mistypes a command. Therefore concentrate on those features which avoid the need to memorise and type commands.

Suggested answer
(i) The user is able to execute a program or select an operation by using a mouse to move a pointer over an icon or a menu option and clicking a mouse button.
    A comprehensive menu system is supported which only allows users to select valid options.

(ii) It is slower or more time consuming to do a simple task because a greater number of operations are required. It takes up more immediate access store (main memory). It takes up more disk space.

2 A *multi-user, multi-tasking, virtual memory* operating system is installed in a minicomputer system. The operating system supports *multiprogramming*. The minicomputer is used for both *batch* and *interactive* work.

(a) Explain the differences between:
    (i)   multiprogramming, multi-access and multi-tasking;
    (ii) interactive and batch programs.   (5)
(b) (i)   Describe the *two* main functions of the scheduler in such an operating system.
                                                            (2)
    (ii) Describe *two* different events that lead to the scheduler being invoked.   (2)
    (iii) Describe *two* of the objectives of the scheduler when assigning job priorities in this system.   (2)
    (iv) Describe a suitable scheduling algorithm and explain how it satisfies at least one of these objectives.   (4)
(c) Explain the term virtual memory.   (5)
                                                             (AEB)

Tutorial note
A clear understanding of scheduling is required: in particular, an understanding of the meaning of the terms 'function' and 'objective'. *Function* should be interpreted as answering the question 'what task is performed?' An *objective* is a target or goal which is aimed at or which is striven to attain. Scheduling is about organising a supply of processes so that the hardware resources are kept busy as much as possible. This ranges from admitting batch jobs into the computer to picking the best process to execute next according to some criterion or criteria satisfying one or more objectives.

Suggested answer
(a) (i)   Multiprogramming is the apparent simultaneous execution of two or more programs.
           Multi-access is when two or more users are able to communicate with the computer at any time.
           Multi-tasking is the concurrent execution of two or more related processes between which communication is possible.
    (ii) With an interactive program the user is in two-way communication with the program.
           With a batch program the opposite is true. The user is required to submit in advance a specification of the requirements for the job, including the data and commands. When processing begins it proceeds without user intervention from beginning to end.
(b) (i)   It is the function of the scheduler to select the next batch job to be admitted to the system and to determine the order in which processes in the system should run.
    (ii) The scheduler is invoked when an interval timer interrupt occurs to indicate time slice expiry and when a process requests an I/O transfer.
    (iii) Two objectives of a scheduler are
          •   to keep processor and other system resources busy;
          •   to ensure each process gets its fair share of use of the processor and other system resources.
    (iv) In the round-robin scheduling algorithm, processor time is allocated to N runnable processes on a rotating-priority basis with every process offered, in turn, the same fixed time slice.
           By allocating a fixed amount of time in turn to each runnable process the processor time is distributed fairly.
(c) Virtual memory is a memory management technique transparent to the user which permits the execution of processes which are only partially loaded into main memory because the total process address space requirement exceeds the physical memory capacity. This is achieved by dividing each process into a number of fixed-size pages. Main memory is also divided into the same fixed-size pages. A page management table for each process keeps track of which pages of a process are resident in main memory.

3 On a single processor machine the scheduler program for a particular multiprogramming, multi-user operating system which supports both *interactive* and *batch* processing maintains a *list of currently active jobs* and a *list of inactive jobs*.

The *inactive list* consists solely of *batch jobs* whereas the *active list* contains a mixture of *interactive* and *batch*. New *batch jobs* are added to the *inactive list*. The scheduler transfers *batch jobs* from the *inactive list* to the *active list* when appropriate.

A job on the *active list* may be running, runnable or suspended; if it is running it will be at the front of the list. When a job is completed it is removed from the *active list*.

(a) Distinguish between *interactive* and *batch processing*.   (2)
(b) State *three* items of control that will need to be specified by a job control language for *each* batch job.   (3)
(c) Describe *two* situations that would lead to a job in the *active list* being suspended.   (2)
(d) With the aid of a diagram/s describe appropriate data structure/s for storing the list of active jobs.   (2)
(e) The operating system groups all information that it needs about a particular active job into a data structure called a process descriptor. Describe *three* distinct items of information of an active job that will need to be stored in this structure.   (3)
(f) Give *three* factors on which the transition from the *inactive list* to the *active list* depends.   (3)
(g) Describe *two* different events that lead to the scheduler being called upon.   (2)
(h) With reference to the *active list*, briefly explain the method of round-robin scheduling.   (3)

(AEB)

Tutorial note

A clear understanding of batch processing and scheduling as applied in a multiprogramming situation where batch and interactive processes coexist, is needed. An understanding of the meaning of the term *suspended* and what causes a process to be suspended are required. A suspended process is one that cannot proceed in its execution, even.if offered the processor, because it is lacking some other resource, e.g. a hardware device other than the processor or some data. The purpose of a process control block (process descriptor) is also explored.

Suggested answer

(a) See 2.(a)(ii)
(b) The user it is being run for (for accounting purposes). The job's priority and the resources required, e.g. Pascal compiler.
(c) One situation is when a job requires data which is not already in main memory then an I/O operation must be initiated. This will involve a delay because I/O operations cannot take place instantaneously. Another situation is when a job in the course of its execution is held up because an expected message has not yet arrived from another job which it is in communication with via a mechanism known as interprocess communication.
(d) A circular queue with a head pointer which points to the job currently running and a tail pointer which points to the place in the queue where rescheduled jobs and new jobs are to be added.

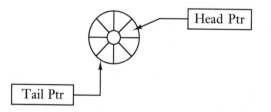

(e) Three items are Process ID, location in memory of job and status, i.e. running, runnable or suspended.

(f) Three factors are:
- the mix of processor and I/O-bound jobs currently active;
- termination of a batch job in the active list allows another batch job to run;
- the proximity of a deadline for a batch job in the inactive list.

(g) Two events are:
- time slice expiry;
- I/O request.

(h) Each runnable process is allocated a fixed quantum of execution time. The runnable processes are picked to execute on the processor for this length of time, in turn, repeatedly or until they no longer become runnable.

4 Computer controlled greenhouses and computer controlled nuclear power stations would both be run using *real-time* operating systems.
(a) Outline and explain *one* important difference in the requirements of these two examples of real-time systems. (2)
(b) Suggest a suitable operating system for producing gas bills. State *two* characteristics of the real-time control operating system, which distinguish each from the other. (4)
(*AEB*)

Tutorial note
In this question the real-time systems are control systems. In such systems, the operating system supports the monitoring of the state of the system which is to be controlled. Monitoring means collecting data. The data is then processed sufficiently quickly to be able to affect the state of the system. In a system in which changes of state occur slowly the monitoring doesn't have to be constant.

Suggested answer
(a) In the case of the nuclear power station monitoring must be constant whereas for the greenhouse, regular is sufficient.
(b) A suitable operating system would be a batch system. In the case of the real-time operating system the nuclear power plant is under the control of the processor at all times. This is in contrast to a batch system where the data is collected off-line over a period of time and only becomes under the control of the processor when it is ready for processing. In the real-time system the collection of data is followed almost immediately by some output which has an effect on the process being monitored. In a batch system there is often a very long delay between collecting the data and receiving the results of processing this data.

5 (a) What is meant by distributed processing?
(b) Give *one* example of distributed processing. (3)
(*AEB*)

Tutorial note
Distributed processing involves more than one processor but it is not parallel processing. The key to answering this question is therefore to distinguish, clearly, parallel from distributed processing. In distributed processing the processors are at physically separated locations. The distribution of the processing tasks is done without the user needing to be aware of or needing to specify which processing unit is carrying out a particular piece of work. Hence the description, transparent.

Suggested answer
Distributed processing is the sharing of data processing, transparently, between processors situated at different locations. An example of distributed processing is a file server.

6 (a) Briefly explain a multi-access computer system. (3)
(b) Spooling is used in multi-access systems.
(i) What is spooling?
(ii) Explain the purpose of spooling in a multi-access system. (4)
(*NEAB*)

Tutorial note
Spooling is a technique used to speed up communication between devices which operate at differing speeds. Output to a printer, for example, may be spooled to disk, which is a high speed device. The output files are then printed using a queuing system when the printer is free.

Suggested answer
(a) A multi-user system is one in which several independent simultaneous user terminals are on-line to the same processor.
(b) (i) Spooling means sending output to a temporary file on a shareable device (e.g. disk). The complete file is then sent to the required peripheral (e.g. a printer) when the peripheral is free.
    (ii) Spooling is useful in a multi-access system because each user can send output without having to wait for the actual peripheral to become free. The user can then continue to work while the output is being printed. It also allows several people to share the same printer without their being muddled up.

7 In a typical file operating system a file specification consists of *a pathname, a file name*, and *a file extension*. Explain with the aid of an example the purpose of each of these *three* components. (6)
(*NICCEA*)

Tutorial note
One purpose of an operating system is to hide the hardware details from ordinary users. A file is a logical construct which the operating system provides so that users can reference their data symbolically, i.e. by file name, rather than disk block address.

Suggested answer
The operating system allows users to organise and reference their work in units of storage called files. A user references a particular file symbolically by file name, e.g. Mick.Exe. The .Exe part of the example file name is called the file extension and it is usually chosen to reflect the purpose of the file. In this example it indicates that Mick.Exe is an executable file. In a multi-level directory system the same file name may be used for several different files but not in the same directory. To uniquely identify a particular file by file name, the full path from the root directory to the directory containing the file name must be specified. This path is the pathname. For example, if Mick.Exe is in a subdirectory of the root called Mick, then the pathname is \Mick\Mick.Exe; with \ being the root directory and Mick\ the Mick subdirectory.

8 Explain how the concept of paging can provide a process with more internal memory than is physically available. (6)
(*NICCEA*)

Tutorial note
This question is about the technique of virtual memory.

Suggested answer
By splitting a process into many small fixed size blocks called pages and doing the same to main memory it is possible to execute the process with some pages, but not all, resident in main memory. Studies have shown that code references are usually very localised to just a few pages at a time. A table called the page management table holds a record of which pages are resident and which are not. This table also provides the mapping from logical page number, which instructions use, to physical page number which is required to reference the relevant page in main memory. Pages are brought in on demand from secondary storage where they reside, and pages are removed when not required. Thus, even though there may not be enough internal memory to hold a process in its entirety, this is unimportant because it becomes unnecessary to do so with a paged approach.

9 Before the data in a data file can be accessed the file must be opened. Describe the sequence of operations performed by the operating system when opening a file.

(4)
(*NEAB*)

Tutorial note
Opening a file means providing the means to be able to transfer data to or from the file. In order to open a file the location of its first disk block must be known. This information is obtained from the file's directory entry. As access to a particular file may be restricted the file's access rights must be obtained, as well. As the disk is a block-oriented device, an area of memory at least equal in size to a disk block must be set up to hold a block in transit between file and application.

Suggested answer
First, a directory must be searched for a match with the given file name. If found, then the next step carried out by the operating system is to check, using the recorded file access rights, if the user has permission to use this file and if so, how, e.g. read only. The operating system also checks to see if the file is already in use and, if so, whether its access rights allow the file to be shared. If the user is allowed access then the operating system will obtain from the directory entry for the file its precise location on secondary storage and allocate a buffer in main memory.

10 In a command-driven operating system, errors can occur when a user miskeys a command.
For example
*deleet somefiel
instead of
*delete somefile
Explain why such errors are unlikely in an operating system with a graphical user interface, for example, a WIMP interface.

(2)
(*SQA*)

Tutorial note
The incorrect example illustrates two problems that arise with command-line interfaces. The first is that there is always the potential for commands to be mistyped. The second is that the exact spelling and structure of the command-line need to be remembered. Graphical user interfaces (GUIs) can be commanded without the need to type a command-line. Secondly, the user does not have to rely solely on his or her memory to invoke a command. The GUI represents commands via pull-down menus, list boxes, option buttons and picture objects called icons. These present only valid commands to the user, so it is very difficult for a user to enter an incorrect command.

Suggested answer
Firstly, in a graphical user interface the set of valid commands and file names are presented visually to the user. It is thus very difficult for the user to choose a non-valid command. Secondly, miskeying a command is avoided by using a mouse in place of a keyboard to select a command and file name by controlling an on-screen pointer to point at the required objects and clicking a mouse button.

11 A computer has a single process operating system with a command-driven user interface. When the operation to load a file from disk is requested, each of the following operating system layers is used:
- the command language interpreter;
- the file management subsystem;
- the memory management subsystem;
- the input/output system.

Describe the role of each layer in this operation, stating errors that each layer might have to deal with.

(8)
(*SQA*)

Tutorial note

The allocation of marks suggests a split of two marks for each operating system layer, one for a description and one for an error. A key feature is required for each layer. For command-line interpreter, this is identifying the load command and separating this from the file name. For file management this is the mapping of file name to disk block addresses. For memory management, this is allocating main memory space to the file. For input/output this is effecting the actual transfer from secondary storage to main memory. This question could be answered in a rather superficial manner, e.g. 'the command-line interpreter interprets the command entered'. Such an answer will gain little credit. The examiners are expecting candidates to demonstrate depth of knowledge, therefore, terms such as 'lexically analysed command line' should be used or a description used which implies something similar. The concept of a memory map is important to the memory management task, etc.

Suggested answer

The command-line (driven) interpreter lexically, analytically and semantically analyses the command-line, reporting errors such as illegal character or command non-existent.

The file manager searches the directory for a match with the given file name and obtains the block address of the first block and the size of the file. If there is no matching file name then the file manager reports an error.

The memory manager uses a map it maintains of free memory and the file size to find the required amount of memory space, marking this space as taken. If there is insufficient memory space then an error is reported.

The input/output system commands hardware to read blocks, possibly using DMA access.

The I/O system will report an error if the data is corrupted while reading or transferring.

12 Graphical user interfaces often make use of *icons*.
   (a) State *four* different classes of object that could be represented by an icon. (2)
   (b) Mouse operations can be semantically different depending on the icon selected. Give an example of a mouse operation and explain how it can be semantically different depending on the icon selected.   (2)
                                                                                        (SQA)

Tutorial note

Objects are 'things' which the computer manipulates. By *different classes of object* the computer means different types of object.

Semantically different means having a different meaning or effect.

Suggested answer

(a) An icon may represent
   • a program or application which the system can execute;
   • a group of several applications whose window of icons has been reduced to a single icon;
   • a directory;
   • a document file.
(b) To start an application, its icon would be selected by clicking a mouse button when the mouse pointer is pointing at the application and then clicked again to execute it. If the icon is not an application but a file, e.g. a document file, then by holding down the mouse button with the mouse pointer on the icon it is possible to drag a copy of the file icon into an application and for the application to use the file, e.g. print it.

PROGRAMMING CONCEPTS

Units in this chapter

Chapter objectives

After working through the topics in this chapter, you should be able to:

- describe the features of a high-level language such as assignment, selection and iteration;
- explain the use of procedures and parameter passing;
- explain what is meant by recursion, its advantages and disadvantages;
- discuss criteria for selecting a programming language for a particular task;
- explain the advantages of structured programming techniques;
- distinguish between declarative and imperative languages;
- describe the principles of concurrent programming and synchronisation;
- explain the concept of objects and inheritance in object-oriented programming;
- interpret and use syntax diagrams and Backus–Naur Form to express language syntax;
- distinguish between compilers and interpreters;
- state the tasks performed in lexical analysis, syntax analysis, semantic analysis, code generation.

11.1   LOW-LEVEL AND HIGH-LEVEL LANGUAGES

Computer languages may be classified as being either **low-level** (such as Assembly language) or **high-level** (such as Pascal, BASIC, PROLOG or 'C').

The characteristics of low-level languages are:

- They are machine oriented; an assembly language program written for one machine will not work on any other machine using a different processor chip or architecture.
- Each assembly language statement generally translates into one machine code instruction. Hence, programming is a lengthy and time-consuming business.

Assembly languages are useful in situations where the program needs to operate as fast as possible and/or occupy as little memory as possible, and where there is a need to manipulate individual bits and bytes. A typical example of this is a **device driver,** i.e. a program which allows the computer to interface with an external device such as a printer.

The characteristics of high-level languages are:

- they are *not* machine oriented; they are **portable** which means that a program written for one machine can be re-compiled and run on a different type of machine (possibly with a few minor alterations).
- they are *problem oriented*; many different high-level languages have statements and data structures which make them well suited to a particular class of problem, for example scientific or engineering problems, business problems, computer-aided manufacture and robotics, etc.
- statements in high-level language resemble mathematical equations or English statements and tend to be easier to learn and faster to code than assembly language programs. Each statement in a high-level language generally translates into several machine code statements.

Special- and general-purpose languages

There are literally hundreds of different languages that have been written specifically for use with various types of problem. **COBOL,** for example, was designed for writing data processing applications in business and commerce, whereas **FORTRAN** was written for scientific applications. C was developed as a language in which to write operating systems, though it is also used now for a wide range of applications such as real-time control applications. **PROLOG** was developed for artificial intelligence applications.

Special features of COBOL which make it suitable for business applications are:

- good file handling facilities, with built-in commands for creating and accessing indexed sequential files;
- SORT verb so that records in a file can easily be sorted into a specified sequence;
- good validation facilities so that both valid and invalid input data can be entered and dealt with appropriately;
- screen painting facilities for quickly designing input screens.

Special features of FORTRAN which make it suitable for scientific and engineering applications are:

- wide range of built-in mathematical functions such as sqrt, log, tan, cos etc.;
- double precision arithmetic for very accurate calculations;
- scientific data types such as complex, floating point, real;
- multi-dimensional arrays;
- libraries of scientific subroutines are available to perform hundreds of different mathematical, statistical or engineering calculations.

Special features of C which make it suitable for control applications are:

- machine register access and manipulation of bits directly;
- programmer can specify times at which certain actions are to take place;
- timeouts can be coded which specify what action to take if a signal is not received within a specified time limit;

- statements are provided to monitor sensors and control actuators (which make something happen);
- ability to support concurrent programming, when more than one action needs to be carried out simultaneously.

Special features of PROLOG which make it suitable for artificial intelligence applications are:
- It can define facts and rules.
- It can automatically search for a solution in many ways. The program can try one route and, if unsuccessful, backtrack and find another route.
- The programmer has only to specify the facts and rules, not how they should be applied. New facts and rules can be added easily.

Selecting a programming language

When a program or complete suite of programs needs to be written for a particular problem, selection of the language may be based on:
- which language has special facilities most appropriate to the problem;
- whether a choice of a particular language would substantially reduce development time;
- whether the programmers have the time or expertise to master a new language;
- whether a suitable compiler exists for the hardware the firm intends to use.

11.2 FEATURES OF A HIGH-LEVEL PROCEDURAL LANGUAGE

A typical general-purpose high-level procedural language such as BASIC, Pascal or C has the following features:

Data assignment statements

(Pascal is used as the sample language in the examples; other languages have similar statements.)
Examples of assignment statements are

        X := Y + Z;
        A := 30;

These statements are called assignment statements because they assign a value to a location in memory; in the examples above, the values in memory locations Y and Z are added together and the result placed in X, and the value 30 is placed in A.

Input/output statements

An example of an **input** statement is
        Read (X,Y);
which causes the computer to read two values from the keyboard or disk, for example, and place the values in memory locations X and Y.
   An **output** statement such as
        Writeln ('The value of X is', X);
causes a text string and the contents of X to be displayed on the screen, e.g. The value of X is 25.

Selection statements (conditional statements)

A selection statement (conditional statement) is typically one in the form *if..then..else.* e.g.
        If (Choice = 'North')
            Then Writeln ('You have just fallen into my trap')
            Else Writeln ('Good choice');

The conditions that can be checked are known as **Boolean** conditions (after a famous logician named George Boole); the conditional operators being =, <> (not equal), >, <, >= (greater than or equal) and <=.

e.g.   If (A <= B) Then C := B − A;

A 'case' statement is a useful way of allowing several options to be taken;
       Case Choice Of

       'N' : Writeln ('You have just fallen into my trap');
       'W' : Writeln ('Pick up the box');
       'S' : Writeln ('This is a dead end');
       'E' : Writeln ('Now wait for the sunrise');
    End; {Case}

Note that the same effect could be achieved with If.. Then.. Else statements but the Case statement is a neater form of selection statement when there are more than two possible outcomes of the condition to be tested.

Iteration (repetition) structures

Programming languages generally offer several ways of performing loops (i.e. executing the same series of steps more than once).

The **While** loop checks a Boolean condition before entering the loop, so that the loop is not performed at all if the condition is false. For example,

       Readln (Mark);
       While Mark <> −1 Do
         Begin
           Total := Total + Mark;
           Writeln ('Please enter next mark, −1 to end');
           Readln (Mark);
         End; {While}
       Writeln ('Total of all marks is', Total);

If the mark read in at the first line is equal to −1, the statements in the loop will not be executed at all and the next line to be executed will be

       Writeln (`Total of all marks is`, Total);

The **Repeat** .. **Until** loop checks the Boolean condition at the *end* of the loop and therefore the loop is always performed at least once. For example,

       Repeat
         Writeln ('Please enter Y or N');
         Readln (Reply);
         If (Reply <> 'N') And (Reply <> 'Y')
           Then Writeln ('Invalid reply; you must enter Y or N');
       Until (Reply = 'Y') Or (Reply = 'N');

The loop prompts the user for a reply, checks that it is either Y or N, and if not, displays an error message and repeats the statements until the user enters a valid response. If a **While** loop was used instead of a **Repeat** .. **Until** loop, the programmer would have to ensure that Reply was set to something other than Y or N before this section of code was reached, or it would be skipped.

The **For** loop (For .. Next loop) is used when the loop is to be repeated a fixed number of times. A counter is automatically incremented each time the loop is performed. For example,

       For Count := 1 to 20 Do
         Begin
           Writeln ('Line', Count);
           (*any number of statements can be placed in the loop*)
         End;

This will display
Line 1
Line 2
Line 3
etc. as Count is automatically incremented.

Subroutines and parameters

Large programs need to be split up into smaller sections of code which are known as subroutines or subprograms. In Pascal there are two types of subroutine known as **procedures** and **functions**. They are very similar but are called in a slightly different way. A procedure is given a name and called by simply writing the name, followed by any **parameters** to be passed, written in brackets. Parameters are the means of passing information to and from a procedure.

This is also expressed by describing the parameter list as the **interface** between the calling program and the procedure.

The following (very simple!) procedure calculates the average of three numbers and passes the result back to the main program from which it is called.

```
Procedure CalculateAverage (A, B, C: Real; Var Average: Real);
  Begin
    Average := (A + B + C) / 3;
  End;
```

The main program could include statements such as:

```
Readln (Num1);
Readln (Num2);
Readln (Num3);
CalculateAverage (Num1, Num2, Num3, Result);   {Call statement}
Writeln (`The average is`, Result);
```

(Note the comment written in braces {} in the program segment above; comments may be placed anywhere in a program and have no effect on its running).

The statement used to transfer execution to the procedure is referred to as the **Call statement**, and the number, type and order of parameters must exactly match the parameters in the procedure heading.

Functions may be used when a single result is to be returned, as in the above example for calculating an average. The result is returned in the function name, so that a function for calculating the average of three numbers could be coded as follows:

```
Function Average (A, B, C: Real):Real;
  Begin
    Average := (A + B + C) / 3;
  End;
```

To call the function, the programmer writes:

```
Result := Average (Num1, Num2, Num3);
```

Many languages such as Pascal have several 'built-in' functions such as

Sqrt   returns the square root of an argument

Sqr   returns the square of an argument

Trunc   truncates a type *Real* value to an *Integer* value. For example, X:= Trunc(5.8) puts X equal to 5.

Parameter-passing mechanisms

There are two different methods of passing parameters generally known as **call by value** and **call by address**.

The order and number of parameters in the call statement and the procedure heading must match. In the above example, the contents of Num1 is copied to the variable A, contents of Num2 are copied to B and contents of Num3 are copied to C. This is called **calling (passing) by value** since the actual values are passed to the subroutine. However, this process is one way only so cannot be used for Result, which *receives* a value from the subroutine. This parameter is passed by *reference (address)*, meaning that only the address of the variable Result, not its actual value, is passed to the procedure. When Average is calculated in the procedure and control passed back to the main program, the result is waiting in Result because this is in fact the identical memory location. In Pascal, the programmer indicates that a parameter is to be passed by reference by putting the keyword **Var** in front of the variable name in the procedure heading.

Block structure, local and global variables

Pascal is said to be a **block structured** language. A block consists of a *declaration* part, in which variables, data types and constants are declared, and procedures and functions written, and a *statement* part, consisting of statements such as assignment statements, selection and iteration statements (ifs and loops) and calls to procedures and functions.

The entire program constitutes the outermost block, which contains other blocks which in turn contain other blocks and so on. Variables declared in the outermost block are called **global** variables and can be used throughout the entire program and any procedures called; variables declared within an inner block (e.g. a procedure) are called **local** variables and can only be used within that block. This is expressed by saying that the **scope** of an identifier includes the block in which it is declared and all blocks included within it.

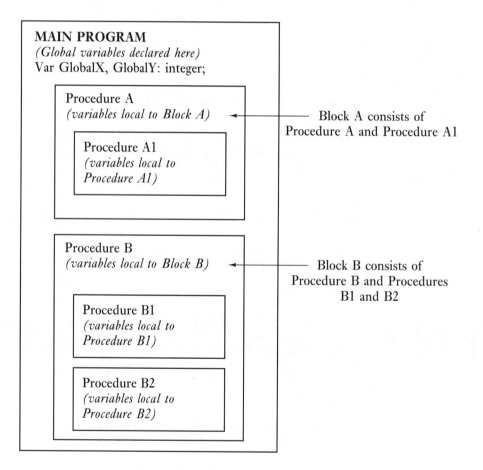

Figure 11.1:   A block structured program

Recursion

A **recursive routine** is one which calls itself, and the process is called **recursion**. In order to understand how a recursive routine works, it is necessary to know that each time a subroutine is called (whether it is recursive or not) the return address (i.e. the address of the next instruction to be executed after completing the subroutine) and the values of any parameters in the subroutine are stored on a last-in first-out data structure known as a **stack**. When the subroutine is completed, the top address on the stack (the one most recently stored) is 'popped' (taken off the stack) and so the computer knows which instruction to go to next. Stacks are described in more detail in the next chapter.

The following is an example of a recursive routine, which displays the numbers 1,2,3,4 in that order.

```
Program RecursionExample;
    Var Abc : Integer;
    Procedure PrintList (Num : Integer);
        Begin
            Num := Num −1;
            If Num > 1
                Then PrintList (Num);   {Here's the recursive call}
            Writeln (Num);              {Line A}
        End; {Procedure PrintList}

{****** Main Program *****}
Begin
    Abc :=4;
    PrintList (Abc);
    Writeln (Abc);                      {Line B}
End.
```

The values 4, 3, 2 are stored in turn as the procedure is called and called again before being allowed to reach its conclusion. Finally Num becomes 1 and Line A is executed. The values 2, 3 and 4 are then successively written at Line A, Line A and Line B.

The *advantages* of recursion are:

- When the solution to a problem is essentially recursive (such as tree traversal which is explained in the next chapter), it enables the programmer to write a program which mirrors the solution.
- Recursive solutions are often much shorter than non-recursive ones.
  The *disadvantages* of recursion are:
- If the recursion continues too long, the stack of return addresses may become full (i.e. no available memory is left) and the program will crash.
- Recursive routines can be difficult to follow and to debug.
- Recursive routines are sometimes very slow in execution owing to the overheads involved in repeatedly calling the subroutine, and storing and retrieving return addresses and parameters.

11.3 PROGRAM DESIGN AND TESTING

Program design aims

Over the past 20 years or so, hardware costs have decreased dramatically, but software costs on the other hand have continued to rise in line with labour costs. Effort put into good program design can often save costly maintenance and debugging costs later on. The aims of program design may be summarised as:

- *Reliability:* the program must always do what it is supposed to do.
- *Maintainability:* the program must be easy to change or modify if this becomes necessary.
- *Readability:* the program must be easy for another programmer to read and understand.
- *Performance:* the program must do its job fast and efficiently.
- *Storage saving:* the program ideally must occupy as little memory as possible, especially if it is a very large program.

Structured programming

Structured programming is a method of writing programs which leads to programs which are clear in their construction, easy to read and thus maintain, and easier to write and test. The ideas embodied in structured programming are closely related to **top-down, modular** programming. Using this method of program design, the main components of a program are first identified, and each main component is then decomposed into smaller, more manageable components. This process continues until each component or module is small enough to be easily comprehensible.

In a structured program:

• Only three basic constructs are used; *sequence* (one instruction after another), *selection* (e.g. If..Then..Else statements) and *iteration* (e.g. While loops).
• Each program module is generally no more than one page and is easily comprehensible.

The advantages of **modular programming** can be stated as:

• Individual modules can be separately tested.
• Modules can be kept in a module library and reused in other programs.
• Long programs that are split into modules are easier to read, debug and maintain.
• The modular approach means that several people in a team of programmers can each work on separate modules, thus shortening the total development time for a large project.

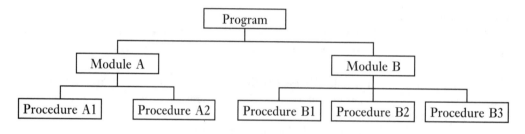

Figure 11.2: The top-down, modular approach

Program errors

A program may have any or all of four types of error:

• **Syntax error**: a statement in the program violates a rule of the language; this could be a simple misspelling of a keyword, a missed punctuation mark, or a wrongly formed statement. For example,

  Writteln ('This statement contains 2 syntax errors);
  (misspelt keyword and missing quote-mark)

• **Semantic error**: violating rules of the language, for example by specifying the wrong number or type of parameters in a subroutine call, or trying to assign a real value (one with a decimal point) or a string of characters to a variable which has been declared as an integer; e.g.

  Num1 := 'John Robert Sharpe' {Num1 being an integer variable}

• **Logic error**: the program runs but gives the wrong answer or performs wrongly in some way. For example, the programmer writes

  Net := Gross + Tax;

when the statement should have been written

  Net := Gross − Tax;

• **Run-time error**: the program has no logic or syntax errors (though possibly weaknesses in not anticipating exceptional circumstances and catering for them), but 'crashes' during execution. This may be caused, for example, by attempting to open a file on a floppy disk which is not in the drive, or division by zero caused by the user entering 0 when the program expected a non-zero number, or entering a character when a number was expected.

The first two types of error will be detected by the compiler, which will usually pinpoint the error and give a suitable (though sometimes puzzling) error message.

Logic errors and run-time errors are detected by rigorous testing, with data for which the expected answers have been calculated. A test plan should test all unexpected occurrences.

Debugging a program

Once testing has established that a logic error exists, locating it can be a long and frustrating job. Various debugging aids and techniques which can be used in this process are described below:

- Single-stepping through the program: using a function key or other means, the programmer can execute one line at a time, so that the path through the program can be traced.
- Setting breakpoints: the programmer can allow execution to proceed up to a certain point and then single-step from that point.
- Displaying contents of specified variables in memory: these can be displayed on the screen so that the programmer can trace their changing values as execution proceeds.
- Dumping (i.e. printing out) and examining the contents of a file before and after updating.
- Dumping and examining the entire contents of memory at a specified point during execution.

Designing test data/test cases

Program testing is best performed at three different levels:

1. Components (subprograms) need to be individually tested to ensure that they conform to specifications.
2. When combined to form a program, the components must not act in unexpected ways, so each program module must be tested.
3. The suite of programs as a whole must be tested to ensure that all programs integrate correctly.

Although program testing in theory should be exhaustive with every possible route being tested, with a large program this is impractical as it would mean performing perhaps millions of tests. At a minimum, the test cases should be selected to ensure that:

- Every statement in the program is executed at least once.
- The effectiveness of all sections of code which detect invalid input is tested.
- The accuracy of all processing is verified.
- The program operates according to its original design specifications.

There are three general categories of test data:

1. normal data – data that the program is designed to handle;
2. extreme values – valid data at the limits of acceptability;
3. exceptional or invalid data – the programmer must assume that users sooner or later will attempt to enter invalid data, and the program must not as a consequence 'crash' or give wrong results.

11.4 TYPES OF HIGH-LEVEL LANGUAGE

Generations of computer language

The term 'generation' of computer language is used to categorise the various computer languages that have evolved over the last 50 years. The generations of high-level language may be defined as follows:

- **first generation** (1940s): machine code;
- **second generation** (early 1950s): assembly language;
- **third generation** (1950s to present): high-level languages such as Pascal, FORTRAN, COBOL;
- **fourth generation** (late 1970s onwards): 4GLs include a whole range of languages which tend to be easier to use than other languages, and are said to be **non-procedural** because the programmer often has to specify only what is to be done without having to specify how to do it. An example of a fourth generation language is structured query language (SQL), widely used to query and manipulate data held in databases. The basic retrieval facility in SQL consists of three clauses in the general form

> **Select** ...
> **From** ...
> **Where** ...

e.g. to display the names of all female students in a table:

> **Select** Student_Name
> **From** Student_Table
> **Where** Sex = 'F'

Procedural (imperative) and declarative languages

High-level languages such as Pascal, COBOL and C are all examples of **procedural** languages, (also known as **imperative** languages) where the program consists of a sequence of instructions which the computer will execute in a specified order.

PROLOG is an example of a different type of programming language known as a **declarative** language. It has the following characteristics:

- The program statements consist of a number of facts and rules about a particular subject.
- Program statements may be written in any sequence, making it easy to add new facts and rules.
- Executing a Prolog program involves stating a goal to be achieved and allowing Prolog to determine whether the goal can be achieved with the given facts and rules.
- The route through the program does not have to be explicitly stated by the programmer; if Prolog fails to achieve the goal using one route through the program, it has the ability to **backtrack** and try another route until either the goal is achieved or there are no further routes to try.

PROLOG is particularly well suited to the **construction of expert systems** which embody the facts and rules about a certain field of knowledge (e.g. medical diagnosis) and then enable a user to query it to obtain an answer to a particular problem. It is also suited to the **processing of natural language** (trying to get a computer to understand ordinary English, Chinese or Urdu) because each of these languages has its own syntax rules which can be stated in the program to help the computer decide whether a group of words makes a sentence, and what it means.

EXAMPLE

A set of rules is being developed for inclusion in a knowledge base which will deliver advice on whether a person may legally drive a certain class of vehicle. The following partially completed knowledge base embodies some of these facts and rules. (They have been numbered for easy reference.)

```
1       age (edward 20)
2       age (robert 19)
3       age (flora 17)
4       age (emma 17)
5       age (andrew 16)

6       minimum_age (motor_cycle 16)
7       minimum_age (car 17)
8       minimum_age (heavy_goods_vehicle 20)

9       passed_test (edward heavy_goods_vehicle)
10      passed_test (andrew motor_cycle)
```

11   passed_test (emma car)

12   has_provisional_licence (andrew)

13   has_provisional_licence (robert)

14   permitted_to_drive (X V) If passed_test (X V)

15   permitted_to_drive (X V) If has_provisional_licence (X) And
            age (X A) And
            minimum_age (V L) And
            A >= L

In this syntax:

fact   1   means that Edward is 20 years old;

fact   6   means the minimum age for driving a motor-cycle is 16;

fact   10   means Andrew has passed the driving test for a motor-cycle;

fact   12   means that Andrew has a provisional driving licence;

rule   14   means that a person X may drive a vehicle V if person X has passed the test for a vehicle of class V;

rule   15   means that a person X may drive a vehicle V if person X has a provisional licence and is old enough to drive a vehicle of class V.

The query

?permitted_to_drive (flora car) means 'is it true that Flora is permitted to drive a car'

The program would first look at rule 14 and then scan the facts to see if Flora has passed the test. The answer is 'no', so rule 15 is examined. The facts are scanned again to check if Flora has a provisional licence. No relevant fact is found so the program returns the answer 'no'.

The query

?permitted_to_drive (robert motor_cycle)

will return the answer 'yes' using Rule 15 and facts 2, 6 and 13.

The query ?permitted_to_drive (emma V)

will return the answer 'car' using rule 14 and fact 11.

Object-oriented programming

In object-oriented programming, the programmer uses **objects**. An object is a data item with all the processing possible on the data item attached to it. The process of attachment is usually referred to as **encapsulation**. Any changes to the structure of the data stored by the object, or the functions to be performed by the object only require changes to the code encapsulated in the object.

For example, a bank account has associated with it the name and address of the customer and the current balance. To be able to use this as a data object, functions (known as methods) are provided to initialise an account, change the name of the customer, get the current balance, credit an amount and print the details of the account.

If it is decided to add a new function to debit an amount (rather than crediting a negative amount), all that is needed is to add the new method to the Account object.

Inheritance

Suppose the bank were to introduce a new class of account for special customers who deposited an initial balance of over £500. This account is to be known as a Gold Account and is to pay interest to customers on their daily balance. The Gold Account, as well as having all the functions of an ordinary account, needs to store extra *data* such as interest rate and date interest added, and extra *functions* such as Add interest to account.

Object oriented languages allow the programmer to create an object for the Gold Account which *inherits* all the properties of Account, but also has additional properties of its own.

Concurrent programming

In the traditional **von Neumann** machine, programs and data are held in memory and instructions are fetched and executed one after another. However, there are many circumstances in which it is necessary or desirable to perform several instructions *simultaneously,* using multiple processors. For example, a computer controlling a nuclear power station may need to monitor hundreds of processes simultaneously, or a computer controlling a robot may need to control its various components (e.g. arms and legs) simultaneously in a synchronised manner. Another use of concurrent programming is to divide up a task such as processing a graphical image; if a different processor is assigned to processing each pixel on the screen, processing will be speeded up enormously.

Synchronisation

One problem with parallel processing is that of **synchronising** the activities of all the processors, as some instructions need to be completed before others may begin. An analogy can be drawn with having several people constructing a building – the windows cannot be installed until the brickwork is done, but several windows can then be fitted at the same time.

EXAMPLE

How can parallel processing be used to speed up the execution of the following instructions?

        A:= 10;
        B:= 6;
        C:= 3;
        D:= A+ (B*C);
        E:= A− B;

Answer: The first three instructions can be carried out in parallel, but the last two cannot be done until the first three are completed, when they can be executed in parallel. The pseudocode constructs ParBegin and ParEnd may be used to show this as follows:

        ParBegin
          A := 10;
          B := 6;
          C := 3;
        ParEnd
        ParBegin
          D := A + (B*C);
          E := A − B;
        ParEnd

11.5 DEFINITION OF PROGRAMMING LANGUAGE SYNTAX

Syntax diagrams

One way of expressing the syntax rules of a language is by drawing syntax diagrams to define the correct format of every statement and identifier. For example, suppose that in a particular language, an identifier (e.g. variable name) must start with a letter and may be followed by either letters or digits. The corresponding syntax diagram may be drawn as in Fig 11.3.

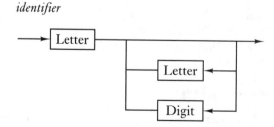

Figure 11.3: Syntax diagram for an identifier

Backus–Naur Form (BNF)

BNF is a special type of language (a **meta-language**) with its own set of rules which is used for defining the syntax or grammar of a computer language.

The common symbols used are

- $<$ $>$ used to enclose a syntactic category;
- ::= used to mean 'is defined by' or 'consists of';
- | used to mean 'or'.

For example

$$<digit> ::= 0 \mid 1 \mid 2 \mid 3 \mid 4 \mid 5 \mid 6 \mid 7 \mid 8 \mid 9$$
$$<binary\_digit> ::= 0 \mid 1$$

A BNF definition may be recursive. The identifier as described above in the syntax diagram may be defined using BNF as

$$<identifier> ::= <letter> \mid <identifier><letter> \mid <identifier><digit>$$

The process of ascertaining whether a given statement is valid, given the BNF definition, is called **parsing**. For example, the identifier A12 is valid because

- A is a letter, and is therefore a valid identifier;
- A1 is an identifier followed by a digit, and is therefore a valid identifier;
- A12 is an identifier followed by a digit, and is therefore a valid identifier.

A1_2 is **not** a valid identifier in this language because the symbol _ is neither a letter nor a digit.

11.6 COMPILERS AND INTERPRETERS

There are two types of translator for converting a high-level language such as Pascal into machine code; **compilers** and **interpreters**.

A compiler translates a complete program into object code before it is executed, whereas an interpreter analyses the source code statement by statement as execution proceeds, decoding each statement and calling routines to carry out each instruction. No object code is stored by an interpreter, which means that a statement has to be translated each time it is used – if the statement is part of a loop performed 1000 times, translation will take place 1000 times.

Advantages of a compiler

1. A compiled program will almost always run faster than an interpreted one, as no translation is taking place at the same time.
2. The object program (the machine code generated by the compiler) may be saved on disk and run whenever required without being recompiled, or requiring the user to have the compiler.
3. Commercially produced software can be sold in the form of object code, thus preventing purchasers from listing the source code and making modifications to it (perhaps with the intention of selling the modified version as their own product).

Advantages of an interpreter

1. Interpreters are very convenient for program development since making modifications does not mean that the whole program has to be recompiled, which can take a considerable time for a large program. Many interpreters will allow a program to run up to the point where an error occurs, let the programmer fix the error and then continue from that point.
2. An interpreter is simpler to write and cheaper to buy.
3. An interpreter generally occupies much less memory than a compiler.

Cross-compilers and cross-assemblers

Cross-compilers and cross-assemblers are translators which enable a program to be compiled or assembled on one machine and executed on a different type of machine. This is sometimes useful if, for example, program development is being done on a mainframe computer for a program which will eventually run on a microcomputer, or in the development of embedded processor programs.

The stages of compilation

The compilation process has four main phases:
1. lexical analysis;
2. syntax analysis;
3. semantic analysis;
4. code generation and optimisation.

(Syntax analysis and semantic analysis are sometimes regarded as a single phase.) The stages are shown diagramatically in Fig 11.4.

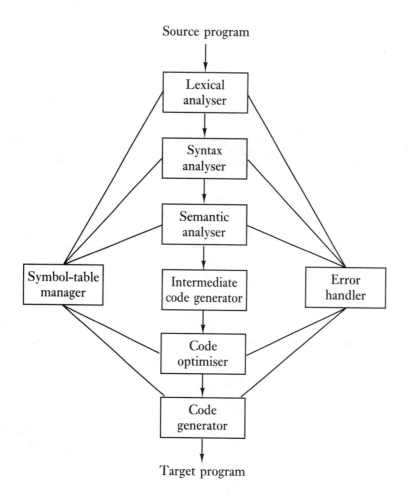

Figure 11.4: The compilation process

Lexical analysis

Lexical analysis performs the following functions:
1. All comments and superfluous spaces are removed.
2. Some simple error checking is performed. For example:
   (a) if the language imposes a limit on the length of identifiers or string constants, the lexical analyser will determine if the identifier is too long;

(b) an illegal identifier such as 2ndYear (illegal in Pascal because identifiers must start with a letter) or Ten% (contains an illegal character) will be flagged as an error;

(c) an attempt to assign an illegal value to a constant, such as (in Pascal);

> Const
>> Name = Lucius Percival;
>
> (The name should be enclosed in quotes.)

3. All keywords, constants and identifiers used in the source code are replaced by 'tokens' (unique symbols). Keywords will be replaced by a single item-code and identifiers by a pointer to an address in the symbol table.

4. All identifiers are placed in a symbol table.

The symbol table

The symbol table plays a central role in the compilation process. It will contain an entry for every keyword, identifier and assigned value in the program. It will also contain information about each of the entries, typically:

- the *kind* of item (simple variable, structured variable such as array, procedure, keyword etc.);
- the *type* of item (integer, real, char, etc.);
- the *run-time address* of the item or its *value* if it is a constant;
- other information such as the bounds of an array, information about parameters passed to a procedure.

Accessing the symbol table

Since the lexical, syntax and semantic analysers all spend a great proportion of their time looking up entries in the symbol table, this activity has a crucial effect on the overall speed of the compiler. The symbol table must therefore be organised in such a way that entries can be looked up as quickly as possible.

The symbol table is commonly organised as a **hash table**; i.e. the position of entries in the table is calculated by applying a hashing algorithm to the identifier. In cases where two identifiers produce the same address, the 'synonym' (the identifier that causes the collision) may be put in the next available free space in the table.

Alternatively, a symbol table may be organised as a **binary tree** (see Chapter 12).

Syntax and semantic analysis

Syntax analysis is the process of determining whether the sequence of input characters, symbols, items or tokens form a valid sentence in the language. An example of a syntax error in a Pascal program is

> X := (Y + Z / 3 ;

because it is not a correctly formed statement in the language – the closing bracket is missing.

Semantic analysis is concerned with the meaning or interpretation of words in the context in which they are used. It is possible to write a syntactically correct statement such as

> A := B + C;

which is semantically invalid if say, A is an integer variable and B and C are character variables, or have not been declared at all.

In natural language (such as English) a sentence may also be syntactically correct but semantically meaningless. For example 'Terry ate a banana' has meaning and obeys the rules of the language, whereas 'A banana ate Terry' obeys the rules of the language (the syntax) but not the semantics.

Code generation

This is the final phase of compilation when machine code is generated. It may include an optimisation stage when the code is amended to make it run as fast as possible; for

example the machine code equivalent of an instruction
        A := A + 1;
may be altered to the equivalent of
        Inc A (i.e. increment A)
because this instruction is executed faster.

Linking

The object code produced by the compiler may consist of separate modules of machine code which are related to each other by call and return addresses. In addition the program may use library routines held separately from the main program block. An object program library is a collection of routines stored in such a way that any routine can be selectively extracted for use in another object module. Object program **libraries** may be classified as

- **system**: a collection of built-in language-defined routines, e.g. in Pascal Writeln and Readln;
- **public**: a collection of generally useful routines which are not standard to the language but likely to be required by many programmers, e.g. graphics routines;
- **private**: a collection of routines written and stored in library form for a programmer's own use.

The function of the **linker** or **linkage editor** is to link all the modules together by putting the appropriate machine addresses into all external call and return addresses.

Chapter summary

This chapter has covered the characteristics of high-level and low-level languages, described the facilities of a typical high-level language, and the process of designing and testing a program. Imperative languages such as Pascal are written differently from declarative languages such as Prolog, used for example in programming expert systems. Object-oriented languages use objects consisting of a data item and the procedures ('methods') which act on it. Concurrent programming languages allow the simultaneous execution of more than one statement using several processors.

Compilers and interpreters are both programs used to translate source code into executable form, but a compiler goes through several phases before producing a complete object code program, whereas an interpreter translates and executes a program one line at a time.

Illustrative questions

1 (a) Describe three features commonly offered by high-level languages that are not normally found in low-level languages. (3)

(b) State two circumstances in which it would be more appropriate to use a low-level language than a high-level language. (2)

(EDEXCEL)

Tutorial note
The wording of part (a) suggests you should be describing statements available in high-level languages that are not available in low-level languages, rather than describing the characteristics or advantages of a high-level language, so think before you answer!

Suggested answer
(a) High-level languages offer
- several different ways of performing loops, such as While..EndWhile, Repeat..Until, For..Next;
- If.. Then.. Else structure instead of simple test and branch instructions;
- input and output procedures such as Readln, Writeln.

(b) Use a low-level language when the code needs to occupy as small a space as possible in memory, or when it needs to run as fast as possible.

2 High-level languages usually allow procedures with parameters.
Explain what is meant by the term parameter passing and why procedures with parameters are beneficial in programming. (4)
(*EDEXCEL*)

Tutorial note
A good way of answering this is to give an example of a procedure with parameters.

Suggested answer
Parameter passing means passing values or addresses of variables between the module which calls the procedure, and the procedure itself.
e.g. to call the procedure GoToxy, which takes two parameters and positions the cursor at the desired x and y coordinates on the screen, the programmer writes

GoToxy (5,19)

to position the cursor at column 5, row 19.
  Procedures with parameters are beneficial because:
• The procedures can be stored in a subroutine library and used in any program.
• Using parameters means that the procedure can be made completely self-contained and independent of any variables declared in the program which calls it. For example, no extra variables need to be declared in the main program in order to call GoToxy as described above.

3 Most high-level languages provide a CASE construct.
(a) With the aid of an example explain how the CASE construct operates.
(b) Show how the CASE construct can be implemented using a nested-if structure.
(7)
(*NICCEA*)

Tutorial note
When asked to give an example you should give actual code or pseudocode rather than just explaining in theory how the construct could be used in a given situation.

Suggested answer
(a) The CASE construct operates by allowing one of several paths to be selected depending on the outcome of the condition being tested. For example, a menu of options could be displayed on the screen and the user asked to enter an integer between 1 and 4 to indicate their selection. The CASE construct is then used to branch to the appropriate procedure.

```
Case Option of
    1:  PrintList
    2:  AddRecord
    3:  DeleteRecord
    4:  Exit
EndCase
```

(b) Using a nested if:

```
If Option = 1
 Then PrintList
 Else
  If Option=2
  Then AddRecord
  Else
   If Option=3
   Then DeleteRecord
   Else Exit;
```

4 The program below is written for a computer using parallel processing, and is designed to calculate X as the square root of $A^2 + B^2$. The statements enclosed between **ParBegin** and **ParEnd** are executed in parallel.

```
ParBegin
  ASquared := A * A;
  BSquared := B * B;
ParEnd
XSquared := ASquared + BSquared;
X := Sqrt (XSquared)
```

(a) Why are the last two statements not included between ParBegin ..ParEnd?   (1)

(b) Write code using a similar convention to take full advantage of parallel processing in assigning values of 5 to R, 3.142 to Pi, and calculating the area and circumference of a circle as Pi * R * R and 2 * Pi * R respectively.   (3)

(New question)

Tutorial note

Part (a) depends on an understanding of the concept of synchronisation, where certain instructions must be completed before others can begin. Part (b) requires you to work out which statements can be performed in parallel and which cannot.

Suggested answer

(a) XSquared cannot be calculated until the values of ASquared and BSquared have been calculated.

(b)
```
    ParBegin
      R := 5;
      Pi := 3.142;
    ParEnd
    ParBegin
        Area := Pi * R * R;
        Circumference := 2 * Pi * R;
    ParEnd
```

5 A particular software house has the following items of software at their disposal:
- compiler;
- linker;
- editor;
- subroutine library;
- debugger.

Briefly describe the function of each one.   (5)

(NEAB)

Suggested answer

A compiler translates source code written in a high-level language into machine code.

A linker links separately compiled modules by putting the appropriate addresses in the call and return instructions.

An editor is used to key in and amend source code, and perform functions similar to a word processor like copying or moving blocks of text, saving and retrieving programs.

A subroutine library holds previously compiled, tried and tested routines for use by programmers, to perform common or frequently needed tasks.

A debugger is used to help find logic errors in a program, by enabling the programmer to execute a program one step at a time, dump the contents of variables at various points in the program, etc.

6 (a) Give *three* reasons for using a fourth-generation language (4GL).   (3)
(b) Give *three* criteria a company might use when selecting a 4GL.   (3)

(NEAB)

Tutorial note
The benefits of 4GLs are best understood by comparing the development of a system using say, Pascal, with the use of something like, MS Access – try and relate the question to your own experience. In part (b), you can draw an analogy with the reasons that you might choose any type of product (such as a video recorder).

Suggested answer
(a) Programmer productivity is increased. Systems can be developed in a shorter time. Users can develop and maintain their own systems and hence get the systems they want.
(b) Is the 4GL used by other major organisations?
Does the supplier provide training and support?
Does it have all the necessary facilities?
Is it good value for money?

7 Explain briefly why different categories of data should be used as part of a testing strategy during program development.
(6)
(NICCEA)

Tutorial note
You should be able to answer this question by thinking of the types of data you have used to test your programming project(s). Try and think of three different categories of data.

Suggested answer
The purpose of testing is to ensure that a program processes correct data correctly and copes with incorrect data in a controlled and predictable manner. Therefore test data should include normal data that the program is designed to process, and incorrect data to ensure that the program copes with it. Also, since logic errors are often made at the boundaries of acceptable values (e.g. the programmer writes 'If A<100' instead of 'if A<=100') extreme data at the upper and lower limits of acceptability should be used to ensure that this is processed correctly.

8 For the following applications state, with a reason, which type of programming language, *declarative* or *imperative*, would be most appropriate for programming:
(a) an expert system;
(2)
(b) a payroll processing system.
(2)
(AEB)

Tutorial note
An **imperative** language is also known as a **procedural** language.

Suggested answer
(a) A declarative language would be most appropriate because it allows the facts and rules which are relevant to the situation to be programmed, and then uses these facts and rules to answer queries made by the user.
(b) An imperative language (e.g. Pascal) is suitable for a payroll system because the processing required is procedural and can be specified by a sequence of instructions.

9 For a language to be classified as object-oriented, it must satisfy three requirements. State these requirements.
(3)

(New question)

Suggested answer
The first requirement is the language must support objects that are data structures with an interface of named operations (e.g. calculate, balance, add, subtract). The second requirement is the object must have an associated type or class. The third requirement is for types or classes to have the ability to inherit attributes from supertypes or superclasses.

10 (a) Convert the following syntax diagrams into extended Backus–Naur form.

Variable

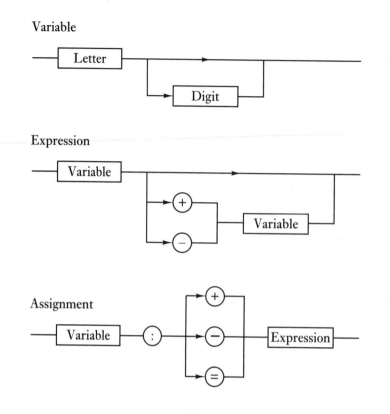

Expression

Assignment

(6)

(b) Using these syntax diagrams list the errors, if any, in the following assignment statements. If a statement has no errors write down 'no errors'.
   (i) tax:=A*B1
   (ii) F:+D
   (iii) G1:=G2+G3+G4   (3)

(NEAB)

Suggested answer
   (a) <variable>::=<letter> | <letter><digit>
       expression ::= <variable> | <variable> + <variable> | <variable> –
       <variable>
       <assignment> ::= <variable>: + <expression> | <variable>: – <expression>
                       | <variable>: = <expression>
   (b) (i) is incorrect. A*B1 is not a valid expression because * is not a valid symbol.
       (ii) No errors.
       (iii) G2 + G3 + G4 is not a valid expression because only two variables are allowed.

11 The process of compilation involves a number of stages (or phases). Name the stage at which each of the following errors would be detected.
   (a) An arithmetic operator has operands of incompatible types.   (1)
   (b) A compiler-created constant is too large to fit into a word of the target machine.
                                                                                (1)
   (c) The name of a variable contains an illegal character.   (1)
   (d) In a language that requires comment statements to be placed between matching special symbols, the terminating symbol is missing.   (1)
   (e) An operand is omitted from an arithmetic expression.   (1)

(AEB)

Tutorial note
Compilation involves four stages: lexical analysis, syntax analysis, semantic analysis and code generation (and possibly code optimisation). You need to know what each one of these stages involves in order to answer this question.

Suggested answer
(a) Semantic analysis.
(b) Code generation.
(c) Lexical analysis.
(d) Lexical analysis.
(e) Syntax analysis.

12 The knowledge contained in the passage below is to be represented in a knowledge-processing language.

'Birds and mammals are air breathing creatures. Air breathing creatures have lungs. Birds have feathers and wings. Mammals have hair. Humans and apes are types of mammal. Chimpanzees and gorillas are types of ape. Bald and Golden are types of Eagle which is a type of bird.'

This information is represented as a set of facts and rules as shown below in clauses 1 to 14. The numbers are for reference only.

1. is_a (mammal, air_breathing)
2. is_a (bird, air_breathing)
3. is_a (human, mammal)
4. is_a (ape, mammal)
5. is_a (gorilla, ape)
6. is_a (chimpanzee, ape)
7. is_a (eagle, bird)
8. is_a (bald, eagle)
9. is_a (golden, eagle)

10. has (bird, wings)
11. has (bird, feathers)
12. has (mammal, hair)
13. has (air_breathing, lungs)

14. has (A, B) IF is_a (A,C) AND has (C,B)

In the above syntax:

capital letters in a clause refer to variables;
clause 1 has the meaning   'A mammal is an air-breathing creature';
clause 10 has the meaning   'A bird has wings';
clause 14 has the meaning   'A has B if it is true that A is a C and it is true C has B'.

(a) What solution(s) would be found to each of the following queries?
  (i) ? is_a (A, eagle)
  (ii) ? has (mammal, B)   (3)
(b) (i) What solution would be found to the following query?
            ? has (golden, wings)
  (ii) By tracing the steps in the search of the knowledge base, describe how you obtained your answer. You may use the clause numbers in your answer.   (5)
(c) (i) It is required to extend the knowledge base to include the following knowledge:
          'Penguins and ostriches are types of bird'
    Devise suitable clauses that can be added to the knowledge base to represent this knowledge.   (1)
  (ii) A new rule, with the meaning 'a creature can fly if it has feathers', is to be added to the knowledge base. Devise a suitable rule and comment on its appropriateness. You should use the syntax used in clauses 1 to 14 above. (3)
                                    (SQA)

Tutorial note

To do well with this type of question, you must know how a goal or query is processed. For each goal or sub-goal, the knowledge base is always searched from the beginning. Sub-goals are created when a rule is encountered. Each fact encountered in the body of a rule becomes a new sub-goal. Values are temporarily assigned to variables in the process, and unassigned when a sub-goal fails.

Suggested answer

(a) (i) Bald, golden
    (ii) Hair
(b) (i) Yes
    (ii) has (golden, wings) is matched with the head of Rule 14, so that A=golden and B=wings. The first fact in the body of rule 14 is_a (golden, C) is searched for a match, which is found at Fact 9, making C = eagle. The second fact in the body of Rule 14, has(eagle, B) is searched for a match which is found at Rule 14, making A = eagle. The body of this rule is_a (eagle, C) is then matched with Fact 7, making C = bird and the body has (bird, B) is matched with Fact 10, making B wings.

    Therefore a solution has been found.
(c) (i) is_a (penguin, bird)
         is_a (ostrich, bird)
    (ii) can_fly (A) IF has (A, feathers)

    The rule is not appropriate because flightless birds do exist – for example ostriches which are mentioned in the database. Also, even if the rule were true, it would be better to state the rule as can_fly (A) IF is_a (A, bird) so that for example the answer to the query

            ?can_fly (eagle)

    could be answered by applying the new rule and fact 7.

13 (a) Distinguish between a compiler and an interpreter. State one advantage and one disadvantage of using a compiler to translate programs compared with an interpreter. (4)

(b) A compiler of an elementary high-level language tokenises keywords and sets up a symbol table containing variables, constants and labels, as illustrated in the table below.

	Index	Symbol
	1	IF
	2	THEN
	3	GOTO
	4	INPUT
	5	PRINT
constants	25	
	.	
	.	
	40	
variables	41	
	.	
	.	
	100	
labels	101	
	.	
	.	
	127	

In this case constants, variables and labels are entered into the first free entry in the appropriate part of the table.

Hence, assuming an empty table, the instructions:

INPUT A

B ← A + 1

would mean that A would be entered at index 41, B at 42 and the constant 1 would be entered at index 25.

The tokenised code produced would be:

4   41

42 ← 41 + 25

(i) What code would be produced by the subsequent instructions?

INPUT C

IF C < B THEN 100

C ← C − B

100 PRINT C   (6)

(ii) With the aid of an example, suggest a type of error which could be detected at this stage. (2)

(iii) A more advanced version of the compiler is designed to handle a large number of variables. The method of inserting variables in the first free space becomes increasingly inefficient. Describe with the aid of a suitable example a method which will allow details of a variable to be accessed quickly. (6)

(iv) State *two* items associated with a variable (other than its name) which need to be stored in a table. (2)

(AEB)

Tutorial note

Part (b) is a question about the symbol table entries put in by the lexical analyser, which tokenises all identifiers, keywords and labels in the manner shown in the question. To answer b(ii) you need to think of an example of a lexical error, *not* a syntax error. In part (iii), remember that the symbol table is commonly organised as a hash table. Be sure to explain how collisions are handled.

Suggested answer

(a) A compiler produces object code which can be stored on disk and run whenever required. An interpreter decodes one line at a time and executes it.

Advantage of a compiler is that the object code will run faster (also that it produces stand alone object code which is more secure because it cannot be read by a programmer).

Disadvantage: it is more difficult to partially test and develop a program. The program has to be recompiled after every change.

(b) (i)   4   43

1   43 < 42   2   101

43 ← 43 −42

101   5   43

(ii) An illegal identifier such as 2A in a language such as Pascal in which variable names must start with a letter, or a variable name that is too long, or a misformed number such as 100.2.67

(iii) The symbol table could be organised as a hash table, with the identifier being hashed to find its address in the table. For example, if there are 200 places in the table, the formula could be:

• Replace each letter in the identifier by its ASCII code.
• Add the ASCII codes.
• Divide by 200 and take the remainder.
• Add 1 to the remainder to give the address.

If two identifiers hash to the same address, the second one could be stored in the next available space in the table, looping round to the first address when the end of the table is reached.

(iv) The address of the variable in memory needs to be stored, and its type (real, integer, string etc.) (Could also say its 'status', i.e. whether it is a single variable or an array), and its scope (local, global).

CHAPTER 12

ALGORITHMS AND DATA STRUCTURES

Units in this chapter

Chapter objectives

After working through the topics in this chapter, you should be able to:

- write and trace through pseudocode algorithms;
- describe how complex data structures can be created from programming primitives;
- illustrate uses for each data structure including multi-dimensional arrays, lists, linked lists, stacks, queues and binary trees;
- describe operations on each type of data structure;
- distinguish between static and dynamic data structures;
- describe how the various data structures can be implemented;
- write algorithms for a sequential search and a binary search;
- write an algorithm for a bubble sort and explain how an insertion sort works;
- explain how to add and delete items from a linked list;
- write an algorithm for printing a linked list;
- write algorithms for adding to and deleting from a stack;
- write algorithms for adding to and deleting from a circular queue;
- write recursive algorithms for traversing a binary tree.

An **algorithm** is a sequence of instructions to solve a given problem.

There are many different methods for writing down algorithms including flowcharts, structure diagrams and pseudocode. **Pseudocode** is an intermediate stage between plain English and the programming language in which the solution will eventually be coded – it enables the writer to concentrate on the steps in the solution without worrying about the syntax rules of a particular language.

Pseudocode algorithms

Typical pseudocode constructs include the following:

If .. Then .. Else .. EndIf
Case .. Of .. EndCase
For .. To .. EndFor
Repeat .. Until ..
While .. Do .. EndWhile
Procedure ...EndProc
Function ...EndFun

There are no hard and fast rules as to how pseudocode statements should be written; an assignment statement to assign the value 10 to X, for example, could be written in any of the following ways:

Assign 10 to X
X ← 10
X := 10;
Put 10 in X.

The following is a simple pseudocode algorithm for a procedure which calculates the average of a set of student marks entered at a keyboard.

```
Average is a real variable.
Count, Total and Mark are integer variables

Procedure Calculate_Average
    Initialise Count := 0, Total := 0
    Prompt for first Mark
    Read Mark
    While Mark Not = −1
        Add 1 to Count
        Add Mark to Total
        Prompt for next Mark
        Read Mark

    EndWhile
    If Total = 0
      Then Display message 'No marks entered'
      Else
         Calculate Average := Total / Count
         Display 'Average mark is ', Average
    EndIf
 EndProc
```

Trace tables

A trace table or dry-run table is simply a method of keeping track of the values of variables as you trace through an algorithm by hand. This is a useful way of checking that you have got the logic of the program correct. For example, suppose a novice programmer had written the pseudocode for the Calculate_Average procedure as follows:

```
Procedure Calculate_Average
   Initialise Mark := 0, Count := 0, Total := 0,
   While Mark Not = −1
      Prompt for next Mark
      Read Mark
      Add 1 to Count
      Add Mark to Total
   EndWhile
   If Total = 0
      Then Display message 'No marks entered'
   Else
      Calculate Average := Total / Count
      Display 'Average mark is', Average
   EndIf
EndProc
```

To test the program, three marks 7, 8, 9 are entered, followed by a 'rogue' value of −1 to signify the end of data entry. A trace table could be drawn up as follows:

Mark	Count	Total	Mark Not = −1	Average
0	0	0	True	
7	1	7	etc.	

Fill in the trace table row by row until −1 is entered. Remember that the condition which causes the computer to execute the while loop is checked just *before* the loop is executed each time. If the condition is *not* true, the loop is exited and execution will continue from the first statement after the loop. The final trace table will look like this:

Mark	Count	Total	Mark Not = −1	Average
0	0	0	True	
7	1	7	True	
8	2	15	True	
9	3	24	True	
−1	4	23	False	5.75

Clearly the wrong answer! The first version of the program has the *Read* statement at the end of the loop, so that the value entered is checked immediately before the loop is executed again. This is the correct version.

12.2 DATA TYPES

Data that is to be manipulated by a computer may be held and organised in several different ways, depending on how it is to be used.

Programming languages such as Pascal allow variables to be declared as integer, real, char (character) or boolean (true or false). These are called **primitive**, **simple**, **unstructured** or **elementary** data types.

A language is said to be **strongly typed** if the type of every object that stores data has to be declared before it can be used. Consequently the compiler can detect and report illegal use of data types. For example, if variables A and B are declared as type real, and C is declared as type string, the compiler of a strongly typed language should detect a type error in a statement such as

   A := B/C;

since C is not a real or integer variable.

Checking done by a compiler is said to be **static**, while checking done when the target program runs is termed **dynamic**.

12.3 STATIC AND DYNAMIC DATA STRUCTURES

Using primitive data types such as integers and characters, **composite** data types or **data structures** such as arrays and records may be built up by the programmer using language-supplied **constructors**, e.g. **Array [...] Of ..., Record.. End.**

Data structures such as arrays are called **static** data structures because they are defined within the program as being of a certain size, and the space is reserved in memory to hold the array. Other data structures such as stacks, queues, lists, linked lists and binary trees are said to be **dynamic** because they can get bigger or smaller during the execution of the program.

When studying these data structures, it is useful to separate the **logical concept** of the data structure from its actual **implementation**, since there are several ways of implementing stacks, queues, linked lists and binary trees.

12.4 ARRAYS AND RECORDS

An **array** is a set of variables of the same type, such as integer or real. Arrays may have several dimensions. In Pascal, a one-dimensional array to hold monthly sales values could be declared as

Sales : Array [1..12] of Real;

The third element of this array would be referred to as Sales[3]. An equivalent pseudocode declaration would be written something like 'Sales is an array of 12 real variables'.

A two-dimensional array to hold 12 values for each of 5 regions could be declared as

Regional_Sales : Array[1..12, 1..5] Of Real;

The sales for the third month and fourth region would be referred to as Sales[3,4].

A **record** is a more complex data structure than an array in that the individual elements may be of different types; a personnel record on a disk file, for example, may have fields as follows:

Name   : String;
Sex   : Char;
Salary   : Real;
Department : Integer;

In order to read a record into memory, space must be set aside to receive it, and the **Record** data structure is used. If several records need to be held in memory simultaneously, perhaps to be sorted into a particular sequence, then an **Array of Records** (a **table**) can be defined.

12.5 SORTING AND SEARCHING

There are several methods of sorting items held in an array in memory into ascending (or descending) sequence. Both alphabetic and numeric items can be sorted in an identical manner; the sort algorithm is the same whether you are sorting integers or strings.

Bubble sort

This is a slow method but simple to understand and useful when there is a small number of items to be sorted. To sort an array of n items, a maximum of $n-1$ 'passes' is made through the array, with each item being compared with the adjacent item and swapped if necessary. A 'flag' can be initialised at the beginning of each pass and set to a particular value (e.g. True) if a swap is made; at the end of the pass it is checked and if it has not been set, the values are already in sequence and no further passes need to be made. The following pseudocode algorithm sorts an array of n items into ascending sequence.

Flag is a Boolean variable, Count is an integer variable and A is an array of N items (could be any type). Temp is a variable of the same type as the items in the array A.

```
Procedure BubbleSort
    Repeat
        Flag := False
        For Count := 1 To N−1
            If A[Count] > A[Count + 1]
            Then
                    Temp := A[Count]
                    A[Count] := A[Count + 1]
                    A[Count + 1] := Temp
                    Flag := True
            EndIf
        EndFor
        Subtract 1 from N
    Until Flag = False Or N = 1
EndProc
```

Insertion sort

The insertion sort algorithm is faster than the bubble sort but is also relatively slow and suited only to sorting a small number of items. Each item is successively inserted into the correct place in the sorted list of previous items. (You may be asked to trace through an insertion sort algorithm but you will not be required to write the algorithm from scratch).

Quicksort

Quicksort is a very fast sort, suitable for sorting a large quantity of items. An item is chosen more or less arbitrarily from the unsorted list which is then divided into two sublists, one containing all the items smaller than the chosen item, the other containing the rest. The two sublists are then each divided in the same way, recursively, until sublists of length one item are achieved. Again, you will not be expected to write a quicksort algorithm.

Binary search

A binary search is used for searching an ordered array, and is much faster than a linear search for arrays of more than a few items. (In a **linear search** of an ordered array, every item is examined in turn until it is found or shown to be absent by finding an item larger than the sought item or reaching the end of the array.)

In a binary search, the ordered array is divided into three parts, a middle item, the lower part of the array and the upper part. The middle item is examined to see if it is equal to the sought item. If it is not, then if it is greater than the sought item, the upper half of the array is of no further interest. The number of items being searched is therefore halved and the process repeated until the last item is examined, with either the upper half or lower half of the items searched being eliminated at each pass.

A pseudocode procedure for a binary search on an array of n items in an array A is given below.

ItemFound, SearchFailed are Boolean variables, Top, Bottom and Midpoint are integer variables and A is an array of *n* items (could be any type). ItemSought is a variable of the same type as the items in the array A.

```
Procedure BinarySearch
    ItemFound := False
    SearchFailed := False
    Top := N
    Bottom := 1
    Repeat
        Midpoint := Integer part of ((Top + Bottom)/2)
        If A[Midpoint] = ItemSought
          Then ItemFound := True
        Else
          If Bottom > Top
            Then  SearchFailed = True
          Else
              If A[Midpoint] < ItemSought
                Then Bottom := Midpoint + 1
                Else Top := Midpoint −1
              EndIf
          EndIf
        EndIf
    Until ItemFound is True or SearchFailed is True
EndProc
```

12.6   LISTS

A list is a collection of data items stored in some sequence, having the following properties:

- Data items may be inserted or deleted at any point in the list.
- Data items may be repeated in the list.
- Lists may contain any type of object.
- A particular list may contain different object types.

Square bracket notation will be used to represent items in a list. For example:

$$Fruit\_Salad = [Apple \quad Banana \quad Orange]$$

represents a list named Fruit_Salad containing three items.

A more complex example of a list containing different types of item (including another list) is:

$$[Fred \quad 36 \quad 3.15 \quad London \quad A \quad [Spurs \quad Arsenal] \ ]$$

Operations on a list

Several useful operations on lists may be defined:

Head(List)   returns the element at the head of the list if the list is non-empty, otherwise reports an error.
e.g. Head([Fred   36   3.15   London   A   [Spurs   Arsenal]]) will return Fred.

Tail(List)   returns a new list containing all but the first element of the original list
e.g. Tail([Fred   36   3.15   London   A   [Spurs   Arsenal]])
returns [36   3.15   London   A   [Spurs   Arsenal]])

Empty(List)   returns TRUE if the list is an empty list or FALSE otherwise. The empty list is denoted by [ ]

Examples: What is the final result returned by the following functions applied to the list
Cities where

Cities = [London Edinburgh Bristol Chester Exeter]?

(i) Empty (Cities)
Answer: FALSE

(ii) Head (Tail(Cities))
Answer: Edinburgh

(iii) Tail(Tail(Tail(Tail(Cities))))
Answer: [Exeter]. Note that the tail of a list is always a list.

A recursive procedure to print a list

```
Procedure T(List)
  If Not Empty(List)
    Then
      T(Tail(List));
      Print(Head(List));
  EndIf;
EndProc
```

The procedure keeps on recursively calling the procedure T(List), not executing the Print
statement until the list is empty and the procedure runs to completion when it begins to
'unwind'. It thus prints the list in reverse order.

An alternative way of representing a list

A list may also be represented as follows:

	[H	T]	where H is the head and T is the tail
e.g.	[1 2 3]	
or	[1	[2 3]]	
or	[1	[2	[3]]]	
or	[1	[2	[3	[ ]]]]	

Note that the list is a recursively defined data structure.

12.7 LINKED LISTS

A linked list is a *dynamic* data structure consisting of a number of nodes. An external
pointer points to the first node, and each node holds data plus a pointer to the next node
in the sequence.

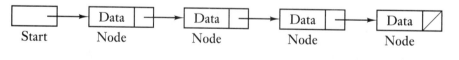

Figure 12.1   A linked list

A linked list may be implemented in some languages such as Pascal and C using dynamic
storage allocation, whereby whenever a new node is required, it is created dynamically (on
the spot during program execution) without having to previously reserve a certain amount
of space for the list. It can also be implemented using records in a file held on disk, or
in memory using a table (array of records). This implementation is static rather than
dynamic, but being relatively straightforward, it will be used to demonstrate the general
principles of adding, deleting and printing elements in a linked list.

Adding and deleting elements

Suppose that a table has been set up in memory with each record in the table containing a data item and a pointer to the next item in alphabetical sequence. A start pointer, Start, points to the first item, and a variable NextFree points to the next available space in the table, and will be incremented when a new item is added. A new name Lee is to be added to the list. The steps can be shown diagramatically as shown in Fig 12.2.

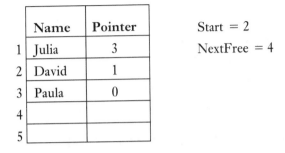

	Name	Pointer
1	Julia	3
2	David	1
3	Paula	0
4		
5		

Start = 2

NextFree = 4

Figure 12.2: A table holding items in a linked list

A new name, Lee, is to be added to the list. The steps can be shown diagramatically as follows:

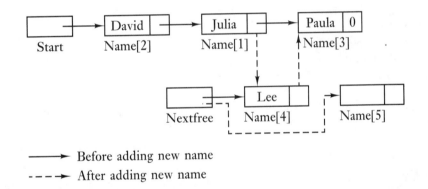

⟶ Before adding new name

- - - ⟶ After adding new name

Figure 12.3: Adding a new item to a linked list

To add a new name, *Lee*, to the list, the following steps need to be taken:
- Put the new name in the space pointed to by NextFree (i.e. Name[4] in this case)
- Adjust pointer in new item (Make Lee point to Paula)
- Set pointer in previous item equal to NextFree (Make Julia point to Lee)
- Increment NextFree.

The modified list now holds the following values:

	Name	Pointer
1	Julia	4
2	David	1
3	Paula	0
4	Lee	3
5		

Start = 2

NextFree = 5

Figure 12.4: The linked list including the new item

To **delete** an element, (for example to delete *Lee* from the linked list above), the pointer in the node immediately before Lee must be altered to the value of the pointer in the node containing Lee. This could be the Start pointer if for example we wanted to delete *David*, the first element in the list. (This algorithm ignores the fact that the space left by the deleted item will not be reusable.)

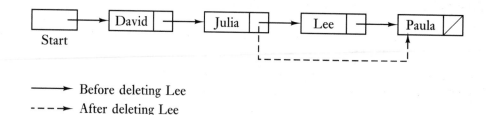

——→ Before deleting Lee

- - - → After deleting Lee

Figure 12.5: Deleting an item from a linked list

Printing the contents of a linked list

To print all the names in the list, follow the pointers, printing each name in turn. In the algorithm below there are assumed to be two arrays, Name[1..n] containing the names, and Pointer[1..n] containing the pointers.

```
Procedure PrintList
    P := Start
    While P<>0 Do
        Print  Name[P]
        P:= Pointer[P]
    EndWhile
EndProc
```

The elements of a linked list may be printed in reverse order using the following recursive algorithm:

```
Procedure PrintReverse(P)
    If P<>0
    Then
        P:= Pointer[P]
        PrintReverse[P]
        Print Name[P]
    EndIf
EndProc
```

Uses of linked lists

A linked list is a useful data structure for keeping data items in a particular sequence as they are added, without having to sort the items. For example in a customer accounts application, all purchases made by a particular customer during a month could be held as a linked list in date sequence, ready for printing on the monthly statement. A file of Start pointers giving the first record for each customer could be separately maintained. A linked list may also be used to implement another data structure called a queue and used in queueing applications (see Section 12.9).

12.8 STACKS

A stack is a *dynamic* data structure which has the special property that it can only be accessed at one end, like a stack of plates in a cafeteria. It is known as a last–in first-out (LIFO) data structure.

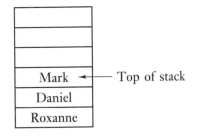

Figure 12.6   A stack

Implementation of a stack

A stack can be represented in memory by an array and two additional variables, *MaxStackSize* holding the size of the array (i.e. the maximum size of the stack) and *Top* holding a pointer to the top of the stack. To initialise the stack the pointer (*Top*) will be set to zero, representing an empty stack. The following pseudocode procedure may be used to add ('push') an element on to a stack:

```
Procedure Push
  If Top = MaxStackSize
    Then Write 'Stack is full'
    Else
      Add 1 to Top
      Stack[Top] := NewItem
  EndIf
EndProc
```

To remove ('pop') an element from a stack:

```
Procedure Pop
  If Top = 0
    Then Write 'Stack is empty'
    Else
      PoppedItem := Stack[Top]
      Subtract 1 from Top
  EndIf
EndProc
```

Uses of Stacks

Stacks are used in many different situations in computing, for example

- to store return addresses, parameters and register contents when subroutines are called. When the subroutine ends, the address at the top of the stack is popped and the computer continues execution from that address;
- in evaluating mathematical expressions held in reverse Polish notation, i.e. a form of notation used by compilers as an intermediate step in translating expressions such as A := (B*C) + D/E.

12.9 QUEUES

A queue is a first–in first–out (FIFO) data structure; new elements are added to the rear of the queue, and elements leave from the front of the queue. A queue can be implemented as an array with a pointer to the front of the queue and a pointer to the rear of the queue. An integer holding the size of the array (the maximum size of the queue) is needed, and it is useful to have an extra variable giving the number of items currently in the queue.

Nigel	Marcus	Davin			

Front = 1   Rear = 3

MaxSize = 6   NumberInQueue = 3

After 2 people have left the queue and 3 more have joined, the queue will look like this:

		Davin	Jon	Ian	Georgina

Front = 3   Rear = 6

MaxSize = 6   NumberInQueue = 4

Now what? Only 4 people are in the queue but the end of the array has been reached. To overcome this problem the queue may be implemented as a **circular queue**, so that when the next person joins she enters at the front of the array:

Bryony		Davin	Jon	Ian	Georgina

Rear = 1   Front = 3

MaxSize = 6   NumberInQueue = 5

Procedures to implement a circular queue

The above queue may be implemented by declaring variables as follows:

```
Q                              : array [1..6] of string;
Front,  Rear,   NumberInQueue  : integer;
```

To initialise the queue:
```
Procedure Initialise
    Front := 1
    Rear := 6 {or Rear := 0}
    NumberInQueue := 0
EndProc
```

To add an element to the queue:
```
Procedure EnQueue
    If NumberInQueue = 6
      Then Write ('Queue overflow')
      Else
        If Rear = 6
          Then Rear := 1      } or Rear := (Rear Mod 6) + 1
          Else Add 1 to Rear
        EndIf
        Q[Rear] := NewItem
        Add 1 to NumberInQueue
    EndIf
EndProc
```

To remove an element from the queue:
```
Procedure DeQueue
    If NumberInQueue = 0
      Then Write ('Queue empty')
      Else
        NewItem := Q[Front]
        Subtract 1 from NumberInQueue
        If Front = 6
          Then Front := 1          } or Front := (Front Mod 6) + 1
          Else Add 1 to Front
        EndIf
    EndIf
EndProc
```

Implementing a queue as a linked list

A queue may be implemented as a special kind of linked list, with each element in the queue pointing to the next item. Items may only be removed from the front of the list and added to the end of the list.

Uses of queues

Queues are used in a variety of applications such as:
- holding jobs waiting to be run by the computer;
- a keyboard buffer, to allow a whole line to be typed and edited while the processor is busy doing something else;
- spooling output on to a disk to await printing.

12.10 BINARY TREES

A binary tree is a data structure illustrated below. Note that each node can have at most two descendants.

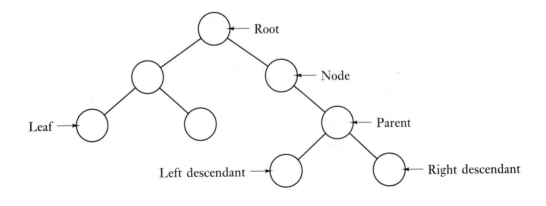

Figure 12.7: A binary tree

Constructing an ordered binary tree

A list of items may be placed in a binary tree structure using the following rules:

1. Place the first item at the root.
2. Take each subsequent item in turn.
3. Start at the root. If the item is LESS than the root, branch to the left, and if it is GREATER than the root branch to the right.
4. Apply the rule at each node encountered; left if less, right if greater.

For example, place the following names in binary tree: Gareth, Robert, Hope, Ashley, Neil, Stuart

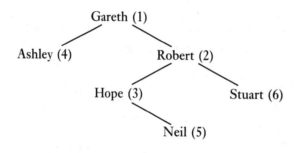

Figure 12.8: Items in a binary tree

(The numbers in brackets indicate the sequence in which the items were placed in the tree.)

Implementing a binary tree

In order to hold this structure in a computer's memory, three arrays may be used, one to hold the list of items and the others to hold left and right pointers. In the above tree, for example, the first item, Gareth, points to the 4th item (Ashley) on the left and the second item (Robert) on the right. The tree is represented by the three arrays shown in Fig 12.9.

	Name	Left Pointer	Right Pointer
1	Gareth	4	2
2	Robert	3	6
3	Hope	0	5
4	Ashley	0	0
5	Neil	0	0
6	Stuart	0	0

Figure 12.9: A binary tree implemented as a table

Traversing a binary tree

'Traversing a tree' means visiting each node of the tree in turn and performing some action on its contents – perhaps simply reading it or printing it out. A tree may be traversed in any of three ways, **pre-order**, **in-order** or **post-order**. *Note that the prefixes pre-, in-, post-, refer to the point at which the root is visited. The left node is always visited before the right node.*

As an example, consider the tree consisting of only three nodes:

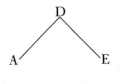

Pre-order traversal

- Visit the root node.
- Traverse the left subtree.
- Traverse the right subtree.

The nodes are visited in the order D A E.
The nodes in the Name tree are visited in the order Gareth, Ashley, Robert, Hope, Neil, Stuart.

In-order traversal

- Traverse the left subtree.
- Visit the root node.
- Traverse the right subtree.

The nodes are visited in the order A D E.
The nodes in the Name tree are visited in the order Ashley, Gareth, Hope, Neil, Robert, Stuart.

Post-order traversal

- Traverse the left subtree.
- Traverse the right subtree.
- Visit the root node.

The nodes are visited in the order A E D.
The nodes in the Name tree are visited in the order Ashley, Neil, Hope, Stuart, Robert, Gareth.

An in-order traversal results in a list in ascending sequence.

Pseudocode algorithm for in-order tree traversal

The algorithm for traversing a tree is recursive – that is, it calls itself. It passes as a parameter the index (subscript) of the current node, the root node being node[1]. The tree is implemented using three arrays; Data[1..6], LeftPointer[1..6] and RightPointer[1..6].

```
Procedure InOrderTraverse (P:integer)
   If LeftPointer[P] > 0
      Then InOrderTraverse (LeftPointer[P])
   EndIf
   Write (Data[P])
   If RightPointer[P] > 0
      Then InOrderTraverse (RightPointer[P])
   EndIf
EndProc
```

The procedure will be called with the statement
    InOrderTraverse (1)

Uses of binary trees

A binary tree is a useful data structure in which to store items which arrive in a random sequence, but which then need to be quickly searched to find a particular item – for example, the dictionary of a word-processor. The items can also be easily retrieved in alphabetical or numerical sequence by performing an in-order traversal.

> ## Chapter summary
>
> This chapter has covered the construction of pseudocode algorithms for sorting and searching data held in arrays, and manipulating elements in data structures such as lists, linked lists, stacks, queues and binary trees. The applications of these data structures have also been covered.

Illustrative questions

1 A computer system is used to store the following examination results data. State a suitable data type for each item of data:
(a) total number of examinations passed by pupils;
(b) average number of passes per pupil;
(c) a pupil's name;
(d) whether a pupil is aged under 16.

(4)
(AEB)

Suggested answer
(a) Integer
(b) Real number
(c) String
(d) Boolean.

2 An array A[0..n] is used for the storage of n values in elements A[1] .. A[n]. The following algorithm sorts the values into ascending order, using A[0] as a temporary workspace.

```
PROCEDURE sort
  BEGIN
    FOR i := 2 TO n
      X := A[i]
      A[0] := X
      j := i − 1
      WHILE A[j] > X
        A[j 1 1] := A[j]
        j := j − 1
      ENDWHILE
      A[j + 1] := X
    ENDFOR
  END
```

Initially A[1] = 4, A[2] = 3, A[3] = 9, A[4] = 6, A[5] = 1 and n = 5.
Trace the operation of the algorithm by stating the contents of the array after each pass.

(6)
(EDEXCEL)

Tutorial note
This is the algorithm for the insertion sort. On the first pass the second item (3) is put into the temporary storage space A[0], and compared with the first item (4). The item 4 is shifted along to make room in A[1] for the item 3. On the second pass, the third item (9) is put into A[0] and compared with the first two items. It is greater than both so no swaps are made. On the third pass, the fourth item (6) is placed in A[0], the item 9 is shifted along to make room for it. On the last pass all items have to be shifted up to make room for the number 1.

In order to answer this question it helps to understand what is happening, rather than trying to follow each line of code. Try it out first with pieces of paper marked with numbers 4, 3, 9, 6 and 1.

Suggested answer

Pass 1:	Array A[0..5] holds	3	3	4	9	6	1
Pass 2:		9	3	4	9	6	1
Pass 3:		6	3	4	6	9	1
Pass 4:		1	1	3	4	6	9

3 Describe two searching techniques. For each technique indicate when its use would be appropriate. (6)

(NEAB)

Suggested answer

A linear search – each item in the list is examined in turn starting with the first item in the list, until either the item is found or the end of the list is reached. This would be appropriate on a short unsorted list or small file of unsorted records each having a unique key field.

A binary search – the list is divided into three parts; a middle item, the lower part of the array and the upper part. The middle item is examined to see if it is equal to the sought item. If it is not, then if it is greater than the sought item, the upper half of the array is of no further interest. The number of items being searched is therefore halved and the process repeated until the last item is examined, with either the upper half or lower half of the items searched being eliminated at each pass.

This type of search is suitable for a large sorted array held in memory.

4 With the aid of a clearly labelled diagram which includes a stack pointer, describe how a previously empty stack would hold these names arriving in the given sequence:

TOM, ALF, TIM, JOE, SAM

Show what the stack would then contain if two of these names were popped (retrieved) from it, and a further name (JIM) added. (4)

(AEB)

Suggested answer

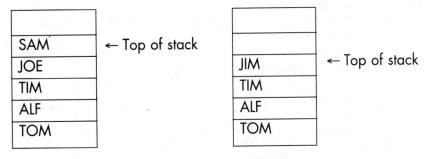

5 An airport departure lounge has, for the benefit of passengers, a number of visual display units in prominent positions which display flight information. Information displayed includes flight number, name of destination airport, estimated time of departure, and reasons for any flight delay. Entries are displayed in order of estimated departure time.

Carefully describe a data structure which could be used to hold this information, and justify the choice you have made. (6)

(EDEXCEL)

Suggested answer

A list could be used, constructed from an array of fixed length records, with each record having fields for flight number, name of destination airport etc. This is a suitable data structure because the list will be short, consisting of a fixed number of entries (suitable for a static data structure). Addition, deletion and changes to existing records are all fast and straightforward. When a departure time needs to be changed, this can be done by first deleting the old record and then adding the new amended one in the correct position in the list.

6 A sort program inputs an unordered list of names and stores them in memory in the form of a binary tree. The following diagram represents this data structure with the first six names entered.

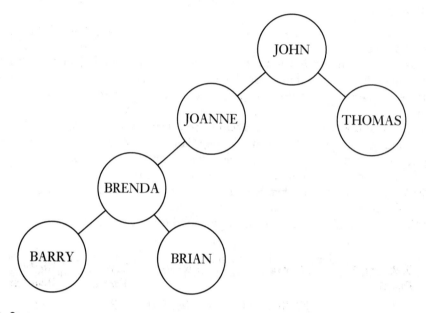

(a) State:
   (i) the name at the root of the tree;
   (ii) the parent of BRIAN.   (2)
(b) Copy the diagram and add nodes for SUSAN, WILLIAM, ANDREW and then JOSEPH, the next four names on the list.   (4)
(c) The table below shows the original six names together with tree-pointers associated with JOHN and JOANNE. An unused pointer has the value 0.
   Copy and complete the table giving the pointer values for *all ten* names. (8)

Subscript Pointer	Name	Parent	Left Pointer	Right Pointer
1	JOHN	0	2	3
2	JOANNE	1	4	0
3	THOMAS			
4	BRENDA			
5	BRIAN			
6	BARRY			

In computer memory this table is stored in the form of a one-dimensional array. Each element of this array is a record comprising a name and three numbers as a character string.

(d) A similar sort program for a list of *integers* uses a two-dimensional array to store the tree structure. Suggest *two* reasons why this program will sort a list of 1000 integers more quickly than the first program sorts a list of 1000 names.   (2)

(AEB)

Suggested answer

(a) (i) JOHN   (ii) BRENDA

(b)

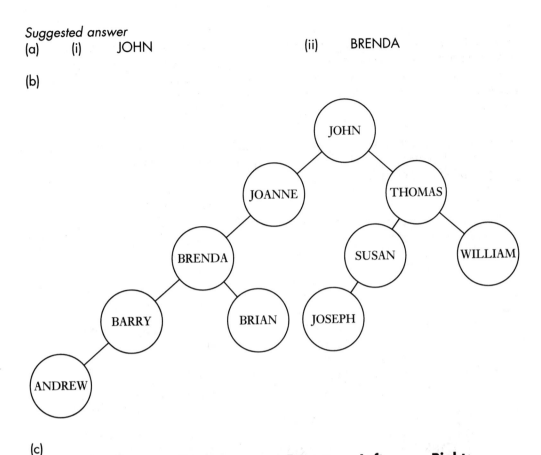

(c)

Subscript Pointer	Name	Parent	Left Pointer	Right Pointer
1	JOHN	0	2	3
2	JOANNE	1	4	0
3	THOMAS	1	7	8
4	BRENDA	2	6	5
5	BRIAN	4	0	0
6	BARRY	4	9	0
7	SUSAN	3	10	0
8	WILLIAM	3	0	0
9	ANDREW	6	0	0
10	JOSEPH	7	0	0

(d) Comparing integers is faster than comparing strings. The pointers will be held as integers and will not need to be converted from character strings.

7 The following section of pseudocode processes a five-digit integer called CODE and then assigns a single character to the variable DIGT.

<u>Initialise</u> W = 2 and NUM = 0
<u>Assign</u> Y = CODE

<u>Repeat</u>
    <u>Assign</u> Z = Y
    <u>Assign</u> the whole number part of Y/10 to Y
    Calculate Z−10*Y and <u>Assign</u> result to N
    Calculate N*W and <u>Add</u> result to NUM
    <u>Add</u> 1 to W
<u>Until</u> W = 7

Calculate the remainder when NUM is divided by 11
                and <u>Assign</u> this to REM

<u>If</u> REM = 0   <u>Then</u> <u>Assign</u> '0' to DIGT
<u>Else</u> <u>If</u> REM = 1   <u>Then</u>   <u>Assign</u> 'X' to DIGT
          <u>Else</u>   Calculate 11−REM and
                  <u>Assign</u> the character code for this result to DIGT

(a) Copy and complete the following dry-run table for this algorithm, given that CODE=14273

W	Y	Z	N	NUM	REM	DIGT

(12)

(b) What is being calculated for the integer CODE, and why is this stored in the computer as a character? (2)

(c) Could the algorithm be successfully used without modification to process four digit codes? Justify your answer. (2)

(AEB)

Tutorial note

The headings for the trace table are provided so you need to 'dry run' the code (execute it) exactly as the computer would, showing how the values of the variables change as each statement is executed.

The choice of variable names, the line 'Calculate the remainder when NUM is divided by 11' and the occurrence of 'X' should provide clues for part (b).

Suggested answer

(a)

W	Y	Z	N	NUM	REM	DIGT
2	14273	14273		0		
	1427		3	6		
3	142	1427	7	27		
4	14	142	2	35		
5	1	14	4	55		
6	0	1	1	61		
7					6	'5'

(b) A modulo-11 check digit is being calculated. It is stored as a character because the check digit may be non-numeric (i.e. 'X').

(c) Yes; the code would be processed as if it had a leading zero.

8 In one system, character strings are stored as linked lists of records. Each record contains a character field and a link field. The following diagram illustrates how a character string, which has an identifier S, contains the word DOG.

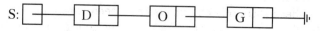

(a) If the character string A contained HAM and the character string B contained LET then the concatenation of A and B would contain HAMLET.
Explain how two character strings can be concatenated. (4)

(b) The function INDEX determines the position of the first occurrence of a character within a character string. Thus, if S contains MISSISSIPPI then
INDEX (S,'I') = 2
If the character does not occur in the string then this function returns value zero.
Describe an algorithm, in pseudocode, to implement the function INDEX. (5)

(c) The function LENGTH determines the length of a character string. Thus, if the character string B contains VIEW then

LENGTH (B) = 4

Describe an algorithm, in pseudocode, to implement a recursive version of the function LENGTH. (6)

(EDEXCEL)

Tutorial note

In the given solution pointer notation is used in part (c) to describe the 'record pointed to by the link field'. However, if you are not familiar with this notation you could use the above phrase instead.

Suggested answer

(a) Null pointer at the end of the first character string is replaced with the start pointer of the second string.

(b)
```
Function Index(S,Char)
    Pointer = 1
    Index = 0
    Repeat
        If S(Pointer) = Char
            Then Index = Pointer
            Else Pointer = Pointer + 1
    Until no more characters or Index<>0
EndFun
```

(c)
```
Function Length(S)
    If S = null pointer
        Then Length(S) = 0
        Else Length(S) = 1 + Length(S^.link)
    EndIf
EndFun
```

(S^.link is the record pointed to by link field of S)

9 Keystrokes at a computer keyboard generate character codes which are temporarily stored in the order in which they are generated in a data storage area known as the *keyboard buffer*. A program which requires keyboard input accesses this buffer and removes one character code at a time. The code which is removed each time is the one which has been in the buffer the longest. New characters arriving may wrap around to the beginning of the buffer.

(a) What name best describes the structure of the keyboard buffer? (2)

(b) The keyboard buffer is designed to hold up to 100 character codes at any one time but during the execution of the program several thousand character codes will enter and leave the keyboard buffer. Describe how the buffer can be best structured to make this possible. Use diagrams to illustrate your answer, clearly showing the full structure for:
   (i) an empty buffer;
   (ii) a full buffer before any characters have been removed;
   (iii) a full buffer after less than 100 character codes have been removed and some new characters have arrived. (5)

(c) Using pseudocode describe algorithms which:
   (i) initialise the buffer;
   (ii) add a character code to the buffer;
   (iii) remove a character code from the buffer.

The algorithm should handle the error conditions generated when an attempt is made to add an item to an already full buffer and when an attempt is made to remove an item from an empty buffer. (13)

(AEB)

Suggested answer
(a) Queue: FIFO
(b) Circular queue or answer implying wrap-around.

    R=Rear pointer   F=Front pointer

   (i) empty buffer:

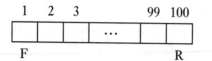

        (need variable SIZE = 0 to show no. of elements in queue)

   (ii)

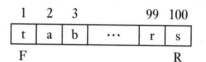

        (need variable SIZE = 100 to show no. of elements in queue)

   (iii)

```
1   2   3           99  100
+---+---+---+     +---+---+
| X | Y | b | ... | r | s |     t and a have been removed, X and Y have arrived
+---+---+---+     +---+---+
  R   F
```

        (R immediately to left of F and SIZE=100)

(c) (i) Procedure InitialiseQueue
           Front := 1
           Rear = 100
           Size = 0
        EndProc

   (ii) Procedure AddToQueue
           If Size = 100
              Then queue full
              Else
                 R := (R Mod 100) + 1
                 Q(R) := NewItem
                 Increment Size
              EndIf
           EndProc

   (iii) Procedure RemoveFromQueue
            If Size=0
              Then queue empty
             Else
                X := Q(F)
                Size:= Size−1
                F := (F Mod 100) + 1
            EndIf
           EndProc

TEST RUN

- To prepare for your mock examinations or final examinations, this section should be tackled towards the end of your revision programme when you have covered all your syllabus topics and attempted the practice questions at the end of each chapter.

- The Test Your Knowledge Quiz contains multiple choice questions on a wide range of syllabus topics. You should attempt it without reference to the text.

- Check your answers against the Test Your Knowledge Quiz answers. If you are not sure why you got an answer wrong, read the points next to the answer and look up any reference to the main text.

- Enter your marks in the Progress Analysis chart. The notes below will suggest a further revision strategy, based on your performance in the quiz. Only when you have done the extra work suggested should you go on to the final test.

- The Mock Exam questions provide a wide spread of question styles and topics, drawn from various examination boards. You should attempt these questions under examination conditions in the time allowed, and without reference to the text.

- Compare your answers to our Mock Exam Suggested Answers remembering that often these are not the only correct answers.

TEST YOUR KNOWLEDGE QUIZ

There are 48 questions to be done in 45 minutes.

1 A mail-merge is most commonly achieved using the following software package(s)
   A. spreadsheet and database
   B. word-processor and graphics package
   C. electronic mail system
   D. word-processor and database.

2 One advantage of a bitmapped graphics package over a vector graphics package is that
   A. The graphic image does not distort when enlarged or shrunk
   B. The graphic image occupies less memory
   C. A photographic image can be imported into a bitmapped graphics package and modified
   D. Bitmap images can easily be transferred from one application to another without distortion.

3 The manager of a leisure centre wishes to estimate the likely effect on profits of a decrease in entry price by examining the consequences of estimated increases in the number of people using the centre. What would be a suitable software package to aid him with the calculations?
   A. An expert system
   B. A spreadsheet
   C. A presentation graphics package
   D. A maths package.

4 The Data Protection Act makes it an offence to
   A. hold personal data longer than necessary
   B. run pirated software
   C. gain unauthorised access to computer programs or data
   D. copy software.

5 A typical use of a WORM (Write Once Read Many) storage device is
   A. archiving data such as copies of invoices
   B. recording music for a CD
   C. storing the operating system of a computer
   D. making regular backup copies of master files held on disk.

6 A suitable method of input for processing credit card applications would be
   A. magnetic ink character recognition (MICR)
   B. optical mark recognition (OMR)
   C. optical character recognition (OCR)
   D. hand-held computer.

7 A point-of-sale (POS) terminal records transactions (sales and returns) on a transaction file which is processed each night after the store has closed. Which of the following data items will *not* be stored on a transaction record?
   A. The transaction type
   B. The price of the item
   C. The quantity sold or returned
   D. The item code.

8 A VDU has just sufficient video RAM to display 256 colours at a resolution of 800×600 pixels. The user wishes to display 65,536 colours. Should she:
   A. increase the resolution to 1024×1024 pixels
   B. decrease the screen resolution to 320×480 pixels
   C. use a larger screen
   D. specify that a smaller screen area is to be used?

9   Which type of file organisation is most suitable for a stock master file holding details of stock items?
   A.   Serial
   B.   Sequential
   C.   Indexed sequential
   D.   Random.

10 Why may it be necessary to hold more than one level of index for an indexed sequential file?
   A.   Because the file is split up and held on separate physical disks
   B.   Because the file contains a very large number of records
   C.   Because the primary key consists of more than one field
   D.   Because the overflow area needs a separate index

11 Records on a random file are stored:
   A.   at addresses calculated by applying an algorithm to the key field
   B.   in the order in which they are input
   C.   anywhere that there is room on the file
   D.   at addresses given by a random number generator.

12 The grandfather–father–son method of updating involves:
   A.   updating the master file in real time
   B.   updating an indexed-sequential file in key sequence
   C.   using two generations of a file in order to create the third generation
   D.   creating a new master file every time an update run is performed.

13 The modulo –11 check digit for the number 2147 is:
   A.   3
   B.   4
   C.   7
   D.   X.

14 What is the objective of a test strategy for a new program?
   A.   To ensure that the program compiles without errors
   B.   To prove that the program has no errors
   C.   To establish which data will allow the program to run without crashing
   D.   To try to provoke program failure.

15 Which of the following is a substantial expense incurred after the installation of a new computer system?
   A.   Transferring data files to new media
   B.   Buying new hardware
   C.   Paying for a maintenance contract for servicing hardware
   D.   Higher electricity bills.

16 Program-data independence in the context of a DBMS means that:
   A.   Changes to the contents of data files do not necessitate changes to the programs
   B.   Changes to the programs do not affect the contents of the data files
   C.   Changes to the programs do not affect the structure of the data files
   D.   Changes to the structure of the data files do not affect the programs.

17 An attribute in the context of a relational database may be defined as:
   A.   something about which data is held
   B.   a column of a table
   C.   a row in a table
   D.   a key field of a table.

18 A foreign key in a relational database table is:
   A.   a primary key of another table, acting as a link field
   B.   unique
   C.   part of a multi-field key
   D.   encrypted for security purposes.

19 A table in third normal form is one which:
  A. contains no non-key dependencies
  B. has only one primary key
  C. is linked to another table by means of a foreign key
  D. has no repeating fields.

20 The number -19 translated into an 8-bit two's complement binary integer is:
  A. 10010011
  B. 11101101
  C. 00010011
  D. 11101100.

21 The number 5.75 translated into a normalised floating point number, with a 10-bit mantissa and a 6-bit exponent is:
  A. 0101110000   000011
  B. 0110110000   000011
  C. 0101110000   000001
  D. 0000010111   000100.

22 The positive binary number 10101111 translated into hexadecimal is:
  A. AE
  B. AF
  C. BE
  D. BF.

23 Two registers involved in the fetch–execute cycle are:
  A. the program counter and the stack pointer
  B. the status register and the program counter
  C. the memory address register and the memory data register
  D. the accumulator and the current instruction register.

24 The address bus of a certain computer has 16 lines. What is the maximum number of addressable memory cells?
  A. 16
  B. 256
  C. 65,535
  D. 65,536.

25 RAM cache is
  A. a small amount of fast memory between main memory and the processor
  B. memory reserved for use by the operating system
  C. the computer's main random access memory for storing programs and data
  D. memory used by the VDU for storing the screen image.

26 Which of the following sources of interrupt has the highest priority?
  A. Division by zero
  B. Memory parity error
  C. Real-time clock
  D. Keyboard key pressed.

27 Two arithmetic left shifts are made on the bit pattern 11001011. What is the result?
  A. 00101100
  B. 00101111
  C. 10101100
  D. 10010100.

28 Which of the following instructions will set the most significant 4 bits of an 8-bit register to zero, while leaving the last four unchanged?
  A. AND 00001111
  B. OR   00001111
  C. OR   11110000
  D. XOR 00001111.

29 Location 600 contains 601, 601 contains 607 and 607 contains 613. What are the contents of register R after the following instruction? (The parentheses indicate indirect addressing.)

> LOAD R, (600)

   A. 600
   B. 601
   C. 607
   D. 613.

30 Relocatable code:
   A. is translated using one type of processor to run on a different processor
   B. is translated using a one-pass assembler
   C. is in a form that can be loaded anywhere in main memory
   D. can be run on a remote processor.

31 A device which combines more than one input signal into a single stream of data which can be transmitted over a single communications channel is known as
   A. a modem
   B. a multiplexor
   C. an optic fibre line
   D. a front-end processor.

32 Which of the following statements is true of a packet-switching network?
   A. The cost depends on the distance transmitted
   B. Data packets for a single transmission always travel by a single route
   C. The size of a packet depends on the number of characters in the message
   D. The cost depends on the number of packets sent.

33 In a token ring network:
   A. messages can be passed around the ring in either direction
   B. several message tokens can simultaneously be passed around the ring
   C. the message is passed to the correct recipient by a central computer
   D. each node has to 'grab' the token at a designated time and send or receive a message.

34 In order to implement video conferencing:
   A. the image must be compressed
   B. an ISDN line must be used
   C. communication must be by radio wave or satellite link
   D. twisted pair cable must be installed.

35 A multi-programming computer is one which:
   A. is capable of running two or more programs apparently simultaneously
   B. has several processors working in parallel
   C. runs only real-time programs
   D. runs only in batch mode.

36 One job of the scheduler is to:
   A. ensure hardware resources are kept free for when they are needed
   B. ensure that one process does not accidentally access another's memory locations
   C. provide acceptable response time to interactive users
   D. select a scheduling algorithm to achieve maximum throughput.

37 The use of virtual memory:
   A. results in faster execution speeds
   B. creates the illusion that a computer has more main memory than it in fact has
   C. ensures that disk space is used efficiently
   D. ensures that all programs are relocatable.

38 A process may be at any time *running*, *runnable* or *suspended*. Which of the following statements is true?
   A. A process will join the queue of suspended jobs if, while it is running, its time slice expires
   B. A process is runnable if it is waiting for an I/O device to become free
   C. A process is suspended if it is waiting for an I/O device to become free
   D. A process is running if it is in memory, waiting for the processor to become free.

39 Which of the following terms best describes the While..Do..EndWhile program structure?
   A. Sequence
   B. Selection
   C. Iteration
   D. Recursion.

40 Which type of language would be suitable for programming an expert system?
   A. Procedural
   B. Declarative
   C. Imperative
   D. Low-level.

41 Which of the following is a suitable language to use to program a device driver (e.g. a printer driver)?
   A. COBOL
   B. Prolog
   C. Pascal
   D. Assembly language.

42 At which stage of compilation will errors (a) and (b) be detected:
   Error (a): the name of a variable has more characters than are permitted.
   Error (b): a closing parenthesis (bracket) is omitted from an arithmetic expression.
   A. (a) syntax, (b) lexical
   B. (a) lexical, (b) syntax
   C. (a) semantic, (b) code generation
   D. (a) lexical, (b) semantic.

43 How many items in the following list will be examined during a binary search to find Ipswich?
   Aldeburgh, Bentley, Colchester, Flatford, Ipswich, King's Lynn, Lowestoft, Manningtree, Norwich, Peterborough, Sudbury, Thetford.
   A. 3
   B. 4
   C. 5
   D. 12.

44 **Head** returns the first element of a list and **Tail** returns a new list containing all but the first element of the list. What is returned by the operation Tail (Tail (Tail (List)))
   where List = [Aldeburgh, Bentley, Colchester, Flatford, Ipswich]
   A. [ ] (*empty list*)
   B. [Ipswich]
   C. [Flatford, Ipswich]
   D. [Colchester, Flatford, Ipswich]

45 A linked list consists of a start pointer and several nodes each containing a Name data field and a Pointer field. The list contains the following items:

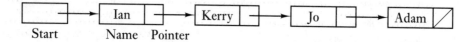

Start   Name   Pointer

What will be printed when the procedure PrintItems is called with the statement PrintItems(Start)?

```
Procedure PrintItems (P)
    If P not equal 0
        then
            P:= Pointer[P]
            PrintItems[P]
            Print Name[P]
    EndIf
EndProc
```

A. Adam Ian Jo Kerry
B. Ian Kerry Jo Adam
C. Adam Jo Kerry Ian
D. Ian.

46 Which of the following data structures is used to hold return addresses when a procedure is called?
A. binary tree
B. stack
C. queue
D. linked list.

47 The following tree is traversed using post-order traversal. In which order are the nodes printed out?

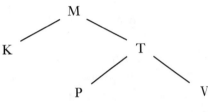

A.   V P T K M
B.   K T P V M
C.   K P V T M
D.   P V T K M

48 The following diagram shows a circular queue containing five items. Which of the diagrams depicts the queue after one item has left and three items P, R and F have been added?

B	S	T	W	A		

Front   Rear

A.

B	S	T	W	P	R	F

Front   Rear

B.

F	S	T	W	A	P	R

Front   Rear

C.

F	S	T	W	A	P	R

Rear Front

D.

S	T	W	A	P	R	F

Front   Rear

TEST YOUR KNOWLEDGE QUIZ ANSWERS

1 D. A mail merge can be done using only the facilities of a word-processor, but is often done using data such as names and addresses stored in a database.

2 C. All scanned images are stored as bit patterns.

3 B. Spreadsheets are ideal for 'What-if' calculations.

4 A. The other options are also illegal but are clauses of other Acts.

5 A. None of the others is a possibility.

6 C. MICR is mainly used for processing cheques, OMR for multiple choice questionnaires etc. Hand-held computers are used by people gathering data in different locations, e.g. reading electricity meters.

7 B. The price will be held on the master file.

8 B. The resolution needs to be decreased to display more colours because of the limited video RAM available.

9 C. The file has to be randomly accessed, and indexed-sequential would be preferable to random for producing stock reports, reorder reports etc. in a particular sequence.

10 B. A large file will require more than one level of index even though it is all on one physical disk.

11 A. The term 'random file' implies that any randomly chosen record may be instantly accessed, not that records are stored anywhere at unknown addresses.

12 D. Using grandfather–father–son, the 'grandfather' file is safely locked away, the 'father' is the current master file, and the 'son' is the new master file which is created by applying transactions to the current master file – which then becomes the grandfather for the next update run.

13 B. Assign weights 2, 3, 4, 5 from right-hand end. Multiply by the digits.

$$\begin{array}{cccccccc} 2 & & 1 & & 4 & & 7 \\ 5 & & 4 & & 3 & & 2 \\ \hline 10 & + & 4 & + & 12 & + & 14 & = 40 \end{array}$$

Divide by 11 giving 3 remainder 7
Subtract the remainder from 11 to give the check digit 4.

14 D. It is impossible to prove the absence of errors, so the aim is to try and locate any errors by thinking up test cases that may cause the program to fail, so that they can be corrected.

15 C. A and B occur before installation, and electricity bills are not a significant cost.

16 D. Program-data independence is one of the major advantages of a DBMS. For example adding a new field will not affect other programs which do not access that field.

17 B. An attribute is something like name, student-number or date of birth.

18 A. A foreign key is used to link two tables together (see Section 5.4).

19 A. This is also expressed by saying that each attribute in a table in third normal form depends on 'the key, the whole key and nothing but the key'.

20 B. $19 = 00010011$. Starting from the right, leave all bits alone up to and including the first 1. Then flip all the rest to give 11101101.

21 A. $5.75 = 0101.11$ The binary point needs to move 3 places left so that the first digit after the assumed binary point is a 1. To compensate, the exponent must be put equal to 3, giving 0101110000 000011

22 B. Break the number up into groups of 4 bits. $1010_{10} = 10_{10} = A_{16}$, $1111 = 15_{10} = F_{16}$

23 C. The PC and the CIR are also involved but not the others!

24 D. The maximum number of addressable cells is $2^{16} = 65,536$. The maximum address is 65535.

25 A. RAM cache is used to improve system performance.

26 B. Memory parity errors need to be dealt with immediately.

27 C. The sign bit is preserved with an arithmetic shift.

28 A. The others do not work.

29 C. The instruction means 'Load into R the contents of the location whose address is in location 600'.

30 C. Relocatable code therefore contains no absolute addresses.

31 B. See Section 9.1.

32 D. Packets of a fixed size may travel by any of a number of different routes, and cost is independent of distance.

33 D. A single token circulates in one direction only. There is no central computer.

34 B. An integrated services digital network (ISDN) line transmits voice, video, and computer data.

35 A. It holds several programs in memory and switches between them. It may run a combination of real-time and batch jobs.

36 C. The scheduler uses (but does not select) a scheduling algorithm to achieve its objectives.

37 B. Disk storage is used as an extension of main memory, typically by swapping pages (fixed-size blocks containing parts of programs) in and out as required.

38 C. A process is runnable if it could use the processor if it were available. It is suspended if it couldn't use the processor because it is waiting for I/O.

39 C. Iteration implies a loop of some kind.

40 B. A declarative language such as Prolog allows the programmer to program the facts and rules associated with the problem.

41 D. The device driver needs to occupy as little memory as possible and run as fast as possible.

42 B. Illegal variable names will be detected by the lexical analyser and a missing bracket is a syntax error.

43 B. There are 12 items in the list. King's Lynn will be examined first and the top half of the list rejected (including King's Lynn). Colchester will then be examined, and the bottom half of the list rejected leaving only Flatford and Ipswich. Flatford will be examined followed by Ipswich.

44 C. Each time Tail(List) is applied the front element is omitted from the resulting list.

45 C. This is a recursive procedure which has the effect of reversing the list.

46 B. A stack (Last-In First-Out) data structure stores the return addresses.

47 C. The direction of traversal is left to right, with the root of each sub-tree visited printed after the left and right nodes.

48 C. Items leave from the front and the front pointer is advanced. As items are added the rear pointer is advanced, returning to the first position when it goes beyond the last position.

PROGRESS ANALYSIS

Place a tick next to those questions you got right.

Question	Answer	Question	Answer	Question	Answer	Question	Answer
1		13		25		37	
2		14		26		38	
3		15		27		39	
4		16		28		40	
5		17		29		41	
6		18		30		42	
7		19		31		43	
8		20		32		44	
9		21		33		45	
10		22		34		46	
11		23		35		47	
12		24		36		48	

Total mark: _____ out of 48

if you scored 1-24

You need to revise basic concepts, learn key facts and definitions and memorise essential knowledge in all topics before you progress any further.

if you scored 25-36

Identify individual topics that need attention and revise these. Make sure you are paying enough attention to the wording of questions so that you don't make careless errors.

if you scored 37-48

Well done – but this is just the beginning! Be sure to identify and revise any topic areas that need more work before you try the Mock Exam Questions.

MOCK EXAM QUESTIONS

Paper 1 (2.5 hours)

Answer ALL questions.

Section A: (Ten short answer questions worth 40 marks)

1   State and briefly describe two different types of program maintenance.   (2)
                                                                          (NEAB)

2   Describe *three* different checks on data as it is entered into fields of a record stored in a database.   (3)
                                                                          (AEB)

3   Officials of an area health authority have made appointments for all two-year-old children living within the area to be vaccinated. Details of the children and their appointments are maintained on a computer file.
    Describe how a word processor could be used to generate personalised letters to send to families to give details of the appointments.   (3)
                                                                          (EDEXCEL)

4   It is claimed that *fourth generation languages* (4GLs) have made computer applications easier to develop. State *three* distinct reasons to support this claim. (3)
                                                                          (AEB)

5   A letter which is stored at each node of a binary tree is printed as the tree is traversed. If the tree consists of just three nodes with the letter D stored at the root, the letter A at the left leaf node and the letter E at the right leaf node, what will be printed when the traversal is
    (i)   in-order?
    (ii) pre-order?
    (iii) post-order?   (3)
                                                                          (AEB)

6   Over the past 40 years, computer systems have developed into essential pieces of office equipment.
    Discuss developments in printer and backing storage technology that have contributed to this.   (4)
                                                                          (AEB)

7   A stand-alone microcomputer is being used for DTP. When the user requests that a document be printed, after a very short delay the user can continue typing even though the printer has not completed its task. Outline the reason why this is possible.   (4)
                                                                          (NICCEA)

8   Distinguish between iteration and recursion. Give one example of the use of each which illustrates appropriately the power of the technique. In each case state why its use is appropriate.   (6)
                                                                          (EDEXCEL)

9   Briefly describe how each of the following methods is used to transfer data to a computer and, in each case, give an appropriate application.
    (i)   MICR (magnetic ink character recognition)
    (ii) OCR (optical character recognition)
    (iii) OMR (optical mark recognition)   (6)
                                                                          (NEAB)

10 The six most significant bits in the status register of a particular computer are defined as follows:

S(ign)   Z(ero)   C(arry)   O(verflow)   I(nterrupt Disable)   B(reak)

Briefly explain how each of these bits in the register might come to be set to 1. (6)

(*NICCEA*)

Section B: (Three questions worth 45 marks)

11 A large credit company has a multi-access mainframe computer system. The computer's operating system employs spooling to manage outputs to the printers.
  (a) Explain the purpose of spooling. (2)
      For each printer a queue is used to implement the spooling routine.
  (b) Show, with the aid of diagrams, how such a queue could be represented inside the computer using:
      (i) an array;
      (ii) a linked list. (4)
  (c) Describe the contents of each element in both representations of the queue. (2)
  (d) Comment on the suitability of each representation of the queue for the implementation of the spooling routine. (2)

(*EDEXCEL*)

12 A company assigns a unique number to each of its employees. This employee number is used as the key-field for processing computer data.

The master file is held on magnetic tape in key-field order.

Each week the master file is updated using a transaction file to create a new master file. The transaction file contains details of new employees, employees who have left the company, and employees whose records have changed.
  (a) Using a systems flowchart or other suitable diagram, illustrate the creation of the transaction file and the subsequent updating of the new master file. (7)
  (b) State, for each stage of the process, *two* error checks which could be included and describe the action which should be taken when errors are detected. (8)

(*EDEXCEL*)

13 The data requirements for a hospital in-patient system are defined as follows:
A hospital is organised into a number of wards. Each ward has a ward number and a name recorded, along with a number of beds in that ward. Each ward is staffed by nurses. Nurses have their staff number and name recorded, and are assigned to a single ward.

Each patient in the hospital has a patient identification number, and their name, address and date of birth are recorded. Each patient is under the care of a single consultant and is assigned to a single ward. Each consultant is responsible for a number of patients. Consultants have their staff number, name and specialism recorded.
  (a) In database modelling, what is:
      (i) an attribute;
      (ii) a relationship? (2)
  (b) State *four* entities for the hospital in-patient system and suggest an identifier for each of these entities.
      Describe *three* relationships that can be inferred from these data requirements. (11)
  (c) A relational database is to be used. Describe tables for *two* of the entities for which you have described a relationship. (7)

(*AEB*)

Paper 2 (2 hours)

Answer ALL questions.

Section A: (9 short questions worth 35 marks)

1 One common business application package is the *spreadsheet*. Give two different reasons why a spreadsheet package is particularly useful as a decision-making tool.
(2)
(AEB)

2 The diagrams below show two possible topologies for linking five nodes in a network.

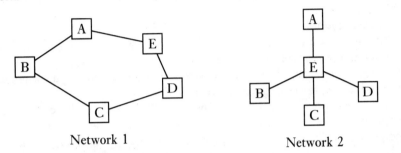

Network 1   Network 2

(a) Name the network topologies shown. (1)
(b) If a node fails, state and explain what the effect would be for users of:
    (i) Network 1;
    (ii) Network 2. (3)
(SQA)

3 State two rights an individual has under the Data Protection Act. (2)
(NEAB)

4 Expert systems are suitable for many different categories of application. Give two different categories, and for each category, one typical application. (4)
(AEB)

5 (a) Express the following decimal numbers in two's complement binary form in 8 bits.
    127   −27 (2)
(b) Explain, using the above as examples, how hexadecimal can be used as a shorthand for expressing bytes that consist of 8 bits. (3)
(New question)

6 Explain why it is usually good practice to develop programs as a collection of separate modules. (5)
(OCEAC)

7 List *three* duties carried out by the database administrator (DBA) in a database management system. (3)
(NICCEA)

8 Describe an appropriate method of data security for the following applications and in each case explain how, in case of loss, your chosen method would allow for the re-creation of the master files:
(i) a batch payroll system;
(ii) a real-time airline seat reservation system. (6)
(NEAB)

9 Describe the operation of the data structure known as a stack and give *one* example of the use of a stack stating clearly the reason for your choice.   (4)

(NICCEA)

Section B: (One question worth 35 marks)

10 A garden centre has invited a firm of computer consultants to advise on the computerisation of its business. The business grows over 300 varieties of plants for sale to the general public. With the consultants' help the centre has been able to identify three key areas that would benefit from computerisation. These are as follows:

- environmental control of climate inside greenhouses, e.g. temperature, humidity, light levels, soil moisture content, and automatic watering of plants growing in the open;
- sales processing;
- a plant information system service for customers, centre staff and the environmental control system.

(a) Describe *three* methods that the consultants may have employed when analysing the requirements of the garden centre business.   (3)

(b) For environmental control many sensors will be needed. The consultants advise connection via a *multiplexor* to a microcomputer operating in *real time* and containing in its interface a single *analogue to digital converter* (ADC).
   (i)   Why is an *analogue to digital converter* required?   (2)
   (ii) What is meant by the phrase 'operating in real time'?   (2)
   (iii) State *two* reasons why a multiplexor is necessary.   (2)

(c) For the plant information service describe, with justification, how plant names and associated information such as plant type can be stored in a database system so that it is possible to look up entries quickly, meeting any of the following conditions:
   - a given plant name;
   - a given characteristic (e.g. red flowers);
   - more than one given characteristic (e.g. red flowers and acid soil).   (3)

For sales processing, the consultants propose that the following data about stocked plants be recorded in a computer-based on-line file, PLANT.DAT, with the following record structure:

       catalogue number
       plant name
       quantity in stock
       current price

Catalogue number is a unique five-digit number.

In addition, the computer is to print catalogue numbers in bar-code form onto labels which are to be attached to each plant for sale. Initially, sales are to take place from a single terminal using a bar-code reader connected to the computer system. The field <quantity in stock> of PLANT.DAT must be adjusted accordingly at the time of each sale.

(d) (i)   Explain *one* advantage and *one* disadvantage to the garden centre deriving from the use of a bar-code reader.   (2)
   (ii) Describe a file organisation for the file, PLANT.DAT, which would enable sales of plants to be processed quickly. Justify your answer.   (4)
   (iii) Describe the basic computer processing that must be done for each item when a sale is made. What use might be made of plant name?   (5)
   (iv) What safeguard would need to be made to the processing if sales are allowed from more than one terminal at any one time? Explain why.   (4)

(e) Describe a sorting algorithm that, when applied to an inappropriately ordered PLANT.DAT file, would enable a price list to be printed in plant name order. (8)

(AEB)

MOCK EXAM SUGGESTED ANSWERS

Paper 1

1 Any two from:
- adaptive maintenance – altering existing software to take account of change in environment;
- corrective maintenance – fixing bugs;
- perfective maintenance – improving software, adding extra features.

2 Any three from:
- verification – must be typed twice or confirmed on-screen;
- validation – range check, format check, length check, check digit;
- unique – must not exist in database already;
- exists – must exist in database already
- protected field – data entry not permitted unless authorised.

3 A mail merge facility in a word-processing package could be used. A standard letter would be created with items such as name, address etc. written in the format 'Dear <Title> <Surname>' to be filled in from the database. This is done automatically when the mail merge is executed, producing personalised letters to each family on the database.

4 Computer applications are easier to develop using a 4GL because:
- I/O form layout often generated automatically;
- data input type checking often handled automatically;
- prototype systems quickly built for user feedback;
- automatic program/report generators available;
- query language/query by example supported;
- relative independence of programs from underlying data structures.

5 (i) ADE
   (ii) DAE
   (iii) AED.

6 *Printers*: from being noisy (daisy wheel and dot matrix), slow and of relatively poor quality, an average office laser printer now costs only a few hundred pounds, produces print of a high quality and is virtually silent in operation. Colour inkjet printers are also inexpensive and can produce colour transparencies for an overhead projector as well as normal printed paper output – useful for presentations. Both these types of printer can produce high-quality graphics, graphs and bar charts which was impossible on early printers.
Backing store technology: the advent of the micro and floppy disks meant that data and software could conveniently be stored and distributed. The capacity of hard disks has risen steadily over the years so that vast quantities of text and graphics can now be stored and retrieved whenever necessary. CD ROMs provide a convenient resource for reference material such as telephone directories, legal cases, catalogues etc.

7 The printer has a buffer, an area of RAM which can store data. The PC checks to see if the printer is ready. If it is, it sends a block of the document, or the entire document to the buffer from where the printer prints it autonomously. While the printer is printing, the PC can continue with user tasks.

8 Iteration means repeating a series of steps using, for example, a For..Next or While..Do..EndWhile statement. Recursion means calling a procedure from within the procedure itself.

Iteration: to set the contents of an entire array of 1000 variables to 0, write:

```
For Count:=1 To 1000
   X[Count] :=0;
```

Iteration is appropriate because the same step needs to be executed 1000 times on different elements of the array X.

Recursion: useful for implementing algorithms which are recursive, such as a binary tree traversal.

9 (i) MICR: Characters (just numbers and a few special symbols) are written using special ink that can be magnetised. The characters are read using a MICR reader. Mainly used for numbers written at the bottom of cheques giving account number, cheque number and bank sort code.

(ii) OCR: Characters are scanned and digitised and software converts the scanned image to text. Many applications including credit card statements/payment slips, scanning text from a newspaper or textbook to be processed using a word-processor into a student handout, etc.

10 S – the last result in the accumulator was negative;

Z – the last result in the accumulator was zero;

C – the last result in the accumulator gave rise to a carry;

O – the last result in the accumulator was too big;

I – the interrupt service routine wishes to temporarily prevent other interrupts from being signalled;

B – the break signal has been received (e.g. Break key pressed).

11 (a) The purpose of spooling is to:
- maximise the use of peripheral equipment;
- avoid some of the problems of resource allocation;
- compensate for the slow operating speeds of peripheral devices in relation to the CPU.

(b)

(i)

	JobQueue	Address
1	Job1	Block 376
2	Job 2	Block 53
3	Job 3	Block 543
4	Job 4	Block 448
5		

FrontOfQueue = 2

RearOfQueue = 4

MaxSize = 50

(ii)

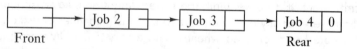

Front   Rear

(c) The elements of the array contain the name of the job and a reference to the location on disk where the output is stored. The elements of the linked list would contain either the actual output, or references to addresses where the output is stored, as with the array.

(d) Since an array is a static data structure it would only be able to hold a set number of output references. The linked list is a dynamic data structure and the actual output could be stored on disk, so only the front and rear pointers would need to be stored in memory.

12 (a)

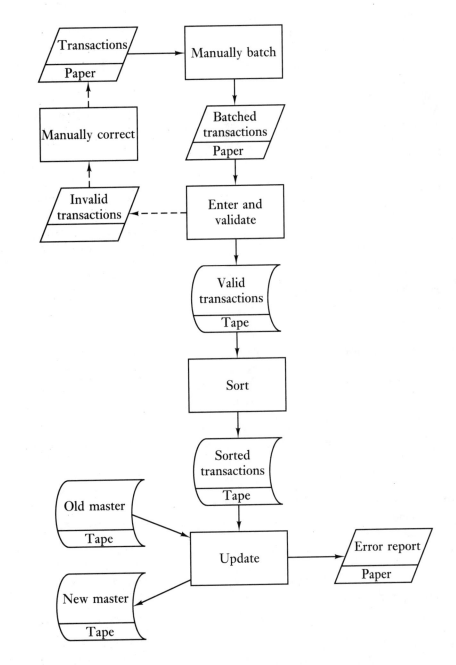

(b) *At the data entry stage*: a batch check on the number of records in the batch, check digit on employee number. Verification (entering the data twice) may be carried out. If any errors detected the original documents should be rechecked and re-entered.
At the update stage: Check that employee to be deleted exists on the file. Check that details of new employee not already on file. A printout of errors should be produced by the computer, and this should be manually checked and the original documents altered and resubmitted.

13 (a) (i) A property or characteristic of an entity/column in a table (NOT field).
(ii) A link or association between two entities.
(b) Four entities are: Ward (identifier Ward Name or Ward number)
Patient (identifier Patient id)
Nurse (identifier Staff No)
Consultant (identifier Staff No)

Three relationships:

occupied by

Ward ——————⟨ Patient

staffed by

Ward ——————⟨ Nurse

responsible for

Consultant ——————⟨ Patient

(c) Tables:

WARD (<u>Ward No</u>, Ward Name, No of Beds)

PATIENT(<u>Patient ID</u>, Patient Name, Address, DOB, Ward No, Staff No)

(or tables describing Consultant or Nurse)

Paper 2

1 Any of the following points:
- ability to present data in a clear and organised fashion/in graphs;
- automatic recalculation;
- 'What if' facility;
- formulae/functions;
- modelling/linking worksheets;
- can import data from other packages.

2 (a) Ring, Star

(b) (i) Ring: No transmission possible between any nodes in the network.

(ii) Star: If the central node fails, all users are affected and are unable to communicate with each other or use data held centrally. If any other node fails, other users are not affected.

3 (see Section 1.9 for full list)

e.g. Personal data must be made available to the individual concerned and provision made for corrections.

Personal data must be accurate and up to date.

4 Categories of application: choose two from list below, or other sensible suggestions:

Analysis and interpretation	Financial planning/DHSS Benefit entitlement
Classification	Insects, flowers
Prediction	Weather forecasting, stock market predictions, iron ore/oil deposits
Diagnosis	Medical problems/computer/car faults
Monitoring and control	Chemical processing plant
Costing	Building costs

5 (a) 01111111   11100101

(b) The two numbers above can be represented in hex as 7F and E3 respectively. This representation is much easier to read on a printout of contents of memory, for example.

6 Any five from:
- program modules are the natural end-product of a top-down design process;
- can be developed independently by different programmers;
- small modules easy to test and debug;
- management can follow programming progress more easily;
- modules may be reused in other applications;
- modular programs easier to maintain.

7 (See Section 5.6.) Design of the database, maintenance of data dictionary, training users.

8 (i) Grandfather–father–son update, with the oldest generation ('grandfather') being locked in a secure place, together with the corresponding transactions. In case of loss, these transactions would be reapplied to the grandfather to create the current master file ('father').

(ii) A RAID system (redundant array of inexpensive drives) could be used where the copies of the master file are held on 2 or 3 different drives at different locations and all transactions applied to all copies of the master file. If one copy is lost, it can be re-created from a good copy. (Alternatively, a nightly backup of the master file could be made, a transaction log of all updates could be made and in the case of loss, the master file would be created from the backup copy and the transaction log.)

9 Items in a stack are pushed and popped from one end only (LIFO). A stack is a suitable data structure for holding return addresses when a subroutine is called, because the last address saved is the first address from which execution must proceed on exit from the subroutine.

10 (a) Interview, examination of existing paperwork, questionnaire, observation.
Any valid analysis technique such as data flow diagrams, system flowchart, decision tables.

(b) (i) The electronic signal generated by a sensor is an analogue of the physical quantity being measured and therefore will range in a continuous manner. As the computer can only operate with discrete/binary signals an analogue-to-digital conversion takes place.

(ii) The sensor data is collected and processed quickly enough for the results of processing to influence the events generating the input data.

(iii) A single analogue-to-digital needs to be shared amongst many sensors and a multiplexor will reduce the input from the sensors to a single output stream.

(c) Use a relational database with a table for the entity. PLANT and associated attributes, having plant name as the primary key, and indexed on other columns such as characteristic. (Alternatively, use an indexed sequential file.)

(d) (i) *Advantage*: avoids miskeyed or mispriced items. Easier to change sale price of plants because they are not individually priced. Faster throughput at checkout.
Disadvantage: Problems when bar-code reader breaks down. Difficult to deal with damaged/muddy/torn bar-code labels.

(ii) *Either*: use indexed sequential organisation with separate index containing entries for highest catalogue number in each physical block.
Or: Hash file: records directly addressed using address calculation algorithm/hashing using catalogue number.
Justification: Bar-code supplies catalogue number only, so therefore a file organisation is required which will provide quick access to other details by catalogue number.

(iii) Read bar-code/catalogue number
Get PLANT.DAT record with this catalogue number
Decrement Quantity in stock
Rewrite record
Get /Display current price and plant name and print on receipt
Update running total.

(iv) The record of the plant being sold will need to be locked to prevent multiple access to the quantity in stock information when it is changed.
When a terminal wishes to record a sale, it makes a copy in memory of the respective PLANT.DAT record, alters the quantity in stock value of this memory copy and then rewrites the original with the updated version. If another terminal simultaneously accesses the same record to update it, the first update will be lost because it will be overwritten by the second.

(e) (Any sorting algorithm is allowable here. Marks are given for defining a data structure such as an array in memory, reading the data into memory, defining the sort key field, and then applying an algorithm such as a bubble sort as shown in Section 12.5.)

INDEX